London's Houses

by Vicky Wilson

London's Houses

Written by Vicky Wilson
Edited by Andrew Kershman
Book design by Lesley Gilmour & Susi Koch
Illustrations by Lesley Gilmour
Cover image: © Benjamin Franklin House
Inside cover images: © Freud Museum, © Emery Walker Trust

Published in 2011 by
Metro Publications Ltd, PO Box 6336, London, N1 6PY

Metro® is a registered trade mark of Associated Newspapers
Limited. The METRO mark is under licence from Associated
Newspapers Limited.

Printed and bound in India.
This book is produced using paper from registered sustainable
and managed sources. Suppliers have provided both LEI and
MUTU certification.

© 2011 Metro Publications Ltd
British Library Cataloguing in Publication Data. A catalogue
record for this book is available from the British Library.

ISBN 978-1-902910-36-9

'And pompous buildings once
were things of use...'

Alexander Pope,
'Epistle IV. To Richard Boyle,
Earl of Burlington', 1731

Acknowledgements

I would like to thank the many house curators
and administrators who have provided me with
help and information in compiling this book.
Thanks also to Dermot Wilson for introducing
me to the joys of many of the houses here and
for his ever-challenging opinions; Tom Neville for
his never-flagging encouragement and perceptive
comments on the text; Andrew Kershman for having
faith in the project's ongoing fascination; and
Lesley Gilmour and Susi Koch for their attention
to every detail of the books's appearance.

Entrance Charges
Entrance charges are listed in the following order:
adult, concessionary, child, family

Contents

West London

West Outskirts

South-west London

South-west Outskirts

South-east London

South-east Outskirts

East London

East Outskirts

Library, Pitzhanger Manor, see p.247

Introduction

Shutting the door on the world outside and embarking on a journey through an historic house releases the magic of time travel. It's an opportunity to recreate imaginatively a specific era peopled by characters whose lives can only be guessed at, or to rerun incidents from a well-known biography in their actual setting. Sometimes teasing out the layers of successive architectural interventions takes on the compulsion of a detective novel; sometimes characters or motifs pop up unexpectedly to create another link in the web of historical interconnections. Emerging to the noise of the 21st-century traffic outside, or to the drone of planes backing up for Heathrow, only emphasises the vividness and immediacy of the experience.

London's houses offer not only an introduction to some of the city's finest buildings and to the lives of some of its more famous inhabitants, but also a broad insight into the capital's architectural and social history. The oldest house presented here is Headstone Manor in Harrow, built c. 1310 and acquired 30 years later by the Archbishop of Canterbury for use as a staging post; the most recent is 2 Willow Road, a piece of restrained modernism built by Hungarian émigré Ernö Goldfinger in 1939. In social terms, the spectrum runs from the destitute who filled the purpose-built workhouse now known as Vestry House in Walthamstow, through servants and the bourgeoisie to the aristocracy and royalty.

The houses fall into two distinct, if occasionally overlapping, categories: those that have been conserved because of famous former inhabitants and those that are of interest because of their architecture. In the first group are the homes of such people as Thomas Carlyle, Charles Dickens, Sigmund Freud, George Frideric Handel, William Hogarth, Samuel Johnson and John Keats; in the second the aristocratic mansions clustered mainly to the west of London and such masterpieces as Queen's House in Greenwich and Spencer House in St James's Park. Overlaps include Horace Walpole's Strawberry Hill, Sir John Soane's houses in Lincoln's Inn Fields and Ealing, Frederic Leighton's house in Kensington and William Morris' Red House in Bexleyheath, as well as the royal residences of Buckingham Palace, Kew Palace, Hampton Court and Kensington Palace.

As the previous paragraph makes obvious, it's a history biased towards the rich and/or famous, most of whom were men. The dwellings of the poor or working class have not until recently been regarded as worthy of interest, though some stately homes have made welcome efforts to recreate the spaces downstairs and research their occupants. As for women, I have focused on their stories as much as possible, for two reasons. First, while information on, say, Thomas Carlyle is readily available, his wife Jane is a much less known (though arguably no less interesting) figure. And second, as sociological surveys sadly show us still to be the case today, the home was more often than not the woman's domain and many bear their imprint.

Few of the buildings featured are actually lived in, but I have found the people who work in these houses often exercise a near-proprietorial interest and are almost uniformly excited by the history and stories that surround them, supplying a fund of unsolicited anecdotes and information. Many buildings are open only as the result of public campaigns and many are staffed by volunteers. Their dedication should be commended, as should the efforts of English Heritage, the National Trust and several local authorities and smaller charities in protecting our architectural heritage.

New entries for this edition include Danson House in Bexley, the Emery Walker House and Kelmscott House in Hammersmith, Benjamin Franklin's house near Charing Cross Station, Kew Palace, and Mansion House in the City. All are witness to a continued determination to preserve such buildings and to make their stories accessible. Other sites have had substantial makeovers, sometimes funded by the trend for spectacular weddings in picturesque settings, sometimes by public grants. Several houses promise refurbishments in time for the influx of Olympics tourists, often making imaginative use of technology to fill rooms with recorded voices or projected images. Do check their websites before visiting as opening hours, as well as admission prices, are regularly revised. Details of wheelchair access are included only (as often) where this is problematic.

I have aimed in this book to give the information I would have found useful when I visited these houses. Sometimes this involves a summary of the architectural history, sometimes a description of the social context, sometimes a snapshot of the lives, loves and work of former inhabitants, occasionally all three. I have tended to restrict biographical detail to the years an individual spent in a particular house rather than attempting an overview. Information from guidebooks and websites has been supplemented by biographies, histories, architectural monographs and so on. Jenny Uglow's *Hogarth: A Life and a World* offers a vivid recreation of a London inhabited by many of this book's key figures; Pevsner's London guides were a constant source of reference for architectural minutiae.

Any book about London has to come up with its own definition of the boundaries of the city. Here I have used the London that appears within the *London A-Z*, with the exception of Charles Darwin's home at Down House, which seemed too important to omit. The book deals only with houses that are open to the public, and of these only houses that are open more than once a year. Another criterion is that the owners have to make available some insight into their building's history, so the many public buildings that were once houses and now function as libraries, community centres or schools are featured only if the visitor is given information about their original architectural state and past occupancy.

I started to write this book because I was fascinated by other people's houses, whether resplendent stately homes or more modest dwellings. A glance at current television schedules indicates the nation perhaps shares my obsession. So support and enjoy these wonderful buildings, campaign for their preservation, and hope that projects in the pipeline, such as the opening of exiled African National Congress leader Oliver Tambo's house in Muswell Hill, will soon come to fruition.

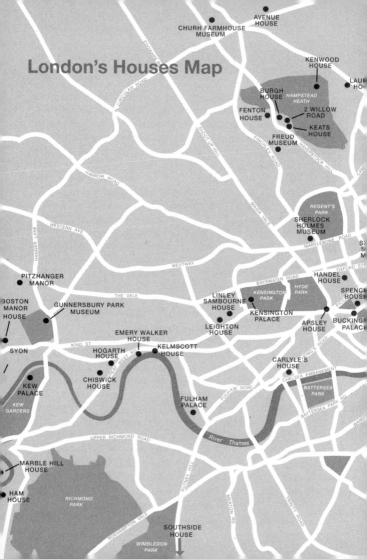

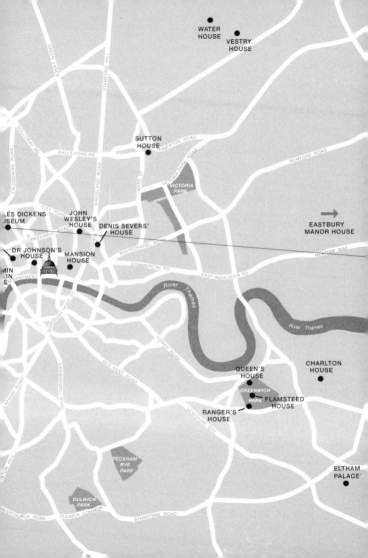

Central

Central

Apsley House

Hyde Park Corner, 149 Piccadilly, London W1J 7NT
Tel: 020 7499 5676
www.english-heritage.org.uk/apsleyhouse
Nearest transport: Hyde Park Corner LU
Open: Wed-Sun 11.00-17.00 (April to Oct), Wed-Sun 11.00-16.00
    (Nov to March)
Admission: £6/£5.10/£3
Wheelchair access: limited

Apsley House

Originally known as No. 1 London because it was the first house
after the toll gates at the top of Knightsbridge, Apsley House is a
relatively modest Robert Adam silk purse turned into a pretentious
sow's ear by Benjamin Dean Wyatt to create a grand residence
for Arthur Wellesley, Duke of Wellington (1769–1852), following
his triumphant return to civilian life after routing Napoleon at the
Battle of Waterloo. Built between 1771 and 1778 for Henry Bathurst,
the 1st Baron Apsley, the house was bought by Wellington's elder
brother in 1807 for £16,000, altered by James Wyatt, and then sold

9

The Waterloo gallery,
Apsley House

to Wellington ten years later for £40,000 – an increase that makes the scale of more recent property-price inflation look modest.

Wyatt's son Benjamin began his transformation of Adam's five-bay house by adding a grand dining room to the rear (the north-east corner) in 1819. In 1828–30, when Wellington was prime minister and had Downing Street as a London base, he built a two-bay extension to the west, running the full depth of the house and beyond, with a double-height picture gallery on the first floor. Adam's red brick was encased in Bath stone and a massive Corinthian portico was tacked on to the centre of the new front elevation. By 1831, the alterations had eaten up £64,000 of the £700,000 Wellington had been granted by parliament for his defeat of the French.

Wyatt's two-bay addition has uncomfortably skewed the plan. You enter through the centre of the portico into the side rather than the centre of the outer hall, ruining any grand scheme for the room. It's a gloomy start, and the space's current use as a ticket office and shop further deprives it of grandeur. John Simpson's darkly romantic portrait of the duke shows a handsome man with pursed lips, a thin face and watchful eyes – charms apparently lost on his aristocratic Irish mother, who sent him into the army at the age of 17 in the belief that her 'ugly boy Arthur' (her fifth son) was 'fit food for powder'. His survival and triumph is celebrated in a painting of the 1836 Waterloo banquet, an annual event that was held in the Waterloo gallery upstairs.

The plate and china room to the left (on the ground floor of Wyatt's 1828 addition) was created by Wellington's son, replacing some small bedrooms. The dazzling array of gold leaf, silverware and china was donated by European allies grateful to the duke for securing Napoleon's defeat. There are also presents from the surviving officers of some of the divisions under Wellington's command during his early career in India (1797–1805). In the inner hall – the entrance hall of Adam's building – hangs an extraordinarily camp, life-size, portrait of the 7th Duke, who bequeathed the house to the nation in 1947 in lieu of death duties. The present duke and his family still occupy some rooms of the property.

At the bottom of the stairs is a 3.5-metre nude statue of Napoleon posing as Mars, the Roman god of war. Commissioned from Canova by its subject (who didn't like the result), it was bought by the British government in 1816 and presented to Wellington. You can't help but feel he must have enjoyed having his former enemy so thoroughly within his power. The Thomas Lawrence portrait of the duke at the top of the stairs, by contrast, depicts him as a dark hero – a model for Heathcliff – against a romantic landscape.

The graceful Piccadilly drawing room retains Adam's delicate gilded frieze and ceiling but has Wyatt's yellow colour scheme and unpleasant carpet. Like the other rooms, it now feels unloved and institutional, its function as a picture gallery with little furniture leaving no sense of its former domestic role. Alongside the many Dutch paintings is David Wilkie's jolly *Chelsea Pensioners Reading the Waterloo Despatch*, commissioned by the duke in 1816 to depict 'a parcel of old soldiers... at a public-house in the King's Road'.

Before the construction of Wyatt's Waterloo gallery along its western wall, the portico drawing room must have been a light and pleasant space, with three windows looking out over Hyde Park. The romantic theme of Adam's chimney piece, decorated with a frieze of Cupid and Psyche, suggests this was once a ladies' drawing room. The current windows under the portico fail to correspond to the internal plan with massive columns at times obscuring the views.

Wyatt's 28-metre-long, top-lit Louis XIV-style Waterloo gallery seems swaggering and heavy-handed after the delicacy of the Adam interiors. Apparently the duke rebelled against his expensive architect by rejecting a £2000 quote for carved wood decorations in favour of £400 spent on gilded plaster putty. Some of the detailing was designed by Wellington's 'confidante' Harriet Arbuthnot, who complained bitterly at the duke's insistence on hanging the walls in yellow damask (the current red was chosen by his son after his death). Many of the pictures, which include several by Velasquez and a Corregio, were given to Wellington by the Spanish royal family following the expulsion of the French from Spain after their defeat at the battle of Vitoria (June 1813).

Stairwell, Apsley House

The yellow drawing room, like the portico drawing room, is compromised by the removal of its original windows. The striped drawing room – a bedroom in Adam's initial scheme – was decorated by Wyatt to evoke a military tent. In the duke's day it was furnished with card and games' tables. Wyatt's grand state dining room – accessed through the charming mirrored octagonal passage – is monumental and oppressive, lined with portraits of European royalty presented to the duke by their subjects.

During his 35 years at Apsley House, Wellington pursued a career as a politician and statesman, with mixed success. His lack of sympathy with the liberal foreign policies of George Canning led him to resign his cabinet post in 1827, when Canning became prime minister. Following Canning's death shortly afterwards, Wellington himself took on the role. His term in office was brief: his backing for the Catholic Emancipation bill lost him much support and his dogged resistance to parliamentary reform led to the fall of his ministry. Wellington's distrust of 'commoners' was so profound that he opposed railways on the grounds that they would encourage the lower classes to move around. His nickname, 'the Iron Duke', probably comes from the bars he put up at Apsley House's windows to protect them from rioters outraged at his refusal to extend the franchise. Wellington's home secretary was Robert Peel and it was the duke who drew up the template for the police force Peel famously introduced. He later served as foreign secretary (1834–35) and then as minister without portfolio (1841–46) when Peel was prime minister.

Wellington proposed to Kitty Pakenham, great-great-aunt of the late Lord Longford, when he was just 24, but was rejected by her family. They eventually married on Wellington's return from India in 1806, by which time he was heard to remark: 'She has grown ugly, by Jove.' Two sons were born in 1807 and 1808. Most biographers seem to agree that the marriage was a mistake and from 1817 until her death in 1831 Kitty lived mainly at their country house of Stratfield Saye in Hampshire. Wellington tended to avoid the place, complaining to Harriet Arbuthnot that Kitty 'made his house so dull that nobody would go to it'.

There is little trace of the personal in this grand museum until you get to the basement, where Wellington's death mask, dressing case and travelling canteen of cutlery at last make him appear human. Perhaps the treatment is appropriate: it seems that while Wellington wanted Apsley House as a showcase, he felt more at home in Walmer Castle, a more intimately scaled residence he used as warden of the cinq ports and in which he died in 1852.

Buckingham Palace

Buckingham Gate, London SW1A 1AA
Tel: 020 7766 7322
www.royalcollection.org.uk
Nearest transport: St James's Park LU or Victoria LU/Rail
Open: daily 9.45-18.00 (Aug & Sept), last admission 15.45,
    pre-booking recommended
Admission: £17.50/£16/£10/under-5s free/family ticket £46

Main entrance, Buckingham Palace

Like Mansion House and Southside House, Buckingham Palace is still very much lived in. So only the state apartments in the west range are open to the public. The palace also houses part of the Royal Collection, an art treasury on a vast scale amassed by various sovereigns. Although the Royal Collection is regarded as held in trust for the nation, visitors may balk at the high entrance fee charged for the privilege of seeing it.

The original Buckingham House was built by Lord Goring in 1633 and rebuilt by John Sheffield, Duke of Buckingham, in 1703–05. It was acquired by George III (1738–1820) shortly after his accession in 1760 through a compulsory-purchase deal made possible because half the property was on royal land. Over the next 14 years William Chambers was hired to remodel it as a family home for the king and his new wife Charlotte, with the ceremonial centre of the court remaining at nearby St James's.

The future George IV (1762–1830) set up his dysfunctional household in Carlton House on Pall Mall in 1783. Two years later he secretly married the Catholic Mrs Fitzherbert, subsequently tenant of Marble Hill House (see page 234), with whom he continued a relationship until 1803. The marriage was declared illegal in 1795 so he could wed his cousin Princess Caroline of Brunswick, whom he banished to Blackheath following the birth of their only daughter, Charlotte, the following year. After his accession in 1820, following ten years as regent, George had Carlton House demolished and sold the site to help pay the cost of converting Buckingham House into a full-scale residential and ceremonial palace. He chose as his architect the ageing John Nash (1752–1835), with whom he had worked on the development of Regent's Park and the remodelling of Brighton Pavilion. In the interests of economy, Nash was forced to retain the core of the old house, which dictated the plan, the ceiling height of the ground floor and the proportions of many of the rooms. Ironically, this celebration of national greatness in the wake of the victories of the Napoleonic wars was far from English in inspiration, since Nash drew many of his architectural references and George IV most of his furnishings from France.

Nash doubled the size of the main block of the old house (now at the centre of the west range) by adding a suite of rooms to its garden side. He then demolished the side wings and replaced them with much grander structures to form a U-shaped plan. The fourth side of the courtyard was enclosed simply by railings, with the monument now at Marble Arch in the centre. On his accession in 1830, George's brother William IV dismissed Nash – who had spent almost three times the sum allocated by parliament, and still hadn't finished the work – and hired the much less inspired William Blore.

In 1837 William was succeeded by his niece Victoria (1819–1901), who became the first sovereign actually to live in the palace, by now almost 80 years in the making. Its shortcomings quickly became apparent after her marriage three years later to Prince Albert of Saxe-Coburg-Gotha and the birth of nine children within 15 years. There was no nursery and no room large enough for a court ball. Between 1847 and 1850 Blore built an east wing enclosing the courtyard to provide apartments for distinguished visitors on the first floor and nurseries on the second, financed in part from the sale of Brighton Pavilion. Between 1853 and 1855 new galleries, a dining room and a ballroom were added to the south-west corner by Nash's pupil, James Pennethorne. Victoria's pleasure in her new home was relatively short-lived. After Albert's death in 1861 she retired to Windsor Castle for 40 years of widowhood and the palace was shut up. Her son Edward VII tackled the interior redecoration and his son George V had the perishable Caen stone façade of the east wing refaced in Portland stone by Aston Webb to give it the insipid beaux-arts profile we know today.

The outline of Buckingham's relatively modest nine-bay house is still apparent in the quadrangle, giving a pleasant sense of domestic scale after the exhibitionism of Webb's 25-bay street elevation. The glory of Nash's golden Bath-stone façades with their finely carved Corinthian capitals and frieze and the elegant double portico is highlighted by contrast with the crude painted stucco of Blore's east wing. The queen's private apartments are in the north

Grand staircase, Buckingham Palace

range; all in all the palace contains 52 royal and guest bedrooms, 188 staff bedrooms, 92 offices and 78 bathrooms in addition to the state apartments. The palace employs more than 800 people.

Paying visitors enter through a door at the side of the central grand hall, part of Buckingham's original house. It is a surprisingly squat room, given drama by Nash's lowering of the floor of the central area. George IV had amassed quantities of furniture, porcelain and works of art, a particularly fruitful source being French palaces whose contents were sold off to raise funds following the revolution. The state rooms were partly designed around his splendid collection, much of which is still in situ.

The entrance to Nash's grand staircase is flanked by two sexy female nudes – Richard James Wyatt's The Huntress (1850) and Jan Geefs' Love and Malice (1859) – that were birthday presents from Victoria to Albert. The staircase itself is surprisingly small in scale and the sinuous gilded bronze balustrade and engraved cupola are jewel-like rather than imposing. The tiny guard room beyond, peopled by statues of Victoria and Albert in Greek fancy dress, their heavy features (and especially his dashing moustache) at odds with their costumes. This again gives some indication of the intricacy of the craftsmanship. Around the lantern, from which hangs one of the palace's several spectacular glass chandeliers acquired by George IV for Carlton House, are studded etched-glass medallions – reminiscent of the ceiling mirrors used by John Soane (see page 58) – which break up the gilding to give a more ethereal effect.

The double-height green drawing room, above the grand hall, forms an anteroom to the throne room. Its most remarkable feature is the highly decorated ceiling, whose complex array of geometric forms, concave and convex coving and domes echoes the Mogul themes Nash elaborated in Brighton Pavilion. The sumptuous throne room has an equally superb ceiling below which – depicting scenes from the Wars of the Roses – runs England's answer to the Parthenon frieze. As in the green drawing room, mirrored doors – their outer edges decorated with hundreds of individually cast and positioned gilt-bronze fleurs de lys – increase the sense of space. The thrones themselves – emblazoned with ER and P, rather like a Ford Capri windscreen – are set behind a spectacular proscenium in the form of two winged female figures holding suspended free-falling swags. The only picture is Angelica Kauffmann's portrait of Augusta, Duchess of Brunswick – sister of George III and from 1807–13 a tenant of the Ranger's House (see page 310).

Throne room, Buckingham Palace

The picture gallery – an internal room between the enfilade from the grand staircase to the throne room and Nash's new additions to the garden front – runs the length of old Buckingham House. Nash's original ceiling design failed either to light the pictures or keep out water; it was modified by Blore and totally remodelled for George V in 1914 in its present barrel-vaulted form. The overall effect is a contrast to the opulence of the Nash rooms that precede it, but the combination of modern ceiling and Grinling Gibbons-style carving is also something of a halfway house, a wasted opportunity to produce a more rigorously modern statement. Among the many paintings are Vermeer's *The Music Lesson* and Rembrandt's *The Ship Builder and His Wife*.

The east gallery is on the quadrangle side of Victoria's 1850s extension. Its ceiling is a delicately etched version of the long gallery's, and is more unified and successful. Ill at ease among the stilted portraits of various official members of the royal family is John Hoppner's lively study of celebrated comic actress Mrs Jordan, for more than 20 years the loyal mistress of William IV – whose debts she would often pay off with her earnings – and the mother of ten of his children. Another abandoned woman is George IV's wife Caroline, painted in 1802 with her young daughter Charlotte. The picture is by Thomas Lawrence, with whom she is alleged to have had an affair.

Queen Victoria's ballroom – 37.5 metres long, 18 metres wide and 14 metres high – is one of the largest rooms in London and undoubtedly impressive. The tapestry-lined west gallery on the garden side leads to the state dining room, envisaged by Nash as a music room but completed by Blore for its present function. The relative coarseness of the detailing speaks of the financial constraints that followed Nash's dismissal. The dominating deep-red walls and carpet deaden the pleasure of the garden views and evoke an atmosphere reminiscent of the oppressive, inward-focused interiors of many a more modest Victorian dwelling.

The blue drawing room, music room and white drawing room – the enfilade Nash added to the garden side of Buckingham House – display a magnificence of proportion and decoration that could scarcely be bettered. The 21 metre-long blue drawing room (so-called because of the wallpaper installed by Queen Mary early in the last century) has a ceiling whose billowing coves and bold console brackets show Nash at his most daring. The central music room with its dramatic bow – still decorated much as Nash intended – is perhaps the best in the house. Its air of light and space is enhanced by the shimmering vaulted and domed ceiling, gilded in a pattern of breathtaking intricacy echoed by the spectacular parquet floor. The ethereal chandeliers are probably the finest in the palace. As in the rest of the rooms on this floor, the five full-height windows in the bow are among the earliest surviving English uses of plate glass, a product developed in the 1820s. The white drawing room – which anywhere else would deserve a paragraph on its splendour but here fades into insignificance – retains its Nash ceiling but was redecorated in the late 19th century.

Blore's relatively modest ministers' staircase, at the foot of which is a Canova sculpture, as at Apsley House (see page 9), leads to the windowless marble hall, running below the picture gallery. Visitors exit to the gardens through the elegant bow room below the music room.

More things to see & do

Shaped by the taste of kings and queens over the past 500 years, the Royal Collection is a vast and important treasury of paintings, sculpture and drawings, furniture and ceramics, and prints and maps. Selected items are displayed in the Queen's Gallery, which mounts exhibitions on themes as diverse as Dutch landscape painting or Antarctic photography. Also sited at Buckingham Palace is the Royal Mews, which houses the state vehicles used for official engagements. And the ever popular Changing the Guard takes place at 11.30 daily from May until the end of July and on alternate days for the rest of the year, weather permitting. For opening times and other information see *www.royalcollection.org.uk*.

Charles Dickens Museum

48 Doughty Street, London WC1 2LX
Tel: 020 7405 2127
www.dickensmuseum.com
Nearest transport: Russell Square LU
Open: daily 10.00-17.00 (the house may close for refurbishment
   from summer 2011)
Admission: £6/£4.50/£3/family ticket £15
Wheelchair access: ground floor only

Charles Dickens Museum

When novelist Charles Dickens (1812–70) leased 48 Doughty Street on 25 March 1837 for three years at £80 a year, the three-storey flat-fronted house, built c. 1807–09, stood in a smart private road closed off by gates manned by porters in livery. It was an impressive step up from the three back rooms he had rented at 13 Furnival's Inn, EC1, made possible by the enormous success of *Pickwick Papers*, which had been appearing in monthly parts for a year. On 2 April the writer celebrated the first anniversary of his marriage to Catherine Hogarth and on 8 April publishers Chapman and Hall organised a dinner to mark the serial's anniversary, giving Dickens a bonus cheque of £500. The Doughty Street household also included Dickens' 16-year-old brother Frederick and the couple's three-month-old son Charles.

The two years and eight months of the family's residency, before moving on to a larger, more upmarket property at 1 Devonshire Terrace, Regent's Park, were far from uneventful. Two more children were born – Mary on 6 March 1838 and Kate on 29 October 1839 – and in addition to completing *Pickwick Papers*, Dickens wrote *Oliver Twist*, *Nicholas Nickelby*, *Sketches of Young Gentlemen*, the first chapters of *Barnaby Rudge*, the farce *The Lamplighter* and several pieces for *Bentley's Miscellany* (the journal he edited and in which *Oliver Twist* and *Nicholas Nickelby* were serialised) as well as rewriting for publication *Memoirs of Joseph Grimaldi*. The most momentous and emotionally scarring event, however, was the death of Catherine's 17-year-old sister Mary, who passed away in Dickens' arms in early May 1837 in one of the upstairs rooms after collapsing following a family visit to the theatre. The play the three had seen was the farce *Is She His Wife?* – an apt title since Dickens was to wear Mary's ring, which he slipped off the corpse's hand, for the rest of his life, planned to be buried next to her and idealised her in a way that can only have contributed to his disillusionment with his marriage to Catherine. Mary was the inspiration for Rose Maylie in *Oliver Twist*, whom Dickens allowed to recover from her serious illness, against his original intentions, and for Little Nell in *The Old Curiosity Shop*.

Opened in 1925 and run by a charitable trust, the Charles Dickens Museum today is endearingly tatty, its state of decoration and atmosphere capturing the feeling of a well-used home rather than a pristine heritage recreation. This was, after all, Dickens' house early in his career, before his rise to fame and fortune, and the scale and decor evoke the informal hubbub of family life rather than the cultivated elegance of, say, John Soane's contemporary residence (see page 58). At the time of writing the museum is hoping to undertake an ambitious refurbishment programme to mark the Dickens bicentenary in 2012. This may involve revamping the current displays and the addition of a visitor and learning centre in the house next door.

The dining room at the front of Dickens' former home is a modest space given character by its curved rear wall and doors. The most striking feature is the superb, overscaled mahogany sideboard Dickens bought late in 1839, presumably with the move to the larger Devonshire Terrace house in mind. Among the memorabilia is the quill pen he used for writing his swan song *The Mystery of Edwin Drood* and the reading glass he kept from 1834 until his death. The morning room at the rear of the house was used by the family as an informal sitting room. The displays here focus on Dickens' family, including several pictures of Catherine as well as photographs of some of the couple's ten children. A portrait of Charles, painted by his friend Danile Maclise in 1839, shows the handsome young writer at his desk, eyes gazing out of the frame as if startled by a sudden and welcome interruption. Among the artefacts are Catherine's engagement ring and Charles' aspirational wedding present to her of a mother-of-pearl visiting-card case. Dickens initially seemed proud of his young wife – letters from their trip to the United States in 1842, a couple of years after they left Doughty Street, describe their social triumph in typically exuberant terms: 'Imagine Kate and I – a kind of Queen and Albert... in newspapers and receiving all who come...' But the relationship gradually soured and in 1857 Charles embarked on an affair with actress Ellen Ternan, who was to be his companion for the rest of his life. His separation from

Catherine was made public in what must have been a humiliating and hurtful manner through an announcement in *Household Words*, the weekly magazine he edited at the time.

At the foot of the stairs hangs the hall clock from Gad's Hill Place, the grand Georgian house near Rochester that Dickens had dreamed of owning when he was a child and in which he lived for the last 12 years of his life. In the basement are reconstructions of the wash house and wine cellar and the still room, formerly a storeroom and informal sitting room for the house's servants, where you can watch a half-hour video about Dickens' life. What used to be the kitchen, at the front of the house, is now a library of first editions.

The first-floor drawing room, at the front of the house, is crammed with furniture, evoking the claustrophobic conditions of Victorian family life, even among the aspiring middle classes. Some of the furniture is Dickens' own; other pieces are similar to items he is known to have possessed. The decor is without sophistication: the lilac paint and wallpaper are believed from documentary evidence to approximate Dickens' colour scheme; the clashing, patterned carpet was chosen because its floral motifs conform to descriptions in Dickens' work. The study at the rear is a repository of memorabilia rather than a reconstruction, though the simple writing table from the garden chalet at Gad's Hill Place at which Dickens wrote his last words will no doubt send tremors up the spines of the many devoted pilgrims. The several fragments of manuscript including *Pickwick Papers* and *Oliver Twist* – pristine but for a few insertions and scorings out – bear witness to the seemingly effortless fluidity with which he could transmit his ideas to paper.

The unatmospheric Mary Hogarth room (second floor, rear) contains information about the various women who played a role in Dickens' life. Included is his first love, Maria Beadnell, a banker's daughter he wanted to marry at the age of 18, but whose parents discouraged the match, and his last love, Ellen Ternan. Among the relics relating to Mary herself is a copy of part XV of *Pickwick Papers*, in which Dickens manages to make light of the tragedy of her death to his readers, explaining that the interruption in the serial's publication is due to 'a severe domestic affliction of no ordinary kind', not, as rumours have it, to his having been 'killed outright... driven mad... imprisoned for debt... sent per steamer to the United States'.

The tiny dressing room at the front of the house, probably used as Frederick's bedroom, contains evidence of the enormously successful series of public readings which Dickens, billed as *The Sparkler of Albion*, engaged in during the last 12 years of his life. Among the memorabilia is a record by his doctor of the increase in his pulse rate after performances. In what was once Dickens and Catherine's bedroom are temporary exhibitions on such subjects as the terrible conditions in factories and schools that the author campaigned against in novels like *Oliver Twist* and *Nicholas Nickelby*, both written in the rooms downstairs.

In Dickens' study hangs *Dickens's Dream*, the melancholy unfinished painting done five years after the author's death by R W Buss, one of *Pickwick Papers'* original illustrators. It shows the author, in colour, seated in his Gad's Hill Place study, surrounded by fairy-scale pen-and-ink sketches of the characters of his imagination, one of whom is sitting on his knee as if begging him to confer her with immortality. The effect is something like that of the museum itself – a mass of borrowings from different sources, through which we hope to come closer to genius, but which perhaps requires someone of Dickens' imagination to bring it fully to life.

Benjamin Franklin House

36 Craven Street, London WC2 5NF
Tel: 020 7925 1405/2006
www.benjaminfranklinhouse.org
Nearest transport: Charing Cross LU/Rail
Open: Historical Experience Shows Wed-Sun 12.00, 13.00, 14.00,
    15.15, 16.15; Architectural Tours Mon, same times as above
Admission: Historical Experience Shows £7/£5, Architectural Tours
    £3.50, children free
Wheelchair access: none

Scientist, inventor, author, diplomat and founding father of the United States, Benjamin Franklin (1706–1790) was a lodger in Craven Street from 1757 to 1762 and from 1764 to 1775. No. 36, a house in which he rented four rooms, was opened to the public in 2006 and is the most extreme example of the trend for using costumed actors, projection and recorded voices to bring the past to life. It techniques are very successful, mainly because the curators have embraced the approach whole-heartedly, with the house's empty spaces animated only by a lone actress, a witty and informative soundtrack, well-selected images and the power of the visitors' imaginations.

Craven Street was built in 1730 on land owned by the fifth Lord Craven. Franklin's landlady, the widowed Margaret Stevenson, moved into No. 36 with her young daughter Polly in 1748. In 1770 Polly married William Hewson, a physician who made important discoveries about the lymphatic system, and two years later

Margaret and Franklin decamped to No. 7 to leave the young couple more room for their expanding family and to allow Hewson to set up a private school of anatomy. After Hewson's death in 1774 from an infected cut incurred while conducting a dissection, the house passed to his sister and her husband.

The construction of Charing Cross Station in 1864 had a huge impact on the area and in 1887 the South Eastern Railway company acquired Craven Street by compulsory purchase. No. 36 was occupied by various tenants including the Empress Hotel. Damaged during the war and let to non-profit organisations such as the British Society for International Understanding, the house suffered increasing neglect. The Friends of Benjamin Franklin House bought the lease in 1976 and were awarded the freehold in 1989, after which an ambitious programme of conservation and restoration began.

One of a row of four-storey three-bay Georgian townhouses, 36 Craven Street has a red-brick façade punctuated by mullioned sashes above a rusticated, stuccoed ground floor and basement. There are two rooms on the main part of each floor plus a rear extension to the lower storeys. The sloping floors and alarmingly tilting staircase are testament to the house's dilapidated condition before its recent renovation. Still, most of the rooms retain their original fireplaces, mouldings and panelling, painted in the green-grey colour thought to have been used in Franklin's time.

Visitors begin their journey in a basement space that was originally part of the back yard. The displays are devoted largely to Hewson, who worked with anatomist John Hunter before a quarrel forced him to set up on his own, probably sharing the lecture theatre of obstetrician Dr John Leake, who lived next door. In the 1990s builders found over 1200 human and animal bones in the basement, including skulls used to practise trepanning. Some of these are on display, alongside Franklin's battered wallet and a letter to his sister, the house's only physical relics of its famous occupant.

After watching a brief film, visitors are led through the ground and first-floor rooms by Polly (played by an actress), who interacts with sophisticated projections and recorded voices of characters including her mother Mrs Stevenson (voiced by Imelda Staunton), Franklin's wife Deborah and son William, and such friends as royal physician Dr Pringle, who accompanied Franklin on his travels, scientist Joseph Priestley, for whom Franklin developed the equipment that enabled the discovery of oxygen, William Strahan, the printer of Dr Johnson's *Dictionary* (see page 46), and, of course, the genial Franklin himself (voiced by Peter Coyote). The two rooms on the first floor were Franklin's own.

Born in 1706 as the fifteenth child of Puritan parents, Franklin left school at the age of ten and two years later was apprenticed to his brother's printing business. In 1725–26 he spent a year in London as a typesetter before returning to Philadelphia to start his own printing house. From 1729 he published the *Pennsylvania Gazette*, winning respect for his well-judged commentaries on local reforms and initiatives.

During the quarter century before he returned to London in 1757 Franklin made an impact on his home country that still resonates today. He invented the lending library in the early 1730s to share books among a group of 'like-minded aspiring artisans and tradesmen who hoped to improve themselves while they improved the community'. In the 1740s and 1750s he set up the colonies' first volunteer fire service, founded the institution that was to become the University of Pennsylvania and established Pennsylvania Hospital, one of the first in the continent. In 1751 he was elected to the Pennsylvania Assembly and two years later he was appointed joint deputy postmaster general of North America, in which role he was to reform the postal service.

Franklin had entered into a common-law marriage with Deborah Read in 1730. The couple had met when they were in their teens but while Franklin was delayed during his first trip to London Deborah married a man who subsequently deserted her. Benjamin and Deborah had a son who died in childhood and a daughter, Sarah, born in 1743. They also brought up William, Franklin's illegitimate son from a previous relationship, who accompanied Franklin to

Craven Street to study law. Father and son were eventually to quarrel over William's rejection of the idea of American independence.

When Franklin arrived in London in 1757 it was as a representative of the Pennsylvania Assembly, charged with trying to end the right of the proprietors of the colony, the Penn family, to overturn legislation and their exemption from paying tax on their land. Having won some concessions, he returned home five years later but was sent back in 1764, this time to petition the king to make Pennsylvania a royal colony rather than a proprietary province.

He almost immediately became embroiled in the furore over the 1765 Stamp Act, which imposed duty on colonial legal documents and newspapers. Though he failed to prevent the act from being passed, his performance as a witness before the House of Commons the following year is widely credited with securing its repeal. From then on Franklin became a leading spokesman for American affairs, working tirelessly for reconciliation between his home and adopted countries, especially as relations worsened when Britain imposed duties on glass, paper and tea. 36 Craven Street acted as a *de facto* American embassy, with Mrs Stevenson welcoming guests as eminent as Whig prime minister William Pitt the Elder.

Franklin was also a dedicated and talented scientist. Among the inventions he made at Craven Street were an improved design for bifocals, which he called 'double spectacles'; the fuel-saving and pollution-reducing Franklin stove, which burns its own smoke; and the glass armonica, an instrument that replicates the sound of rubbing the rims of glasses filled with water, for which musicians as eminent as Mozart composed. Franklin also developed a phonetic alphabet and was the first person to chart the Gulf Stream, when as postmaster general he wondered why mail boats took longer than merchant ships to reach America. While still in Philadelphia he had formed the idea of positive and negative electric charge and devised an experiment to prove that lightning is electricity. His design for a lightning rod, invented while at Craven Street, was installed on St Paul's Cathedral.

'Human felicity is produced not so much by great pieces of good fortune that seldom happen as by little advantages that occur every day.'
Benjamin Franklin, *The Autobiography*, 1817

Franklin's wife Deborah, afraid to cross the ocean, never visited her husband in England and he failed to respond to her pleas to return home as she grew increasingly ill. She died in early 1775. Soon afterwards Franklin went back to America, arriving just after the outbreak of the American revolution. He helped to draft the Declaration of Independence and returned to Europe as ambassador to France from 1777 to 1785, eventually negotiating the Treaty of Paris, which gave America her independence. Though Franklin and his son had brought their slaves Peter and King to Craven Street, by the end of his life Franklin was a staunch abolitionist, becoming the first president of the Society for the Abolition of the Slave Trade. After her mother's death in 1783, Polly and her children followed Franklin to Paris and then to the United States.

This is a long and complex story to tell, and one of the ways the Benjamin Franklin House succeeds is by using Polly to convey information, so enabling political and scientific concepts to be simplified to the point where lay visitors can quickly grasp them. The script's mix of letters, speeches and in particular conversations – most successfully in the downstairs parlour, where Franklin, Polly and Mrs Stevenson are joined for tea by William Strahan and blind musician John Stanley – also means information can be imparted in easily digestible chunks, as the discussion ranges naturally from politics and science to food and family and back again.

The decision not to fill the Benjamin Franklin House's rooms with contemporary or reproduction furnishings or to amass a collection of memorabilia may have been driven partly by practicalities. But the strategy has paid off – both in making 36 Craven Street unique among London's historic houses and in conveying the complex flavours of Benjamin Franklin's time here with the mix of mundane and miraculous, funny and moving found in life itself.

Handel House Museum

25 Brook Street, London W1K 4HB
Tel: 020 7495 1685
www.handelhouse.org
Nearest transport: Bond Street LU
Open: Tues-Wed & Fri-Sat 10.00-18.00, Thurs 10.00-20.00,
   Sun 12.00-18.00
Admission: £5/£4.50/£2/under-5s free and under-16s
   free at weekends

The Brook Street buildings occupied by the Handel House Museum boast blue plaques commemorating two famous musicians: George Frideric Handel, who lived at No. 25 from 1723 until his death in 1759, and Jimi Hendrix, who lived at No. 23 in 1968-69. At No. 25 experts have restored the rooms that formed the major part of Handel's home to their presumed condition in the 1720s, using paint scrapes, an inventory made after the composer's death and the evidence still available in the less tampered-with houses next door. Unfortunately the top-floor flat Hendrix occupied in No. 23 isn't open to the public, but the inaugural Handel House Museum director assured me that the rock guitarist's rooms have been restored to their late-1960s condition of white-painted woodchip walls and scarlet carpet, based on information from the musician's former girlfriend and traces of fabric found between the floorboards.

Handel moved to London in 1712 at the age of 27 and proceeded to dominate the English music scene for almost half a century.

Little is known of his life outside the music world – he didn't marry, had no recorded sexual relationships with men or women, left few letters and kept no diary. Contemporary accounts indicate that he was strikingly handsome in his youth, while his meteoric rise to prominence in Hamburg, Italy and Hanover before the move to London suggests a charismatic personality as well as a prodigious musical talent. As he grew older he became more corpulent, thanks to a 'culpable indulgence in the sensual gratifications of the table', as a biographer put it. Abraham Brown, the lead violinist at performances of *Messiah* in the 1750s, describes how at one dinner party Handel claimed sudden inspiration and retired to the room next door; when one of the guests peeped through the keyhole he was seen quaffing a new delivery of Burgundy vastly superior to the wine served at his table. But such apparent meanness was tempered with public generosity, in particular to the newly established Foundling Hospital (also a favourite charity of his contemporary William Hogarth, see page 179), for which he raised the vast sum of £10,000 in the 1750s through annual charity performances of *Messiah* and his own considerable donations. Biographers also comment on his dry humour, explosive temper and gift for storytelling.

When Handel moved to fashionable Mayfair he must have felt that his position at the pinnacle of the London music scene was secure: he had an annual pension of £400 as music master to the royal family, was music director of the Royal Academy of Music opera company and was composer to the Chapel Royal. Brook Street itself was planned and built between 1717 and 1726 and No. 25 was part of a residential development of four buildings by speculative builder George Barnes. The brick houses were flat-fronted and four storeys high, with the two rooms on each floor arranged around the staircase in a standard L plan with a closet at the back. Handel was the first occupant of No. 25 and his neighbours included Sir John Avery and MP John Monckton. Hanover Square to the east had been laid out in 1714, with several of its houses leased to Whig generals, while Grosvenor Square to the west, developed in 1737, accommodated George I's mistress the Duchess of Kendal.

As a foreign national, Handel would have been unable to buy the house when he moved in, but even after his naturalisation in 1727 he elected to continue to rent. Following his death, the house was taken over by his servant John Du Burk, who may have run it as a boarding house until 1772. In 1905 it was converted into a shop by art dealer C J Charles, who replaced the façade of the first two floors and virtually gutted the interior. Since 1971 the freehold has been owned by the Co-operative Insurance Society, which leases the rooms occupied by the museum to the Handel House Trust.

Handel arrived in England through his connection with George I, whom he had courted in Hanover when the future king was the elector and Handel was Kapellmeister. With *Rinaldo* (1711) the composer had introduced Italian opera to the London stage, and the Royal Academy of Music, which he founded in 1719 with his Italophile patrons Lord Burlington (see Chiswick House, page 162) and Lord Chandos, briefly established London as Europe's opera capital. London's art world at the time was divided between those who wanted to nurture a strong, homegrown British culture for the newly formed United Kingdom with its newly imported Protestant dynasty and those in thrall to the superiority of Italian and French models. In music terms, this translated into a battle between the supporters of Handel's Italian opera and those like Alexander Pope and Jonathan Swift, who deemed the fashion 'wholly unsuitable to our northern climate, and the genius of the people, whereby we are overrun with Italian effeminacy and Italian nonsense.' The rivalry culminated with the staging of *The Beggar's Opera* in 1728 at Lincoln's Inn Fields Theatre. The libretto by John Gay was both a political satire and a parody of the Royal Academy's extravaganzas, and the opera's unprecedented popularity (exploited by Hogarth, who painted at least five versions) proved the last straw for Handel's beleaguered enterprise. The Royal Academy folded and Handel went to Italy to find more singers, returning to form a new venture with John James Heidegger, manager of the King's Theatre. Portraits of George I, Lord Burlington, Pope, Gay and Heidegger can be found in the dressing room here.

In 1733 the Opera of the Nobility was formed by a group of aristocrats headed by Frederick, Prince of Wales. Led by the castrato Senesino, whom Handel had brought to London, most of Handel's singers defected to the rival company, apparently tired of his autocratic zeal. Handel moved to the smaller Covent Garden Theatre, where he continued to put on operas but also experimented with the new semi-dramatic form of the oratorio, usually sung in English and based on a religious theme. He suffered a stroke in 1737 – possibly brought on by the strain of writing and producing three new operas in eight months. In 1739 he moved to the more modest Lincoln's Inn Fields Theatre, where he capitulated to public demand by giving his first all-English season. He left London for Dublin in 1741 to stage two new works, *Messiah* and *Samson*.

Following his return to London, Handel abandoned opera to concentrate on oratorios. In 1744 he hired the King's Theatre for the first complete English oratorio season with tickets sold by subscription, at which he presented *Hercules* and *Belshazzar*. The season was a disaster, and Handel suffered a nervous breakdown. Thereafter he limited his ambitions to Lenten seasons at Covent Garden, with tickets sold for individual performances. Meanwhile he was garnering great public popularity with such patriotic pieces as a *Te Deum* celebrating George II's victory over the French in 1743 in the war over the Austrian succession and *Judas Maccabaeus* (1747), an allegory of the Duke of Cumberland's rout of the Scots at Culloden with a libretto by Hogarth's great friend Thomas Morell. The rehearsal in Vauxhall Pleasure Gardens for the *Music for the Royal Fireworks* (1749), commemorating the end of the war, attracted a crowd of 20,000. But whatever the work's subsequent popularity, the first performance – held in Green Park – was a fiasco, with drizzle turning many fireworks into damp squibs, one of the pavilions set alight and the display's architect arrested for drawing his sword on the event's organiser.

In 1752, following another stroke, Handel lost his sight almost completely, putting an end to composing. With the help of J C Smith the younger, he was able still to revise his works and direct oratorio

Main bedroom, Handel House

seasons, while he continued to perform organ concertos from memory. Despite the many ups and downs in his career he was able to leave an estate of £20,000 – 400 times the annual rent of his desirable Brook Street residence.

The first and second floors of No. 23 Brook Street, accessed from No. 25, now house temporary exhibitions about aspects of Handel's life and work, an activity area for families and items owned by the Handel House Collections Trust as well as a small

Rehearsal room, Handel House

display of photographs of Hendrix. But the journey into Handel's former home begins disorientingly with a trip in a high-tech metal lift to the second floor of No. 25. You arrive in a pleasant room with a large three-bay bow to the side that replaced the original closet in about 1790. The panelling throughout the house is replicated from that still in existence in Nos 27 and 29 and the colour (a grey akin to a modern undercoat) is thought from paint scrapes to have been used by Barnes for the whole development. Areas such as skirtings and doors that got more wear are believed to have been repainted chocolate brown, as here.

Handel used the room at the rear of the second floor as a dressing room. Like the rest of the house, the space is sparsely furnished and hung with portraits based on a specific theme – in this case the London music scene. The three-bay room at the front was the composer's bedroom, its bed and hangings recreated from descriptions in the posthumous inventory. Though state-of-the-art in 1723, the paired curtains would have been noticeably old-fashioned by 1759, when ruches were all the rage. But Handel was apparently more interested in food, drink, good company and art (he owned some 80 canvases including Dutch, Flemish and Italian old masters, two Rembrandts and a Watteau) than in interior decoration, or at least that's the impression given by these somewhat austere rooms. The lively 1756 portrait of the composer with his fleshy face, protruding lower lip and bushy eyebrows in its extravagant frame of gilded bulrushes seems distinctly at odds with the atmosphere of calm restraint that otherwise prevails.

The rear room on the first floor is probably where Handel composed most of his music of this period and the front room takes up the theme of rehearsal and performance. The room is dominated by a 1734 portrait of the somewhat severe-looking Faustina Bordoni, a soprano who joined Handel's company in 1725. Her increasing rivalry with the more established Francesca Cuzzoni, whom Handel had threatened to defenestrate in 1722 when she had refused to sing an aria in *Ottone*, culminated in a public brawl on stage on 6 June 1727 which Gay satirised in *The Beggar's Opera*.

We know that Handel held rehearsals here after he moved to Covent Garden in 1734, perhaps because the new theatre's varied programme meant the auditorium was not always available. The 1759 inventory lists no curtains for the room, possibly because this improved the acoustics. Friends' and neighbours' diaries record being invited to attend rehearsals of new works; violinist Brown recalled 'being heated by a crowded room and hard labour'. The modern reproduction harpsichord (Handel owned a 1612 model made by Hans Ruckers of Antwerp) is used during opening hours by music students and professionals for rehearsals and lessons and the museum organises well-attended concerts. It seems that the opportunity to hear Handel's music in the space where it was conceived has lost none of its popularity with the passage of time.

More things to see & do

Handel House hosts regular live music events with recitals held every Thursday evening and frequently at weekends. Audience numbers are strictly limited, so it is advisable to book well in advance. Booking line: 020 7399 1953. The rehearsal and performance rooms are closed during recitals and visitors to the rest of the house are charged a reduced admission fee.

There is also a changing programme of exhibitions focused on Handel's life and works at No. 23. See *www.handelhouse.org*.

Sherlock Holmes Museum

221b Baker Street, London NW1 6XE
Tel: 020 224 3688
www.sherlock-holmes.co.uk
Nearest transport: Baker Street LU
Open: daily 9.30-18.00
Admission: £6/under-16s £4
Wheelchair access: shop only

Study, Sherlock Holmes Museum

The fictional detective Sherlock Holmes and his stalwart friend and
biographer Dr Watson rented rooms on the first and second floors
of 221b Baker Street from their landlady Mrs Hudson between about
1881 and 1904. This narrative is from the imagination of Arthur
Conan Doyle, but this flat-fronted four-storey house is real. It was

built in around 1815 – not long after Dickens' home in Doughty Street (see page 24) and at the same time as John Nash was developing nearby Regent's Park. Like Dickens' house, 221b Baker Street is built to a standard L plan, though it's noticeably smaller in scale. And the patina of age, to put it kindly, is everywhere apparent: the risers of the stair carpet are holed from all those clumping male feet, while the rug in Holmes' bedroom is practically threadbare.

It's known that 221b Baker Street was registered as a lodging house from 1860 to 1934, and indeed the location – in easy walking distance of the West End and virtually overlooking Regent's Park, which was opened to the public in the 1830s – could hardly be bettered. Today the ground floor, predictably, is a souvenir shop with a separate entrance. However, the original front entrance (somewhat unnecessarily guarded by a policeman in period dress) has been retained, and the mean, gloomy hallway and stairs to the first floor – cold, ill-lit and distinctly grimy – are among the most evocative spaces of any of the houses described here. The cramped front room, a study the two men shared, has comfortable armchairs on either side of a low table in front of the blazing fire, a dining table set for two in the corner opposite the door and Watson's desk with his medical textbooks and doctor's bag filled with a gruesome array of implements. It's obviously several notches down in terms of scale and taste from the lifestyle enjoyed by contemporary Linley Sambourne (see page 147). Unusually for a heritage museum, you're allowed to touch the objects, sharpen your reflections with the aid of Holmes' trusty violin and try on the duo's well-worn hats. The costumed maid will take photographs if asked.

Holmes occupied the back bedroom on this floor, furnished with an uncomfortable-looking iron bedstead and washstand with a pitcher and ewer. The completeness and relative poverty of the contents again give an almost eerily vivid idea of what life might have been like. The second-floor front room (occupied by Mrs Hudson) contains several of the objects that provided vital clues in Holmes' detective work – for instance a piece of plaster smeared with blood that led to the denouement of *The Norwood Builder*:

'With dramatic suddenness [Inspector Lestrade] struck a match and by its light exposed a stain of blood upon the whitewashed wall. As he held the match nearer I saw that it was more than a stain. It was the well marked print of a thumb.'

Here also is a tragic scrapbook of recent letters begging Holmes for help – Stéphanie Duverger in France asks him to trace a missing friend and the Japanese Kanal asks him to prove a friend's death was murder, not suicide.

Watson's bedroom at the rear of the house and the two rooms on the top floor are given over to chilling displays of waxworks depicting some of the more dramatic episodes from Holmes' investigations. The top-floor bathroom has a remarkable (still functional) porcelain toilet and basin decorated with rampant blue flowers.

Dr Johnson's House

Dr Johnson's House

17 Gough Square, London EC4A 3DE

Tel: 020 7353 3745

www.drjohnsonshouse.org

Nearest transport: Chancery Lane LU

Open: Mon-Sat 11.00-17.30 (May to Sept), Mon-Sat 11.00-17.00
   (Oct to April)

Admission: £4.50/£3.50/£1.50/family ticket £10

Wheelchair access: many unavoidable steps

Dr Samuel Johnson (1709–84) rented this gem of a Queen Anne house (built c. 1700 for a city father by the name of Gough or Goff) from c. 1748 to 1759 for about £30 a year. He chose it because of its proximity to the premises of William Strahan, the printer for the *Dictionary* he was to compile and deliver letter by letter. The house is reached through a network of alleys from Fleet Street, at the time part of the thoroughfare connecting Westminster to the City and a bustling conglomeration of shops, theatres, taverns, coffeehouses and chophouses with a somewhat seedy reputation. The double-fronted brick house, on a corner site, was occupied until 1911, when it was bought by Liberal MP Cecil Harmsworth and restored, many of its original features having been saved by years of neglect. The garret suffered severe damage during the Blitz of 1941–42.

Johnson's residency at Gough Square was a time of poverty and continuing financial crises – he was under arrest for debt in 1756 for the sum of £5 18s, which he was able to borrow from the more successful Samuel Richardson, author of *Pamela* and *Clarissa* – and it wasn't until 1762 that the award of a crown pension of £300 per annum brought financial security. The *Dictionary* (contracted in 1746 by a syndicate of booksellers for which he was to be paid £1575 for an anticipated three years' work) took eight years to complete, during most of which his supposed patron Lord Chesterfield (see Ranger's House, page 310) ignored him (patron in the *Dictionary* is famously defined as: '...Commonly a wretch who supports with insolence, and is paid with flattery'). In 1749 actor and theatre manager David Garrick, a former pupil and lifelong friend, staged

Johnson's play *Irene*, which earned him £300, and the gloomy, profoundly personal poem *The Vanity of Human Wishes* was sold for 15 guineas. From 1750 to 1752 he wrote a twice-weekly journal *The Rambler*, often completed amid a roomful of people with the printer's boy waiting at the door, containing essays designed to 'inculcate wisdom or piety [while] refining our language to grammatical purity.' It was not a commercial success. In 1758 he began a weekly series of essays known as *The Idler* which were scarcely more popular.

Johnson's wife Elizabeth (Tetty), a widow 20 years his senior whom he married when he was just 25, died in March 1752. Though the marriage had not been without its problems – she was known for her extravagance and drunkenness and from the late 1740s had refused to have sex with him – he greatly respected her judgement, took pleasure in her skill at reading aloud, was probably never unfaithful and missed her sorely. A bear-like, shambling man, unable to control his rolling head and the near-constant convulsions that shook his shoulders, he became even more slovenly and unkempt and his house disordered and dirty following his wife's death. In 1759 his mother died (he covered the funeral expenses from the sale of the *Candide*-like story *The History of Rasselas, Prince of Abissinia*, which he wrote in a week) and he decided to move to cheaper lodgings in Staples Inn.

Johnson hated to be alone – according to his wife's friend Elizabeth Desmoulins: 'The great business of his life (he said) was to escape from himself; this disposition he considered to be the disease of his mind, which nothing cured but company.' An impoverished friend Anna Williams was staying with the Johnsons when Tetty died and he gave her a home. Two weeks later he took in the ten-year-old Francis Barber, a slave separated from his family and imported to England from Jamaica then given his 'freedom' on his master's death. Francis ran away from Johnson twice during this period – mainly because he didn't get on with Williams – but he eventually became Johnson's long-term manservant and principal heir. Dramatist Arthur Murphy described Johnson's busy home

Staircase, Dr Johnson's House

life: 'He took no exercise, rose about two, and then received the visits of his friends. Authors, long since forgotten, waited on him as their oracle...' When his guests had departed he would go out to a tavern and would usually be among the last to leave. After the move to Staples Inn he would invariably take tea with Williams – one of many female friends he sought out following Tetty's death – on his way home, sometimes arriving as late as five in the morning.

Visitors to Dr Johnson's House enter through a side door into the dining room. The house has several tucked-away cupboards

'His house was filled with a succession of visitors till four or five in the evening. During the whole of this time he presided at the tea-table.' Dramatist Arthur Murphy on Dr Johnson

designed for specific purposes such as the cupboard for candlesticks on the stairway and the cellarette cupboard with six smaller wood-panelled compartments for bottles behind the reception desk. The fortress-like front door – secured by a strong chain with a bar across the fanlight to prevent small children from climbing through to open the locks – demonstrates the lengths to which even people of Johnson's modest means had to go to protect their worldly goods. Johnson and his friends were sure to be armed with stout sticks when they wandered the dimly lit streets at night (Johnson's and Garrick's can usually be seen in the garret), hugging the safety of the walls as they walked.

The parlour is a pleasantly proportioned, squarish room with windows on two sides. Like the rest of the house it has exposed wide floorboards with Turkish carpets, original, delightfully simple door fittings and is sparsely furnished. The entire ground floor is painted a murky brown which experts believe resembles the original decor. The atmosphere is warm and welcoming – no doubt more so than in Johnson's day, when Barber professed himself 'disgusted in the house' following Tetty's death. Among the pictures are a portrait of Barber himself, a copy of a self-portrait by Joshua Reynolds, one of Johnson's closest friends, an unflattering but lively likeness of James Boswell, Johnson's biographer and travelling companion. Johnson would no doubt have approved the print of Chesterfield, which shows a small, bird-brained head perched on a body bloated by the flowing robes that alone confer status.

On the table in the centre of the room is a facsimile of the *Dictionary*, conceived as Britain's response to the national academy-authored dictionaries of Italy and France. Johnson employed six assistants to help him with his task and keep him company; he would read books he considered appropriate for quotation and mark the relevant words and passages, which his assistants would then copy and arrange in alphabetical order. Friends who loaned him books complained they were returned 'so defaced as to be scarce worth owning'. Though the *Dictionary* was criticised for its omissions, sometimes laboured definitions (net is defined as 'anything reticulated or decussated at equal distances with interstices between the intersections') and partiality (see patron, above), the scope of Johnson's achievement can be measured by comparison with Nathan Bailey's vastly inferior 1721 dictionary in the small display case. Virtuous ladies praised him for his omission of rude words ('What, my dears! Then you have been looking for them', was his response) but a quick check (visitors can rifle freely through a facsimile first edition) revealed plenty of words absent from a common spellchecker, including turd ('excrement') and whore ('a fornicatress; an adulteress; a strumpet'), appositely illustrated with a quote from Dryden: 'Tis a noble general's prudent part, / To cherish valour, and reward desert; / Let him be daub'd with lace, live high, and whore; / Sometimes be lousy, but be never poor.'

At the base of the stairs is a 1915 watercolour of Johnson by Max Beerbohm, one of the house's first governors. The first floor, painted pale green throughout, attains a wonderful flexibility by having the walls of the rooms to either side of the spacious landing made up of panels that can be closed to make three discreet spaces. The room above the parlour has over the mantelpiece an amateur-looking picture of John Wesley (see page 72) preaching in Old Cripplegate church, with Johnson, Boswell and Williams in the congregation. Other images include engravings of a mop-haired Garrick posed dramatically, sword aloft, as Richard III and of Johnson in his travelling clothes for his expeditions with Boswell. The drawing room opposite has a portrait of the near-blind Williams (by Reynolds' sister Frances) looking patient and expressionless. The manuscript collection (displayed in rotation) includes such items as accounts, IOUs and a letter in Johnson's surprisingly clear, unpretentious hand to the young Hester Thrale, one of his closest friends for the last two decades of his life.

The library on the second floor is dominated by a portrait of a regal-looking Elizabeth Carter, a blue-stocking poet and classical scholar who contributed two editions of *The Rambler*. Also in this room is a rare image of Johnson when young – a change from the two famous portraits of the bewigged scholar by Reynolds and

Opie. In the will room opposite is a recreation of a literary party at Reynolds' house that shows Boswell in the shadows, Johnson as if pausing to find words, Reynolds, Garrick, the elegant Edmund Burke, Oliver Goldsmith *et al* – members of the Literary Club Johnson founded in 1764 which is still in existence today.

The garret where the work on the *Dictionary* took place spans the width of the house. Johnson was said to have worked at an 'old crazy deal table', his body precariously balanced on an even older wooden armchair which eventually lost an arm and a leg. The room is dominated by *Johnson Doing Penance in the Market Place at Uttoxeter*, which depicts the bizarre incident when he stood bareheaded in the rain for an hour to atone for a 'sin' committed 50 years earlier, when, swollen with pride from his Oxford student life, he had refused to open his father's bookstall.

Dr Johnson's House is worth visiting for the charm of the building alone, a rare example of a town house in this area. Given its former inhabitant's strained circumstances and the fact that he lived before the Victorian mania for collecting took hold, few of his personal possessions have been preserved, so it's a case of soaking up the atmosphere rather than delighting in objects touched by his hands. Even so, there are times when less might have been more, as in the brick on the first-floor landing – presumably stolen from the Great Wall of China – presented to illustrate a quote from Boswell's biography in which Johnson expresses his desire to visit this marvel.

Mansion House

Walbrook, London EC4N 8LB
Tel: 020 7397 9331
Nearest transport: Mansion House LU
Open: guided tours Tues 14.00 from the Walbrook entrance (Sept to
   July), check as tours may be cancelled at short notice
Admission: £6/£4

North and west elevations, Mansion House

One of the grandest surviving Georgian town palaces in London,
Mansion House was built by George Dance the Elder in 1739–58
as a residence, workplace, court of justice and ceremonial stage
for the Lord Mayor during his year in office. Its vast scale and the
opulence of its interiors give new meaning to the phrase 'working
from home'.

The north elevation, facing the Bank road junction, has changed
little over the past quarter of a millennium. The monumental nine-
bay façade, clad in Portland stone with a rusticated ground floor, is
fronted by a grand temple portico approached by flights of steps on
each side. The elaborate carving on the vast pediment – an allegory

showing the City of London (wearing a turreted crown) trampling on envy and receiving the benefits of plenty brought by the River Thames – is by Robert Taylor, architect of Danson House (see page 319). Dance's initial plan had suites of rooms surrounding a central courtyard. A dancing gallery and hall for entertainments ran the full width of the building at front and back respectively, both topped by attics that rose above the rest of the structure and were nicknamed the Mayor's Nest and Noah's Ark. The kitchen and servants' quarters were on the ground floor, and the state rooms and private apartments on the first and second floors.

Some 50 years later, George Dance the Younger, mentor to Sir John Soane (see page 58) and designer of the John Wesley complex (see page 72), was brought in to roof over the courtyard, which had proved damp and impractical, and dismantle the attic above the hall, now in a dangerous condition. The other attic was demolished in 1842–43 and in 1846 a porch, which serves as today's underwhelming main entrance, was built on the west side. A fourth storey, now containing meeting rooms and offices, was added in the 1930s.

Visitors enter through the Walbrook hall, originally intended as a stable and then used as storage space, to the vaulted inner and waiting halls, originally servants' quarters. These relatively simple, low-ceilinged spaces are poor preparation for the huge scale and ceremonial grandeur of the rooms above. The monumental saloon or salon was once Dance's open courtyard, framed by colonnades at each end that still have their original elaborate plaster ceilings and rococo wall trophies. The octagonal lantern dates from the major restoration work in the early 1990s; the magnificent crystal chandeliers were introduced in 1875 after their predecessors, which were carried to and fro from the Guildhall as necessary, were broken in transit.

The long parlour to the west, with its deeply coffered ceiling based on the Banqueting House by Inigo Jones, is used for dinners and business meetings. Until the courtyard was roofed, the room would have been lit from both sides and the windows that once looked on to the open space are now mirrored to maximise the light. The imposing marble chimney piece at the south end is original.

Designed and still used for banquets and able to seat 350 people, the Egyptian hall runs the width of the rear of the building. The younger Dance replaced its attic with a lower-level coffered barrel vault, but as you gaze upwards beyond the towering double-height Corinthian columns and gilded frieze it's hard to imagine it could have been more lofty. Though the architecture appears decidedly Roman to us, Palladio had published an illustration of an 'Egyptian' hall based on a description by Vitruvius of a space with a clerestory and flat ceiling supported by two orders of columns, one above the other. The form and name became popular in the 18th century and was used by Dance the Elder in his design. The fussy gallery, which destroys some of the monumentality but provides useful storage space for catering equipment, was installed during the 1930–31 refurbishment, though it is thought to replicate the elder Dance's original. The seventeen larger-than-lifesize statues in gilded niches date from the mid 19th century.

On the opposite side of the salon from the long parlour are the interlinked north and south drawing rooms, created in their present form in the 19th century and more intimate in scale than the other state rooms. The walls of both are hung with paintings from the Harold Samuel collection of 17th-century Dutch art.

The Lord Mayor – who unlike the bankers he represents is elected and unpaid – is the ambassador for London's financial-services sector. (To date there has been only one female representative, Dame Mary Donaldson in 1983–84.) Most incumbents live at Mansion House, in private apartments on the second floor. On the first floor, sometimes visible through open doors from the salon, are offices for staff and the room where the Lord Mayor himself works and receives visitors. The 45 employees continue their business as tours progress, making Mansion House unique in this book in welcoming visitors into the everyday life within its walls.

Sir John Soane's Museum

13 Lincoln's Inn Fields, London WC2A 3BP

Tel: 020 7405 2107

www.soane.org

Nearest transport: Holborn LU

Open: Tues-Sat 10.00-17.00, first Tues of month 18.00-21.00, guided
tour Sat 11.00

Admission: free; guided tour £5

Wheelchair access: limited at present

Sir John Soane was one of England's most influential and original architects, his projects including such prestigious commissions as the remodelling of the Bank of England, the Houses of Parliament and Westminster Law Courts as well as a string of country houses for the aristocracy of his day. But we have his sons John and George and their time-honoured rebellion against an autocratic, pushy parent to thank for this museum, in a story that bears out the truism 'from rags to riches and back again in three generations'.

Born in 1753 to a provincial bricklayer, Soane came to London at the age of 15 to seek fame and fortune as an architect, beginning as a pupil in the office of George Dance the Younger, designer of the John Wesley complex (see page 72). He soon made his mark and in 1784 married Eliza Smith, the niece and ward of City builder George Wyatt, thereafter dreaming of founding an architectural dynasty along the lines of the Dances. His country house Pitzhanger Manor in Ealing (see page 247) was purchased in 1800 with the idea that it would be an ideal home for a budding architect, but John and George refused to play ball. Both married women who brought no wealth or social connections (George by his own admission out of spite towards his parents), and George, a grimly unsuccessful novelist and later intermittently acclaimed dramatist, began a lifelong feud with his father. Soane's bitterness and disappointment is given full rein in a paper he wrote in 1812, in which he imagines a future antiquarian speculating on the museum's origins and concluding that it was the work of a great architect who suffered for his originality, was abused by his kin and died of a broken heart.

Sir John Soane's Museum

The museum is a wonderful labyrinth studded with treasures. At the time of writing it was about to undergo a major improvement programme, 'Opening Up the Soane', due for completion in 2014, which would see the recreation of a suite of rooms on the first floor and improved access arrangements. The present building's history began in 1792, when Soane, using a legacy from his wife's uncle, bought and demolished the 17th-century house that stood at 12 Lincoln's Inn Fields and built a new family home, with his office on the site of the stables at the back. In 1808 he bought No. 13 and rebuilt the stables to form a single-storey extension linked to No. 12; in 1812 he rebuilt the front of No. 13 as a residence and moved into it, renting out No. 12; in 1824, nine years after his wife's death, he bought and rebuilt No. 14, the back as an extension of the former stable blocks, the front as a residence which he rented out. By this time the building was clearly intended as a display case for his growing collection of paintings, architectural drawings and antiquities, a museum that would surpass the nearby British Museum, for which the commission for rebuilding had annoyingly been given to one of his rivals, Robert Smirke Jr. In 1833, by Act of Parliament, Soane disinherited George (the sickly John had died in 1823) and bequeathed his house and its contents to the nation as a museum 'for the inspection of amateurs and students in painting, sculpture and architecture'. But he didn't quite renounce his dynastic aspirations in that he requested John's son to take on the role of curator and hoped that once a national institution to teach architecture had been established, the museum would revert to the family line and an architect would be born.

Soane made many enemies and was involved in many controversies in the course of his career. Described by a pupil as having 'an acute sensitiveness, and a fearful irritability, dangerous to himself if not to others; an embittered heart, prompting a cutting and sarcastic mind; uncompromising pride, neither respecting nor desiring respect; a contemptuous regard for the feelings of his dependants; and yet himself the very victim of irrational impulse; with no pity for the trials of his neighbour and nothing but frantic despair under his own', he was not easy to live with. His marriage to Eliza – a popular, intelligent and well-informed woman with a good head for business – was a love match and she acted willingly as his emotional support and confidante. But the marriage became increasingly strained in the decade before her death in 1815 as relations between Soane and his sons worsened and Soane was reported to be seen too frequently in the company of a certain Norah Brickenden. Following Eliza's death, Mrs Sally Conduitt took over as housekeeper at Lincoln's Inn Fields, replacing Soane's wife as hostess and to some extent as his companion until his death in 1837. His cruelty to George and to John's widow Maria continued unabated: in 1827 he refused George's pleas for money to buy medicines for his 16-year-old daughter, who subsequently died, and didn't even answer his letter asking that she might be buried in the family vault.

In 1792 Lincoln's Inn Fields was a good address, with easy access to shops and markets, galleries and theatres, the Bank of England and the Royal Academy. But Eliza found the unhealthy climate and lack of outdoor space for the children, aged seven and four when they moved, oppressive. Soane was often away overseeing jobs and she and the boys spent most of the holidays with his family in Chertsey or at Margate, where they socialised with the high society that frequented the then-fashionable Isle of Thanet. (Eliza moved with ease between her roles as hostess for her architect husband's wealthy clients and friend and supporter to the impoverished family of his bricklayer brother.) Though Soane had begun Lincoln's Inn Fields with the enthusiasm of a 40-year-old architect who at last had the chance to design a house that would express his own tastes and act as a showcase for his abilities, subsequently he was to bury himself in the project as a distraction from the many unhappy periods in his professional and family life.

The museum is immediately recognisable by its façade – a revolutionary departure for a Georgian terraced house – which boasts a three-storey loggia in Portland stone decorated with incised Greek key patterns and topped by statuary. It has been suggested that the elevation was a mocking response to the portico

'Some in Poems have raised fine architectural Edifices, but most rare have been those who have discovered... that they have built a Poem. All this you have accomplished.'
Isaac D'Israeli writing to Soane, 1836

of the Royal College of Surgeons at No. 41 – another commission for which Soane was gallingly overlooked, this time in favour of Dance, with whom Soane had fallen out seemingly irrevocably in 1805–06 after he had allegedly schemed to take the professorship of the Royal Academy from his mentor.

The library/dining room at the front of No. 13 is painted Pompeiian red – possibly to match a sample of plaster Soane lifted from the ruins during his formative two-year travelling scholarship to Italy from 1778. It's a colour that has since graced many an Islington drawing room. Despite being home to some 50 urns and vases, this worn and somewhat dusty space appears elegant and uncluttered thanks in part to the architect's trademark use of mirrors, particularly the one between the front windows, which when the blinds are up makes the wall look like a continuous plane of glass, and those above the bookcases on the west wall, which reflect the ceiling paintings. The furniture (invitingly curved leather chairs and a simple leather chaise of the type coveted by architects to this day) was made for Soane. A portrait by Thomas Lawrence shows the master looking benign and kindly.

The study and dressing room leading to the rear of the house are so small there's an Alice in Wonderland feel about them, as if it's you who has grown, not the scale that has shrunk. There's a pleasing continuity, though, in the beautiful polished wood used for the desk and the built-in washbasin, while the Roman fragments stretch up to the ceiling. These are the rooms of a sensualist. The view of the sculpture courtyard from the east window gives the impression of a ruined temple discovered among London's prosaic brick-faced backyards, an incongruous mix of worlds that perhaps reflects the way the heady idealism inspired by Soane's scholarship to Rome – a time he described as the happiest of his life – was crushed by the disappointing realities of London architectural practice.

Squeeze through a narrow corridor and suddenly the space changes from calm elegance to chaos. At this point turn right for the picture room at the rear of No. 14, where the stars of the show are undoubtedly paintings by Hogarth (see page 179) of *A Rake's*

Bust of Soane beneath the dome, Sir John Soane's House

Progress and *An Election*. Again the clash of cultures is visible in the contrast between the serene Rafael cartoon fragments above and these very English portraits of debauchery and corruption – from the sublime to the ridiculed. Ask a steward to pull out the panels and don't take no for an answer. The north wall swings open to reveal a series of Piranesi drawings of Paestum and the south wall is hinged twice, first for J M Gandy's watercolour perspectives of Soane's fantastic visions and the second time for a view into the yard and monk's parlour below.

The monk's parlour (also in No. 14) satirises the contemporary passion for all things gothic. Soane invented the character of Padre Giovanni – allegedly buried in the yard in a tomb which in fact holds the remains of Eliza's dog Fanny – and created a melancholic atmosphere for his rooms through restricted space, sombre colours and stained glass. You descend the narrow staircase and emerge from the corridor into the light of the crypt at the rear of No. 13, which houses a disturbing collection of prototype tombs, predominantly for women and children, designed by Soane's close friend John Flaxman. Wander and wonder. In the sepulchral chamber is the sarcophagus of Pharaoh Seti I, which Soane bought in 1824 for £2000 after the British Museum refused to cough up. He celebrated the acquisition with three evenings of parties with some 900 guests including the prime minister, Samuel Taylor Coleridge and his great friend J M W Turner. Yellowed by the London air, it is perhaps another candidate for forcible repatriation along with the Parthenon frieze. Above it in the double-height space float dismembered bodies like an episode of *Casualty* set in stone. The many sculptural fragments above the sarcophagus can best be appreciated from upstairs, where a colonnade leads to the dome beneath which a bust of poor old Soane faces forever a plaster cast of the Apollo Belvedere, considered the most perfect representation of male beauty. The cramped viewing conditions offer an unparalleled opportunity to examine what's under the figleaf as long as you look up at the right moment.

The new picture room on the ground floor of No. 12 was not designed by Soane. The breakfast parlour of No. 12 – decorated in a much lighter and more modest style with a *trompe l'oeil* trellis on the ceiling to give the impression of a garden room – has been restored to conform to a painting by Gandy of 1798 that shows Soane and his wife taking tea while their two young sons, dressed with stifling formality, do their best to amuse themselves. The breakfast parlour of No. 13 is almost a résumé of the mature Soane style – a beautifully proportioned, near-square room with a trademark pendentive dome inset with mirrors, a central lantern, a mirror reflecting the window with its view of sculptures and fragments, highly polished wood, books, and drawings of a Roman villa (a bizarre contrast with the portraits of Fanny the dog).

The oval staircase leads to the first-floor drawing room of No. 13, painted a fashionable if slightly grubby yellow and sparsely furnished, giving a feeling of spaciousness and light. Until 1834 the loggia was an open balcony. Typically for this patriarchal household, Eliza Soane is represented by a small pencil sketch by Flaxman while Soane and his two sons have full portraits. The elder son's obvious physical resemblance to his father must have made his inability to follow in Soane's footsteps all the more difficult to swallow.

Spencer House

27 St James's Place, London SW1A 1NR
Tel: 020 7499 8620
www.spencerhouse.co.uk
Nearest transport: Green Park LU
Open: Sun 10.30-17.45, 1-hour guided tours only (except Jan & Aug)
Admission: £9/£7/under-10s not admitted
Wheelchair access: limited

West façade, Spencer House

The part of Spencer House open to the public is a glittering recreation of the state rooms of one of London's most ambitious private palaces. Built in 1756 by the 1st Earl Spencer, the house was stripped during World War II of most of its chimney pieces, doors, skirting mouldings and architraves, which were installed in the family seat at Althorp. The building was restored in the late 1980s by its current occupants, RIT Capital Partners plc, under the chairmanship of Lord Rothschild. Many of the 18th-century works of art have been returned on loan while others have been copied from the originals.

The 1st Earl inherited his immense wealth while he was still a minor. At a ball to mark his coming of age in 1755 he secretly married 18-year-old Georgiana Poyntz and almost immediately set about building a London house to display his art collection, host lavish entertainments and as a 'paean to connubial bliss'. (The diamond buckles on his honeymoon shoes were valued at £30,000.) He chose as his architect William Kent's pupil John Vardy, who designed the external elevations and ground-floor rooms using motifs from imperial Rome. In 1758 Vardy was replaced by James 'Athenian' Stuart, possibly at the suggestion of Colonel George Gray, who like Spencer was a member of the Society of Dilettanti, a group of aristocrats dedicated to promoting 'Roman Taste and Greek Gusto'. Stuart had been sponsored by the society to compile the first accurate survey of the antiquities of Athens and thus the *piano nobile* at Spencer House became one of the first informed applications of Greek ornament to an English domestic interior. Subsequent alterations to the ground floor were made for the 2nd Earl by Henry Holland, the fashionable architect of the Prince Regent's palace, Carlton House. The 2nd Earl's sister Georgiana was the wife of the 5th Duke of Devonshire, owner of Chiswick House (see page 162).

The Palladian elevation of Spencer House to St James's Park is stunning: a rusticated ground floor topped by a plain upper storey of seven bays separated by Doric columns supporting a five-bay pediment crowned by statues of Bacchus, Flora and Ceres:

Palm room, Spencer House

'the embodiment of hospitality, supported by those of beauty and fertility'. Next door, presumably on an infill site created by bomb damage that highlights Spencer House's lucky escape, towers a robustly brutalist block of flats by Denys Lasdun.

The tour begins in a room intended by the 1st Earl as a family dining room. Relatively modest in scale, it is entered through double doors into an apse with a gilded coffered ceiling inspired by the Temple of Venus in Rome. The apse was originally designed to hold the sideboard, with double doors on either side; Holland transformed it into the entrance to the circuit of grand ground-floor rooms and installed the mahogany doors copied here. His alterations are also to the fore in the adjacent library – another modestly elegant room, with a delicate acanthus-leaf frieze – designed to house the 2nd Earl's book collection.

The main dining room – the central space in the west front overlooking the park – is a magnificent contrast in style and scale. In Vardy's original design the walls were embellished with 12 pilasters and niches but Holland replaced these with the grand gesture of a central space screened at each end by massive scagliola Ionic columns. Vardy's adjacent palm room surpasses even this. A rectangular space opens into a trefoil-plan alcove with a statue of the Medici Venus at its centre. The coffered central dome and the half-domes of the apses are exquisitely gilded but the main impact derives from a series of gilded columns in the form of palm trees – symbol of marital fertility – with fronds spilling out to fill the upper walls.

The change of mood on the first floor is signalled by the way Vardy's unadorned lower stairwell gives way to Stuart's upper storey of Ionic pilasters linked by garlands. The music room is relatively restrained, the geometric simplicity of its architraves and chimney piece a contrast to the swagger of the ground floor. Above the library is Lady Spencer's room. The panels in the pink, blue and gold ceiling were intended to receive paintings, but Stuart, a painter by training who was said to prefer 'an easy and convivial life to the exacting routine of a busy architects' office', failed to get round to them in the eight years he spent on the project.

The great room above the dining room was used for receptions, balls and as a picture gallery. The four medallions in the cove of the ceiling – supported by putti and the Spencer griffins – represent Bacchus, Apollo, Venus and the Three Graces, symbolising the pleasures for which the space was intended. Here all restraint disappears and the elaborate green and gold coffered ceiling and intricately carved door surrounds and chimney piece make for an uninhibited display of wealth, all the more dazzling because of the newness of the restoration. It is the painted room beyond, however, that is Stuart's masterpiece. Almost every surface is decorated with urns, nymphs, wreaths, flowers and scenes on the themes of love and marriage including a Venus whose features are believed to have been modelled on Lady Spencer's.

The Spencer family lived for at least part of the year at Spencer House until the end of the 19th century, when it was let to tenants by the 5th Earl as an economy measure. The 6th Earl moved back in 1910 and in 1926 the 7th Earl had the house redecorated before leasing it to the Ladies' Army and Navy Club.

John Wesley's House

49 City Road, London EC1Y 1AU

Tel: 020 7253 2262

www.wesleyschapel.org.uk

Nearest transport: Moorgate LU/Rail or Old Street LU/Rail

Open: Mon-Sat 10.00-16.00, Sun 12.30-13.45 (closed Thurs 12.45-13.30 for services)

Admission: free

Wheelchair access: ground floor only

Founder of Methodism John Wesley (1703–91) lived in this house for only the last 12 years of his long life – or more accurately, the last 12 winters, since even in his late 80s he spent some ten months each year on the road, having clocked up about 250,000 miles and 40,000 sermons in the course of his lifetime.

Wesley's first London base was a ruinous cannon foundry 200 metres down the road; after 40 years, the lease was running out and the Corporation of London was keen to acquire the land for development. The site of the proposed new complex, designed by George Dance the Younger, the mentor of John Soane (see page 58), was opposite an existing nonconformist burial ground but was otherwise surrounded by fields. It was to consist of a terrace of five dwellings on the roadside with a courtyard and chapel behind. Wesley found Dance's designs for the dwellings too elaborate and asked him to scale down the ornamentation and materials to the 'perfectly neat but not fine' aesthetic of the chapel. In the end, only one house and the chapel were built, between 1778 and 1779, by local preacher and builder Samuel Tooth.

The hushed atmosphere of the house today is misleading: in Wesley's time it accommodated several preachers, sometimes with families in tow, a housekeeper (sometimes the wife of one of the preachers), a manservant and a live-out maid and cook (Wesley's wife had left him in 1751). After his death, it became the residence of the superintendent ministers of the chapel and their families. Later residents had to endure a stream of pilgrims, many of whom asked to see Wesley's bones, so in 1891, when funds became

John Wesley's House

available, a new superintendent minister's house was built on the opposite side of the courtyard and in 1898 the first floor of Wesley's house was opened as a museum. In 1934 artist Frank Salisbury and minister George McNeal instigated an ambitious renovation plan and Salisbury donated the portrait to be found at present in the front room of the basement. A great deal of structural work was undertaken over the next half century and after an extended period of closure the house was reopened in 1981 by Margaret Thatcher – to the disgust of many Methodists, who reasonably enough saw her policies as an attack on the working-class congregations from which the movement had since Wesley's time drawn its support. The museum's first professionally trained curator was engaged in 1991 and after much research the house was restored to the condition it is in today.

The cobbled courtyard planned by Dance is today dominated by a statue of Wesley. The neoclassical chapel at the rear has a museum of Methodism in the basement; Daniel Defoe, William Blake and John Bunyan are buried in the cemetery opposite. Visitors enter the simple four-storey house, built of brick with stucco and stone dressings, via the trade entrance into the basement kitchen with its huge fireplace and dresser. The front room contains displays of Wesley's personal possessions including a diminutive gown (he was only 5 feet 4 inches tall) and shoes (size 41/2), a sturdy umbrella, spurs, a nightcap, a travelling writing case and communion set and a pair of spectacles.

The ground floor has a dining room at the front, its table laid with a simple meal of bread and cheese. The stone-white walls are believed from records and paint scrapings to be near the colour of the original. Though visitors, particularly Americans, are impressed by the austerity and 'poverty' Wesley endured, the Oxford-educated scholar in fact enjoyed an income and standard of living in line with his middle-class contemporaries. The smaller back parlour was where the preachers would have spent the evenings reading and chatting – as in a latter-day episode of *Father Ted*. The unusual semi-glazed built-in cupboards are thought to have been requested by Wesley.

The first floor was occupied by Wesley when he was in residence. The drawing room/study at the front has a wonderful glazed bookcase full of his own books and a Queen Anne bureau with secret drawers in which he is said to have kept letters hidden from his wife. Wesley used the 'electrical machine' in the corner to administer a primitive form of electric-shock therapy to patients seeking treatment for depression from the free dispensary at the foundry. The 1788 portrait by William Hamilton (possibly posed for in this room) shows a man with one hand leafing through a Bible, but whose intent gaze follows the direction of the other hand in reaching out to the world. The bedroom where Wesley died and in particular the prayer room leading off it – a small space added by Wesley himself and simply furnished with a chair, a kneeler and a low bureau on top of which are a candle and a Bible – are surprisingly moving. Wesley would rise at 4am and spend several hours here thinking and praying, hence the room's nickname 'the powerhouse of Methodism'. On the second floor are one of the rooms in which visiting preachers were accommodated and a room commemorating the work ongoing in the house following Wesley's death.

John Wesley's House is a shrine of a quite different order from the houses of, say, Dickens or Dr Johnson. Though some might ask whether the cost involved in creating and maintaining a bricks-and-mortar memorial to a man who preached largely out of doors, disdained material comforts and introduced what amounted to a social-welfare programme is appropriate, lesser mortals seem to need graven images, and the many thousands of believers who flock to Wesley's altar no doubt derive a thrill and some comfort. And despite being an atheist, I found the pervasive sense here of lives lived to a transcendent purpose surprisingly alluring.

Fenton House, see page 90

North

North

2 Willow Road

2 Willow Road, London NW3 1TH

Tel: 01494 755570 (Infoline)

www.nationaltrust.org.uk/2willowroad

Nearest transport: Belsize Park LU

Open: Thurs-Sun tours at 12.00, 13.00 & 14.00 and non-guided visits
15.00-17.00 (March to Oct); Sat & Sun only (Nov), times
as above

Admission: £5.50/£2.75/family ticket £13.75/joint ticket with
Fenton House (see page 99) £8

Wheelchair access: please contact property for information

Modernist architect Ernö Goldfinger's first house, completed just
before war broke out in 1939, became his home for almost 50 years
until his death in 1987. The keys to its success are an exacting
attention to detail, with each element designed for its specific

2 Willow Road

location and function, and the potential for flexibility – what once was the nursery became rooms for Goldfinger's ageing mother; the servants' quarters were converted into a flat in which both his sons and their families lived at different times.

The intimacy and elegance of Goldfinger's house and its purpose-designed furniture may come as a surprise to those who know only the architect's much maligned 'concrete jungles': the Ministry of Health's Alexander Fleming House (1962) at Elephant & Castle; the housing schemes focused on Balfron Tower (1965) on the northern approach to the Blackwall Tunnel and Trellick Tower (1973) in north Kensington. However, though these developments were held up in the 1980s as prime examples of modernist arrogance and contempt for human values, Goldfinger (whose personal arrogance his friends readily acknowledged) was to some extent rehabilitated in the 1990s as the sculptural drama, constructivist heroics and above all fine detailing of his schemes were appreciated. Apartments in Trellick Tower – made uninhabitable because of social not architectural factors – now command high prices.

Born in Budapest in 1902, Goldfinger moved to Paris in 1920, where he participated in a near-revolution at the conservative Ecole des Beaux-Arts by asking Auguste Perret, one of the first architects to explore the artistic possibilities of reinforced concrete, to set up a studio. He and his wife Ursula Blackwell, a painter who studied with Le Corbusier's one-time collaborator Amédée Ozenfant, left for London in 1934, the year after their marriage and the birth of their first child Peter (Liz was born three years later and Michael in 1945). The family moved into Berthold Lubetkin's utopian Highpoint 1 in Highgate and Goldfinger set up a studio in Bedford Square. Business was far from brisk – his only executed building was a house in Essex for the painter Humphrey Waterfield, though he also designed a showroom and some toys for the educational toy firm Paul and Marjorie Abbatt and his only furniture to reach the production line, some storage cabinets for Easiwork. 2 Willow Road was financed by his wife's capital from food manufacturer Crosse & Blackwell.

In Paris Ernö and Ursula had numbered among their friends surrealists Max Ernst and Roland Penrose (whose collages hang in the dining room), so it's hardly surprising they were attracted to Hampstead, which in the 1930s had replaced Chelsea as the London centre for left-leaning artists and writers. (Goldfinger was a signatory of the English surrealist group's call for the government to lift the arms embargo to republican Spain and in 1942 held a fund-raising 'Aid to Russia' exhibition at Willow Road that included work by Hampstead artists Henry Moore, Barbara Hepworth and Ben Nicholson.) The first design for the Willow Road site, a four-storey block of flats and studios, was rejected by the LCC, and a campaign to outlaw the design-as-built was initiated by Tory MP Henry Brooke. But the target was a foolish one – Goldfinger's modest row of three brick-clad houses is far less radical than such local schemes as Wells Coates' Isokon flats (1934). As the architect himself pointed out, the plan was 'a modern adaptation of the eighteenth-century style... far more in keeping with the beautiful Downshire Hill houses round the corner than their [florid Victorian] neighbours in Willow Road... As for the objection that the houses are rectangular, only the Esquimeaux and Zulus build anything but rectangular houses.'

Though Goldfinger supported the modernist call for cities characterised by 'espace, soleil, verdure' – apparent in Willow Road's plentiful windows and Heath-side location – he was no fan of Le Corbusier's nostalgic Mediterranean vernacular of smooth white walls, which he dismissed as 'kasbah' architecture. Indeed, he was a great admirer of London's Georgian squares and terraces, and Willow Road, with its brick cladding, stone coping and classical internal arrangement of a first-floor *piano nobile*, can be seen as a modern reinterpretation of the traditional street. Like Perret, he believed in the open expression of materials and structure, so here the reinforced-concrete floor slabs and supporting columns are clearly visible on the outside. The concrete frame, which relies on the cylindrical well of the internal spiral staircase for extra strength, was calculated by Ove Arup, at the time working for J L Kier. (Though

'You know what importance I attach to building my first house, and one specially for you… We must think seriously how to conceive this house so that it does not become a weight which one drags after one for years or a chain that attaches us to one place.'
Ernő Goldfinger to Ursula Blackwell, 1931

at the back of the house two concrete columns run from basement to second floor, at the front the top storey is supported on thin steel stanchions behind the ribbon window.) The family occupied the central house (No. 2); No. 3 was presold to civil servant Stephen Wilson and furnished to his specifications; No. 1 was rented to classical scholar R P Winnington-Ingram. The contract price for No. 2 was £2751 6s 1d at a time when a suburban semi cost just £800.

Unusually for the time, Willow Road had two built-in garages, one with an inspection pit, and the guided tour begins with a well-presented video screened in one of them, now hung with photographs of the architect's work. Snapshots of Ernö at a student fancy-dress party show him to have been startlingly handsome; later cine film captures a tall, dark-haired, imposing figure with the confident bearing and glamour of a filmstar. Peter and Liz talk of a childhood filled with parties and dinners; associates and friends describe a demanding nature tempered by extreme generosity, a love of argument and a fiery temper. Rumour has it that Ian Fleming, who played golf with Ursula's cousin, borrowed the Goldfinger name for his arch-villain.

The small entrance hall, like the rest of the house, is hung with pictures, many of which are inscribed with personal dedications. The door at the rear led to bedrooms for the chauffeur, cook and au pair, the kitchen and the laundry (now the custodian's flat). The walls on either side of the front door are made up of textured glass panels set into a grid of wooden shelves filled with souvenirs – as well as art, Ernö and Ursula collected knick-knacks and the kind of anthropological artefacts Ozenfant and his contemporaries used as inspiration. Typical of Goldfinger's capacity to rethink every detail from scratch and produce an elegant and economical solution is the letterbox: a clear glass flap (completely unobtrusive, through which you can see when mail has arrived) on the inside of one of the compartments hinged at the top for opening.

2 Willow Road has a footprint of 1000 square feet (93 square metres), though the fact that many of the rooms are interconnected, avoiding the need for corridors, and the only space given over purely

to circulation is the compact spiral stair, makes it seem larger. You climb the cantilevered reinforced-concrete cork-covered treads, holding the rope balustrade, to the semi-open-plan first floor. At the front, separated when required by folding floor-to-ceiling partitions, are the dining room and studio; at the rear (where the floor level is lower – hence the very low ceilings of the entrance hall, cloakroom and flanking garages) are the living room (separated by folding partitions from the studio) and study. For parties – as at Dr Johnson's House (see page 46) – the whole area could be opened up. The use of colour – a cubist palette of mustard yellow, terracotta, poster red and dirty blues that get lighter as you progress through the house – is startling: the doors off the staircase are bright red gloss; the rear wall of the dining room, on which hangs a black-and-white Bridget Riley, is terracotta.

The dining-room furniture, created by Goldfinger for the Highpoint flat, is another reinterpretation of traditional forms. There's a sideboard whose doors slide back at the touch of a finger to reveal drawers individually crafted for cutlery and other implements; a large table with a lino-clad plywood top set on a heavy cast-iron industrial base; and tubular-steel and plywood chairs with reclining backs. The only discordant note is the pair of elaborate silver candlesticks – a present from Ernö's mother.

Originally the kitchen was downstairs and food was delivered by dumb waiter to an adjacent servery. Later this was transformed into a tiny fitted kitchen, where Peter remembers his mother 'rustling up endless meals'. It's a windowless galley shoehorned into the leftover space between the stairwell and party wall into which, by dint of careful planning, are squeezed a washing machine, oven, microwave, coffee-maker, etc. Ernö and Ursula's children gave the house and its contents virtually intact to the National Trust in lieu of paying inheritance tax, and here – as you gaze at the Ambrosia creamed rice, Cafe Hag and ketchup that still fill the shelves – the sense of the place as a time capsule is strongest.

There's little evidence in the house that Ursula used her studio much for its original purpose, and it seems that Ernö took it over completely following his retirement in 1977. Alongside his desk with its pivoting drawers crammed with a mess of rubber bands, light bulbs, a hole punch, and so on, are personal files with such headings as 'Obituaries', 'Questions political and social' and 'Interviews'. Built-in cupboards contain household tools, cameras and artist's materials; beneath the raised platform leading to the living room – lit to serve as a dais for models – are enviably large plan-chest drawers. A strikingly simple Ozenfant pencil drawing of a mother and child is inscribed 'Pour mon ancienne élève Ursula Goldfinger'.

The oak-ply-lined living room, with a full-length balcony overlooking the garden, is a comfortable, homely space furnished with an assortment of chairs, some of which have needlepoint covers made by Ernö's mother to Ursula's designs. The fireplace is set into a convex-curved wall – to throw out the heat – with bookshelves ingeniously fitted into the space between the front of the curve and the party wall behind. Among the collection of personal artefacts are a pebble painted by Max Ernst, which inspired Goldfinger to paint some of his own; an intricate mechanistic pen-and-ink drawing of a head dedicated to the couple by Eduardo Paolozzi, with whom Goldfinger worked on the iconic 1956 'This Is Tomorrow' exhibition; and a striking photograph of Ursula – as tall and handsome as her husband – by Man Ray. Around the sofa is a wooden frame holding books at the bottom and demarcating a gallery space for a changing display. Alongside a Duchamp, a Riley and a Jean Arp hangs a picture of a car drawn by one of the couple's grandsons. The adjoining small study contains Ernö's library.

The second floor has a top-lit landing and two bathrooms in the middle sandwiched by the nursery at the front and the main and spare bedrooms at the rear. The austere main bedroom (above the dining room) is almost filled by a low bed (Ernö believed that higher civilisations, such as the Japanese, slept nearer the ground) flanked by simple wall-mounted metal anglepoises. The party wall with the spare room is made up of a row of fitted cupboards (incidentally providing a sound barrier) with different sections accessed from one side or the other or from the landing (the linen cupboard).

The en-suite bathroom is the site of yet more masterful rethinking: a built-in dressing-table/cupboard with mirrors at the back and on the doors, glass shelves and an array of family snaps tacked on the walls; a washbasin bracketed to hang clear of the wall for easy cleaning; a bidet (the height of European sophistication); a separate toilet lit with its own skylight. Both the tip-up bed and the washbasin in the spare room can be concealed in cupboards when not in use. Among the furnishings here is a kitsch ashtray in the form of a pair of goggles.

The nursery could be subdivided into three – originally the two ends were for the children, with the nanny (suffering an acute lack of privacy) in the middle. A servery similar to the one on the first floor allowed meals to be eaten upstairs. The end walls were left in natural grey plaster so the children could draw on them (Peter remembers carving a hammer and sickle); their heights are marked in pencil on the partitions. Alongside the modernist, unpainted-plywood dolls' house Goldfinger designed for Liz are examples of the educational toys he produced for Abbatt.

The extent of the journey Goldfinger travelled to enable him to conceive of Willow Road is poignantly illustrated by a photograph of the nursery when it was occupied by his mother Regine in the 1960s – claustrophobically stuffed with heavy, ornate Austro-Hungarian furniture and portraits. But the evolution of the house from the 1930s to the 1980s tells a story of changing social pressures and aspirations too. It is inconceivable today that a young married couple, even with a considerable fortune, would contemplate filling a house this size with three live-in servants, expect to have their meals cooked and sent upstairs on a tray and to be driven wherever they wished at a moment's notice. By the end of the couple's life, however, the cooking was done by Ursula and the space had been juggled to accommodate four generations. That it did so successfully is a tribute to the capacity of Ernö – still popularly reviled for placing ideals above human understanding at his death – to 'think seriously', inventively and humanely about a family's needs.

Avenue House

East End Road, London N3 3QE
Tel: 020 8346 7812
www.avenuehouse.org.uk
Nearest transport: Finchley Central LU
Open: Tues-Thurs 14.00-16.00
Admission: free

This eclectic house – its façade an ugly asymmetrical stuccoed mishmash, its rear a sprawling if picturesque mix of rustic Italianate tower, romanesque arches and gothic windows – was built in 1859 by the Reverend Edward Philip Cooper. He inherited the land from the Allen family, owners of the Bibbesworth estate, whose manor house was what is now the Sternberg Centre on East End Road.

In 1874 the house was bought by Henry Charles 'Inky' Stephens, son of Dr Henry Stephens, inventor of the famous ink. 'Inky' Stephens continued to develop the family business as well as becoming MP for Finchley in 1887. He bequeathed his house to his constituents

Avenue House

on his death in 1918 and it was opened to the public some ten years later. In 1989 it suffered a major fire and since its restoration in 1993 it has operated as a venue for meetings and functions.

The only part of the house officially open to the public is a small room housing the Stephens collection. However, other areas can occasionally be glimpsed if they are not in use. Stephens extended the house in 1884, adding the drawing room at the east end. Presided over by a portrait of the man and his horse, this space is dominated by its fussy windows and kitsch mock-medieval ceiling. The elegance of the original drawing room (the salon) is still suggested by the fine proportions, semi-circular bay to the garden, original panelling and fireplace. An idea of Stephens' laboratory, above the drawing room, can be gained from photographs within the collection showing an arts-and-crafts wood-panelled room with a built-in inglenook. And don't miss his most successful addition, a charming stableblock to the east of the house with a fairytale French gothic tower topped by a dovecote.

Bruce Castle

Lordship Lane, London N17 8NU

Tel: 020 8808 8772

www.haringey.gov.uk/leisure/brucecastlemuseum.htm

Nearest transport: Bruce Grove Rail, Wood Green LU or Seven Sisters
   LU then 123 or 243 bus

Open: Wed-Sun & summer bank hols 13.00-17.00

Admission: free

Bruce Castle takes its name from the family of spider-watcher Robert de Bruce, who owned the land on which it sits before it was confiscated when he joined the war for Scottish independence at the end of the 13th century. The house as it stands today – a seven-bay, three-storey red-brick manor with two full-height polygonal end bays and an elaborate central porch – comes across as a feeble, small-scale imitation of Charlton House (see page 291) that eloquently makes the point that when it comes to architecture, 'Try, try, and try again' may not be the best strategy. Inside, the demands of generations of schoolboys and a century of public ownership have destroyed any grandeur the interior may once have possessed.

We know that in 1514 the site was occupied by a simple courtyard house owned by William Compton, groom of the bedchamber to Henry VIII; a tower in the grounds, possibly built as a falconry, dates from about this time as does some of the brickwork in the west bay. The house was radically remodelled between 1682 and 1684 by Henry Hare, the 2nd Lord Coleraine, following his second marriage to the rich and powerful Lady Sarah, Duchess of Somerset (his first wife is said to have been so ill-treated that she killed herself and her son by jumping off the balcony). One room deep and nine bays long, with wings at each end extending to the rear, Henry's new house had the E-plan south front we see today. His grandson – another Henry – extended his home to the east at the beginning of the 18th century and added a range of rooms along the north front to give the present heavily pedimented rear façade, its ground-floor windows set within arches, perhaps intended as a loggia. James Townsend, an MP married to the second Henry's illegitimate daughter Henrietta Rose,

Tudor tower, Bruce Castle Park

remodelled the uppermost storey to its current profile, replacing the pitched roof and gables of the south front with a flat roof and parapet to give the house a more Georgian look.

Subsequent owners have included former MP John Eardley Wilmot, who helped refugees fleeing first the American War of Independence and then the French Revolution, and the Hill family, who extended the house to the rear in 1860 to accommodate a progressive boys' boarding school run without corporal punishment according to a system of self-discipline developed by co-founder Rowland Hill. Hill left teaching in 1833 and was subsequently the originator of the penny postage system. Soon after the school's closure in 1891 the house was sold to the council; it opened as a museum in 1906.

The large entrance hall ran the full depth of the first Henry's house; the room beyond, which has information about the development of the building, was the centrepiece of the north range added by his grandson. The two main rooms that make up the east wing are now an inventor centre and local-history exhibition space; the museum's historic postal collection is displayed in a small anteroom by the main staircase; the polygonal east bay houses 1930s office equipment. The bay and room to the west are a kitchen and café. A large, impressive room above the entrance hall is a further exhibition space.

More things to see & do

The Green Flag Award-winning Bruce Castle Park covers 8 hectares and dates back to the early 11th century. A large 400-year-old oak stands close to its centre and a tree trail identifies different species and points out other trees thought to be over 200 years old. Details are available from the museum.

Burgh House

New End Square, London NW3 1LR
Tel: 020 7431 0144
www.burghhouse.org.uk
Nearest transport: Hampstead LU
Open: Wed-Fri & Sun 12.00-17.00, Sat Art Gallery and café only
Admission: free
Wheelchair access: ground floor only

Burgh House

The front half of this imposing five-bay, three-storey red-brick Queen Anne house, nestled among council flats in a quiet Hampstead lane, was built in 1703, probably by wealthy Quakers Henry and Hannah Sewell. The spa at Hampstead Wells, whose foul-tasting, iron-impregnated waters were bottled at the nearby Flask Tavern, was beginning to be developed and the spa's physician Dr William Gibbons lived at Burgh House in the 1720s. He doubled the size of the property by extending it to the rear.

Subsequent occupiers include Whig politician Nathaniel Booth (in residence 1743–59), upholsterer Israel Lewis (1776–1822), who was a friend of Keats (see page 108), and the Reverend Allatson Burgh (1822–56), from whom the house takes its name. Burgh – author of *Anecdotes of Music, Historical and Biographical* and like neighbour James Fenton (see page 99) actively involved in the successful 1829 petitioning of parliament for the withdrawal of a private bill that would have permitted the lord of the manor to develop Hampstead Heath – let the house fall into a state of extreme disrepair. Following his death, it was used by the Royal East Middlesex Militia as a headquarters and officers' mess. In 1884 it was rented out to Thomas Grylls, an acclaimed stained-glass designer responsible for the rose window in the poets' corner at Westminster Abbey.

In the 20th century the house was lived in by art expert George Williamson, Captain Constantine Benson, a director of Lloyds bank who purchased it at auction for £4750 in 1925 (less than double the price paid by Burgh a century earlier), and retired diplomat George Bambridge, husband of Rudyard Kipling's daughter Elsie. It was bought by the council in 1946 and used as a community centre; following a public campaign in the mid 1970s to prevent it from being turned into commercial premises, it was restored and leased to the Burgh House Trust, which runs it as a community arts centre and local-history museum.

Today the front door leads directly into a reception area that occupies the two right-hand bays of the Sewells' house; originally this would have been a narrow hallway and a self-contained, squarish room. Lined with 18th-century panelling probably from nearby Weatherall House, the music room to the left – which occupies the two bays on the other side of the door plus a three-bay single-storey extension – was created in the 1920s. To the rear (in the Gibbons addition) are a library, decorated in Georgian style, and an art gallery.

The pleasingly simple staircase with its original barley-twist balusters leads to panelled bedrooms containing displays about the history of Hampstead. Alongside the expected stories of Constable and Keats is a corner devoted to the Isokon flats in Lawn Road designed in 1934 by Wells Coates, with a bar created by Walter Gropius and Marcel Breuer that became a popular meeting place for the modernist artists and architects who gravitated to Hampstead in the 1930s, many of them German refugees (see 2 Willow Road, page 79). This too was a worthy focus of a public campaign to preserve an equally significant part of the area's history. It was refurbished at the start of the 21st century to include a number of affordable flats for local key workers; unfortunately there is no public access.

More things to see & do

Hampstead Museum was founded in 1979 by Christopher and Diana Wade and the collection now holds more than 3000 objects relating to Hampstead art and life. A permanent display on the first floor traces the area's history from prehistoric times to the modern day and there is also a schedule of changing exhibitions in the Christopher Wade Room on the first floor and the Peggy Jay Gallery on the ground floor, as well as a programme of events and talks. Museum entrance and many events are free. See *www. burghhouse.org.uk.*

The pleasant Buttery Café serves meals and snacks and has both indoor and courtyard seating.

Rear façade, Church Farmhouse Museum

Church Farmhouse Museum

Greyhound Hill, London NW4 4JR

Tel: 020 8359 3942

www.churchfarmhousemuseum.co.uk

Nearest transport: Hendon Central LU

Open: Mon-Thurs 10.00-13.00, 14.00-17.00; Sat 10.00-13.00,
    14.00-17.30; Sun 14.00-17.30

Admission: free

Built in c. 1660, only 15 years before Christopher Wren's Flamsteed House (see page 302), this charming red-brick farmhouse gives an insight into the lives of the rural middle-classes away from the elegance of the court and its acolytes. The house was the tenanted property of the Powis family – lords of Hendon manor – until 1756, when actor David Garrick bought the manor and the farm was sold to a Mr Bingley. Some ten years later ownership passed to Theodore Henry Broadhead, whose descendants kept the farmhouse until 1918, mostly letting it to tenants. The freehold was then sold to George Dunlop, whose father Andrew had been the lessee from 1870. The property was acquired by Hendon Council in 1944 and from 1951–55 it was restored as a local-history museum. The space is now divided between reconstructions of 19th-century life and galleries for temporary exhibitions.

Though surrounded today by leafy Hendon suburbia, Church Farm boasted more than 80 hectares of land at the peak of its productivity, mostly devoted to making hay for the London market in fields fertilised symbiotically by dung swept up from the city's streets. Hendon produce was in high demand – according to John Middleton's *View of the Agriculture of Middlesex* (1798), the area turned out the best hay in the county – but by the mid 19th century suburban housing was beginning to replace the fields (Hendon station was built in 1868 and the Underground reached Golders Green in 1907). Within half a century, factory work had superseded a millennium of agriculture as the main form of employment.

The original three-bay house, two-and-a-half storeys high and one room deep, had two rooms on each floor with a central chimney stack in the large room to the east. The attic was used to store grain and the cellar as a dairy. The original front door was probably at the back, facing the farmyard. Most of the two-room rear extension was added before 1754; the staircase was installed in the late 18th or early 19th century; the front porch and west bay date from the late 19th century. The 35-centimetre-thick walls are of Flemish-bond red brick and most of the roof tiles are original. The most striking architectural feature is the dramatic chimney stack with its six grouped shafts.

Though the upper floor is used as an exhibition space, the integrity of the rooms has been retained so it's not difficult to imagine these as light-filled (if cramped) bedrooms. The sagging wooden beams and bowed floors (with notices warning that no more than 15 people should occupy the room at any one time) add atmosphere. The fireplaces are Victorian. The ground-floor extension has a display of 19th-century laundry equipment including washing dollies, mangles and flat irons. The kitchen is set up as it might have been in the 1820s, its huge walk-in fireplace sporting an array of implements that resemble medieval instruments of torture. The small central oak-panelled dining room is furnished with an oval table and Windsor chairs dating from the 1850s.

Hendon Council bought Church Farm in 1944 intending to demolish it for redevelopment. More enlightened views prevailed, however, and today's affluent suburbanites have been offered a glimpse into the village life of an alien past. Unfortunately at the time of writing, local-authority funding was once more under threat, so the museum's future again looks uncertain.

Fenton House

Windmill Hill, London NW3 6RT

Tel: 01494 755563/020 7435 3471

www.nationaltrust.org.uk/fentonhouse

Nearest transport: Hampstead ⊔⊔

Open: Wed-Fri 14.00-17.00; Sat, Sun & bank hol Mondays
    11.00-17.00 (April to Oct)

Admission: £6/£3/family ticket £15; joint ticket with 2 Willow Road
    (see page 79) £8

Wheelchair access: ground floor only

A two-storey, red-brick house, Fenton was built in about 1686, possibly by the master-builder father of its first owner William Eades. Subsequent inhabitants were typical of Hampstead's professional middle-classes: lawyer Sir George Hutchins (in residence 1689–1706); Quaker linen and iron-ore merchant Joshua Gee (1706–30), one of the original mortgagees of Pennsylvania and part of a consortium of six British businessmen who raised £6000 to get William Penn out of debt, using the state of Pennsylvania as security; admiral's widow Mary Martin (1857–65), who added a clock to the east front, giving the house for a time the name of Clock House; and tobacco importer John Hyndman (1765–86). In 1793 the house was bought by merchant Philip Fenton, who with his nephew James had made a career in Riga exporting goods to England; James, his wife Margaret and their seven children lived at Fenton until James' death in 1834. Later occupants include merchant Richard Hart Davies (1834–42), lawyer Thomas Turner (1842–56), gas engineer George Trewby (1884–1920) and electrical engineer Robert Brousson (1922–36). The last private owner, Lady Katherine Binning, left the house to the National Trust in 1952. It now holds a collection of porcelain and pictures assembled by herself, her mother Millicent E Salting and her uncle George Salting, and the early-instrument collection of George Benton Fletcher.

   The house was originally designed to be entered via the elegant south front – seven bays, the outer two blind on the ground floor and the central three projecting slightly and capped by a pediment.

Garden front, Fenton House

The asymmetrical pitch of the roof suggests the house was the work of a master builder rather than an architect; the bold carved wooden cornice under the widely projecting eaves is almost identical to that at nearby Burgh House (see page 93). Moving the main entrance to its present position on the five-bay east front and marking it with an imposing colonnaded loggia slung between the two projecting end bays was probably the idea of James Fenton.

The room that now runs the length of the south front was once a separate morning room and dining room divided by the entrance passage. The bay that occupies the projecting wing on the east front was originally a closet and as elsewhere the tiny windowless room leading off it would have housed a close-stool or toilet. The ghastly striped orange wallpaper, along with most of the decoration in the house, dates from the National Trust's 1970s refurbishment of the property by John Fowler. In the north-west corner of the roughly square, four-room plan is the smaller porcelain room (named for its collection of Meissen and English 16th-century figurines), used at various times as a study, smoking room, sitting room and doctor's surgery during the tenancy of Dr Abercrombie (1937–39). The oriental room to the north-east with its collection of early Chinese ceramics is furnished much as it was when it was Lady Binning's library. Like the other rooms on the east front its basic rectangular plan is enhanced by opening up the former closet, here to create a bay that provides light and a degree of seclusion for a desk and chair.

The staircase – lit by an enormous window that dominates the west front – retains its original 17th-century twisted balusters. The prickly-pear wallpaper clashes hideously with the heavily patterned carpet taken from a design at Hardwick Hall. The Rockingham room (named from the collection of ceramics from that factory) in the north-east corner has a fascinating assembly of 17th-century stump- or raised-work needlework pictures – in King Solomon and the Queen of Sheba (possibly a tribute to Charles I and celebration of the restoration of the monarchy) the heads are three dimensional and the chain-mail is worked in relief.

The blue porcelain room (named for its collection of blue-and-white Chinese china) in the south-east corner was enlarged by James Fenton by replacing the wall of the corridor that led to the mechanism for the clock on the east front with a screen of Ionic columns. From at least 1884 this room was linked to the drawing room in the south-west corner by double doors. The drawing room – decorated in depressing two-tone yellow – retains the panelling and arched alcoves flanking the deep chimney breast installed by the Fentons. The small green room in the north-west corner contains more needlework pictures and pottery.

The attic rooms were probably used originally as bedrooms for the family, with the servants sleeping in outbuildings (Joshua Gee had nine children and James Fenton and George Trewby seven each). To add a further layer to what is already a baffling mix of interests, one room is devoted to a display of illustrations, cover art and toys from James Roose-Evans' 1970s 'Odd and Elsewhere' children's books, which use Fenton House as the setting for an equally baffling series of adventures.

More things to see & do

As well as world-class collections of oriental, European and English porcelain and 17th-century needlework, Fenton House is home to the Benton Fletcher Collection of early keyboard instruments, many of which are played regularly by visiting students. The grounds contain a rose garden, walled garden and 300-year-old orchard with more than 30 varieties of English apple which visitors can taste on the annual Apple Day in late September. See *www.nationaltrust.org.uk/fentonhouse*.

Freud Museum

20 Maresfield Gardens, London NW3 5SX
Tel: 020 7435 2002
www.freud.org.uk
Nearest transport: Finchley Road LU, Finchley Road & Frognal Rail or
    Swiss Cottage LU
Open: Wed-Sun 12.00-17.00
Admission: £6/4.50/£3/under-12s free
Wheelchair access: very limited

Freud Museum

More than any other of London's great men's houses, the Freud
Museum has the unsettling quality of a place of pilgrimage to which
initiates come to pay homage, communing with their long-dead
prophet to bolster their faith. The impression is reinforced by the lack
of written information provided – without the audioguide, no-one
coming through the door out of curiosity will learn much or have their
interest kindled. On the other hand, there's also none of the curatorial
nonsense that assembles anything the great master has touched
and then tries to justify its presence. The strategy was epitomised

in the museum's celebration of the centenary of *The Interpretation of Dreams* in 2000. Objects – some added, such as a bowl of cherries on a table; some already there, such as a cupboard – were captioned with cryptic, allusive dream descriptions taken from Freud's *magnum opus*. Slippage, ellipsis – the onus of interpretation is on you.

20 Maresfield Gardens was the home of father of psychoanalysis Sigmund Freud from 27 September 1938 until his death at the age of 83 on 23 September 1939 and of his youngest daughter Anna (born 1895), known for her controversial work in child psychology, and her lifelong companion Dorothy Burlingham until their deaths in 1982 and 1979 respectively. It opened as a museum, in accordance with Anna's wishes, in 1986.

The red-brick double-fronted two-storey Edwardian house with big dormer windows in the roof opens – like Freud's explorations of the mind – into an unexpectedly extensive and complex array of spaces. Beyond the small entrance lobby in the central bay is an imposing double-height hall that runs half the depth of the house. Freud's study occupies the space running the full depth of the house to the right; behind the hall is a spacious dining room and a conservatory part-designed by Freud's architect son Ernst. (It's now a shop that sells 'Freudian slippers' – 'now you can really put your foot in it!' – alongside learned texts.) Above the dining room is a room devoted to the life and work of Anna Freud; above Freud's study are exhibition and video rooms. The left-hand side of the house is now office and administration space.

Freud was released from Vienna following the Nazi invasion of Austria in March 1938 mainly because the German authorities realised he was too big a fish to fry. Works by Freud and other psychoanalysts had been publicly burned in Germany in 1933 and now, as a condition of his release, the Gestapo demanded that a copy of his complete works stored for safekeeping in Switzerland should be returned and ceremoniously burned and that he should sign a statement declaring he had been treated 'with all the respect and consideration due to my scientific reputation, that I could live and work in full freedom... and that I have not the slightest reason for any complaint' (he signed, insisting on adding: 'I can heartily recommend the Gestapo to anyone'!). In addition he was required to pay large amounts of so-called fugitive tax to prevent his library and collections from being seized, some of which was provided by his pupil Marie Bonaparte, who through her connections to the Greek royal family had already arranged for his stock of gold, then a common insurance against inflation, to be transferred to London by the Greek king. Freud's permitted retinue included his wife Martha, Anna, Martha's sister Minna, two maids and his dog Lün; he was never to know that the four sisters he left behind were incinerated five years later.

London welcomed him with open arms: he was feted in *The Lancet* and *BMJ*; visitors included H G Wells, Chaim Weizmann and a delegation from the Royal Society. According to his biographer and disciple Ernest Jones, he thought the house 'really beautiful' ('too good for someone who would not tenant it for long') and was particularly fond of the garden, which he would enter through the French doors in his study to sit in a comfortable swing couch shaded with a canopy from the unseasonable autumn sunshine. Later, as he succumbed to the cancer of the palate that had dogged him since 1923, involving 33 operations, he had his sick bed moved here and enjoyed the views of the flowers.

Freud's study today – its blinds shut in the interests of conservation – gives a mistaken impression of stereotypical Viennese gloom and of dark, impenetrable secrets. But it's still less austere than might have been imagined: the famous couch, on which even towards the end of his life he conducted up to four sessions a day sitting himself on a green tub chair out of sight, is draped in a richly textured Persian carpet (the stuff of dreams, indeed); Freud's well-worn swivel desk chair takes the playful form of a human figure. An extensive library lines the walls and the collection of some 2000 objects including antiquities from ancient Greece, Rome, Egypt and the orient – arranged by his son Ernst and maid Paula Fichtl to replicate as closely as possible the Viennese apartment in which he had lived for 47 years – is crammed into cabinets and scattered over surfaces rather than displayed, as if the

Study, Freud Museum

enjoyment was in possession not contemplation. (Freud confessed that his passion for collecting was second in intensity only to his addiction to cigars.) In many ways the room seems distinctly Edwardian – the heavily draped table in front of the window, the relentless clutter – especially in comparison with its modernist neighbour and direct contemporary at 2 Willow Road (see page 79).

Freud's Viennese study is captured in photographs in the dining room which also show Vienna's swastika-festooned streets and the familiar severe, bearded face of the master. The 18th- and 19th-century peasant furniture painted with scenes and stylised plants is from Anna and Dorothy's Austrian country cottage.

The mezzanine landing in the light-filled bay above the lobby – whose table displays a Biedermeier elegance characteristic of much of the assembled furniture – was presumably another favourite place to sit. On the top landing is a remarkable portrait by Salvador Dali, who was intrigued by Freud's fascination with myth, that conflates the psychoanalyst's head with a fingerprint. Dali was brought to the house in July 1939 by writer Stefan Zweig. Freud commented afterwards: 'Until now I have been inclined to regard the surrealists, who apparently have adopted me as their patron saint, as complete fools... That young Spaniard... has changed my estimate.'

In the Anna Freud room, behind a green baize door, are assembled the couch and desk from her study, the loom she kept in her bedroom (she used to knit when conducting sessions) and various certificates and family photographs. The father-daughter relationship is described by Jones as 'peculiarly intimate'– from 1918 she was psychoanalysed by her father, while he admitted to becoming increasingly emotionally and physically dependent on her as his illness progressed. (Freud's wife is conspicuous by her absence.) After her father's death, Anna opened the Hampstead War Nursery, which provided foster care for children whose relationships with their parents had been disrupted by the war. Later she worked with orphans from concentration camps. Whereas the aim of Freud's analysis was arguably to help his patients better understand themselves, Anna believed people could be encouraged to become model citizens by strengthening the rational side of their ego, enabling them to control their unconscious impulses. She experimented first with Dorothy Burlingham's children, following their parents' divorce – Rob, whom she had tried to dissuade from being gay, died of alcoholism; Maddy returned to commit suicide at Maresfield Gardens in the 1960s.

But there's little hint of this darker story at the Freud shrine bar the testimony of a member of staff from the Hampstead Clinic for Children, established by Anna in the early 1950s, who hints that emotion and professionalism were as linked here as they must have been in her initiation into psychoanalysis with her father: 'The Hampstead Clinic is sometimes spoken of as Anna Freud's extended family, and that is how it often felt, with all the ambivalence such a statement implies.'

More things to see & do

The Freud Museum hosts an ambitious and imaginative programme of exhibitions and talks responding to aspects of Freud's life and work. See *www.freud.org.uk* for full details.

Keats House

Keats Grove, London NW3 2RR
Tel: 020 7332 3868
www.keatshouse.cityoflondon.gov.uk
Nearest transport: Belsize Park LU, Hampstead LU
Open: Tues-Sun 13.00-17.00 (May to Oct), Fri-Sun 13.00-17.00
   (Nov to April)
Admission: (valid for 12 months) £5/£3/under-16s free
Wheelchair access: ground floor only

'You could not step or move an eyelid but it would shoot to my heart – I am greedy of you – Do not think of any thing but me. Do not live as if I was not existing – Do not forget me... If we love we must not live as other men and women do – I cannot brook the wolfsbane of fashion and foppery and tattle. You must be mine to die upon the rack if I want you... No – my sweet Fanny – I am wrong. I do not want you to be unhappy – and yet I do, I must while there is so sweet a Beauty – my loveliest my darling! Good bye! I kiss you – O the torments!'

This was the letter the 24-year-old John Keats (1795–1821) wrote to his 20-year-old fiancée and neighbour Fanny Brawne (1800–65) a few days after he left for the last time the Hampstead house where he was the tenant (paying £5 per month) of his friend Charles Brown. Plagued by financial worries, family problems, doctor's instructions not to work, and above all an acute awareness of his advancing consumption, he looked to Fanny as an emotional lifeline while at the same time suffering torments at the idea that she might be enjoying the company of others. The tragic ironies of Keats' situation – heir to an unobtainable legacy and reduced to borrowing from friends; a writer whose first two books were so unpopular they lost money, but whose *Odes*, published just months before his death, would be claimed as containing the most perfect poems in English; a consumptive whose medical training gave him an inescapable awareness of his condition – pervade Keats House. Yet the 18 months he spent here included happy times with friends,

Keats House

John Keats, portrait by Joseph Severn, 1819

some productive months of work and the dawn of a love affair that was as passionate and unreasonable as might be expected of any young love.

The eldest of a family of four surviving children, whose father had died when he was nine and mother when he was 15, Keats moved into Wentworth Place in December 1818 following the death from consumption of his younger brother Tom. He had nursed Tom in the lodgings in nearby Well Walk which the three brothers had shared until George's emigration to the United States earlier in the year. As Brown, a 31-year-old merchant who had retired to spend more time on his writing, recalled: 'Early one morning I was awakened in my bed by a pressure on my hand. It was Keats, who came to tell me his brother was no more... At length, my thoughts returning from the dead to the living, I said – "Have nothing more to do with those lodgings – and alone too. Had you not better live with me?" He paused, pressed my hand warmly, and replied – "I think it would be better." From that moment he was my inmate.'

The pleasant stuccoed Regency house – whose modest scale will surprise anyone who has based their expectations on Jane Campion's much hyped 2009 film *Bright Star* – was built as a two-family dwelling in 1815–16 by Brown and his schoolfriend Charles Wentworth Dilke, a literary critic and civil servant. The appearance of a symmetrical three-bay detached house was maintained by having Dilke's entrance in the centre of the main façade and Brown's on the side wall. The house was surrounded by fields and the Heath, and Hampstead was a village favoured by such writers as Shelley, Coleridge and Keats' first champion Leigh Hunt, publisher of the radical *Examiner*, who later moved to Chelsea and was a friend of the poet's exact contemporary Thomas Carlyle (see page 154).

In 1839 Wentworth Place was made into one house and the single-storey extension comprising the Chester room and a conservatory (replaced in 1975) was added by retired actress Eliza Chester. The door between this room and the rest of the house was originally the front door to Brown's residence. Chester had been employed as a 'reader' at Windsor Castle and was nicknamed 'Prinny's last fling' because of the Prince Regent and future George IV's interest in her. Her light-filled room is larger and more pretentious than its predecessors, with gilded mouldings, an elaborate fireplace, a rich red colour scheme and heavy ruched curtains. In 1921, threatened with demolition, Wentworth Place was bought by the Keats Memorial House Fund and offered to the council. Four years later it opened to the public and it is now run by the City of London Corporation.

Visitors enter via a charming veranda through the back door into Dilke's side of the house. The two ground-floor rooms are now knocked into one and contain a display case dedicated to Fanny Brawne that includes the engagement ring she received from Keats, which she wore for the rest of her life, as well as props from the film *Bright Star*. From 1815 to 1816 Keats had studied at Guy's and St Thomas's medical school and his licence from the Society of Apothecaries hangs on the wall.

Keats met the Brawne family – Fanny, her widowed mother and her younger siblings Samuel and Margaret – after Brown rented them his rooms while he and Keats were on a walking holiday in Scotland in the summer of 1818. Keats, troubled by a sore throat, returned to Well Walk early (having covered 642 miles in a couple of months) and met Fanny on visits to the Dilkes. Preoccupied with nursing Tom and beginning work on *Hyperion*, he didn't properly register her presence until November. It was hardly love at first sight, though he was intrigued, describing her as 'beautiful and elegant, graceful, silly, fashionable and strange.' Intelligent, diligent and quick-witted, interested in languages and fashion and with no pretensions to literary appreciation, to Keats' relief she 'liked me for my own sake and for nothing else.'

The Brawnes moved to a nearby cottage on Brown's return and in May or June the following year Dilke – whose portrait shows a robust, jolly young man in contrast with the abstracted asceticism that colours the likenesses of Keats – rented them his side of Wentworth Place. Keats' love letters to Fanny begin in July 1819, when he was forced by Brown's summer letting of his home to stay with his sick friend James Rice in the Isle of Wight and then with Brown in Winchester. The source of the famous 'season of mists and mellow fruitfulness', this summer and autumn were a low point in Keats' life: his brother George was writing from America asking for money but none of his friends could or would repay the total of £230 he had generously loaned out, and he was penniless; his sore throat was getting worse; Rice and he got on each other's nerves; and as well as writing *Lamia* and struggling with *Hyperion*, he was turning a play by Brown, *Otho the Great*, into comic verse as a potential money-spinner. After considering putting his medical training to good use by signing up as a ship's surgeon, he decided instead to try his hand at journalism, moving in October to rooms in Westminster. After a dispiriting few days tramping the streets in search of a position, he returned helplessly to Brown. Fanny and Keats were engaged in December.

The Brown side of the house is noticeably smaller in scale than Dilke's rooms. To the right of the central corridor is Keats' parlour, a modest but pleasantly proportioned space with French windows overlooking the garden, whose tranquillity after the noisy conditions and distress of Well Walk enabled him to write such masterpieces as the odes 'To Psyche', 'To a Nightingale', 'To a Grecian Urn' and 'To Melancholy', completed in a month in April 1819. The two slender bookcases contain volumes he is known to have owned – Burton's *Anatomy*, the works of Molière and Spenser, the *Illiad* and the complete Shakespeare he always carried. The somewhat priggish posthumous portrait by Joseph Severn, who accompanied Keats to Italy in September 1820 and stayed with him until his death in February 1821, shows the room as Keats inhabited it; more poignant are the likenesses of his sister Fanny in late middle age – a reminder of what might have been – and the print of Severn's watercolour of Tom, dead at the age of 19.

Brown's parlour opposite, slightly larger and used for entertaining, once looked out on the Heath and it was here that Brown made up a sofa bed for Keats during his illness of February and March 1820. Hogarth's *Credulity, Superstition and Fanaticism: A Medley* hangs on the wall; Keats complained that it gave him nightmares. Though Brown's clowning and comic verse could become wearisome, he loyally nursed his friend and supported him both emotionally and financially until his death.

What was once Keats' bedroom was enlarged following the conversion of the house into a single unit and the consequent removal of Brown's staircase. Though it contains no original furnishings, it is surprisingly atmospheric. It was here that Keats retreated in February 1820 when after travelling home from London on the outside of a coach – to save money – he caught a chill and experienced the first haemorrhage which told him he had pulmonary tuberculosis. He made a brief recovery in spring – enough for Brown to continue with his plans of letting the house out for the summer – but following a stay with the Hunts in Kentish Town he returned to Wentworth Place, where the Brawnes nursed him until the journey to Italy which it was hoped would restore his health. Severn's pen and ink sketch of the poet drawn less than a month before his death shows a face with fine cheekbones and an aquiline nose, both romantic and beautiful.

Brown's room opposite contains portraits of his stolid parents and a few items he is known to have owned. He was an amateur artist, as well as a writer, and beside the bed is a surprisingly delicate watercolour of a flower. In the summer of 1820 Brown and his maid Abigail O'Donaghue had a son, Carlino. We don't know what happened to Abigail, but from 1822 to 1835 Brown and Carlino lived in Italy and in 1841 they emigrated to New Zealand.

Fanny Brawne married Louis Lindon, a man 12 years her junior, in 1833. The couple had three children and spent much of their lives on the continent. The sparsely furnished Fanny Brawne room contains copies of images from her scrapbooks and some items chosen to evoke her love of fashion. As much as anything else in Keats House, there's a poignancy to our interest in this unremarkable woman whose only claim to fame is that she inspired an unconsummated passion in an aspiring poet who died tragically young.

Keats led a life of relative poverty and died with few possessions to his name. His legacy is in his writing, and it's a shame the facsimiles of his poems and letters that once filled the Chester room here are no longer on display following the house's recent remodelling. It's worth making the effort to read the laminated A4 sheets with typed extracts from his writings that are available in some rooms; the letters, more than anything else, give a sense of the intelligence, wit and exuberance that inspired the loyalty of friends and the love of his Bright Star.

Kenwood House

Hampstead Lane, London NW3 7JR
Tel: 020 8348 1286
www.english-heritage.org.uk/kenwood
Nearest transport: Archway LU or Golders Green LU then 210 bus
Open: daily 11.30-16.00
Admission: free
Wheelchair access: ground floor only

South façade, Kenwood House

'While he aimed at elegance within, he covered the outside of his buildings with frippery... Most of the white walls, with which Mr Adam has speckled this city, are no better than Models for the Twelfth-Night Decoration of a Pastry Cook.' Robert Smirke, painter and illustrator and father of the architect by the same name, in a pamphlet attacking Adam, 1779

Until it was bought in 1754 by newly appointed attorney general William Murray (1705–93) – who commissioned Robert Adam in 1764 to undertake a major redevelopment of the property – Kenwood was a simple brick Queen Anne-style house, two rooms deep and seven bays wide with an orangery to the west. It was built between 1694 and 1704 by surveyor general of the ordnance William Bridges on the site of (and perhaps incorporating) a dwelling built by king's printer John Bill around 1616. Murray had left his native Scotland for England at the age of 13. Though his father and one of his brothers had been imprisoned during the Jacobite uprising of 1715 and another brother was the tutor to the Young Pretender (Bonnie Prince Charlie), William threw himself firmly behind the Hanoverians.

Kenwood, meanwhile, had been in Scots hands since it was bought by John Campbell, 2nd Duke of Argyll – one of several Scots who flocked to London to seek preferment at court following the Act of Union of 1707 – from William, 4th Earl of Berkeley, who moved to the more fashionable Twickenham. By 1746 the house had passed to Campbell's nephew John Stuart, 3rd Earl of Bute, soon to become tutor to the future George III and from 1762–63 the new king's chief advisor and one of England's most unpopular prime ministers. During the early 1760s Bute moved to Luton Hoo, where he was later to employ Robert Adam, whom in 1761 he had persuaded the king to appoint as architect of the king's works. It is therefore probably to Bute – Murray's friend and mentor – that we owe Adam's transformation of Kenwood.

Murray himself – who took the title Earl of Mansfield in 1756 – is regarded as one of the greatest British judges and law reformers of the 18th century, credited with ruling against the rights of slavers over slaves in England. In 1738 he had joined the aristocracy by marrying the 34-year-old daughter of the 2nd Earl of Nottingham and 7th Earl of Winchilsea; his reconstruction of Kenwood must in part have been inspired by the need for a house suitable for entertaining the public figures it was in his interest to cultivate. For whatever his abilities, Mansfield was never forgiven for being a Scot (at a time when his fellow countrymen were perceived to hold undue power and influence) and was repeatedly accused of Jacobite leanings, of being a closet advisor to the king and even a papist. Matters reached a head during the anti-Catholic Gordon riots of 1780, when a mob burned down his Bloomsbury Square house (including his prized library) and pursued him to Hampstead, armed with the townhouse's iron railings. Kenwood escaped a similar fate in part because the landlord of the nearby Spaniard's Inn plied the rioters with free ale, supplemented by barrels set out at the roadside by Mansfield's steward.

Mansfield and his wife had no children of their own but they brought up Elizabeth Murray, the daughter of William's nephew and heir David, 7th Viscount Stormont, and the 'mulatto' Dido Elizabeth Belle, illegitimate daughter of Mansfield's other nephew Sir John Lindsay, a captain in the Royal Navy who possibly took Dido's mother prisoner in the West Indies and brought her to England. David – a former ambassador in Paris and Vienna – survived his uncle by only three years, during which time he hired George Saunders to enlarge Kenwood with the addition of the two single-storey brick wings that flank the entrance front. His son, who owned the house from 1796 to 1840, employed William Atkinson, a pupil of James Wyatt, to oversee an extensive programme of restoration and refurbishment, using many of the same cabinet-makers as the future George IV employed at Carlton House. His heir, the 4th Earl, spent only three months a year at Kenwood, preferring the family seat of Scone, but the 5th Earl – dubbed the most eligible bachelor in London – made the house for eight years around the turn of the 20th century once more the backdrop for glittering social gatherings. Under the 6th Earl it was let to tenants including Grand Duke Michael Michaelovitch (in residence 1910–17), the great-great-grandson of Catherine the Great, who had been exiled from Russia in 1891 following his morganatic marriage to Pushkin's great-great-granddaughter. During World War I the service wing was used as a barracks; from 1917 to 1920 Kenwood was the home of Nancy Leeds, the wealthy widow of an American tin-plate manufacturer, who also rented Spencer House (see page 66).

In 1925 Kenwood was acquired by Edward Cecil Guinness, 1st Earl of Iveagh, who bequeathed it to the nation on his death. (Despite such gifts, the exchequer reaped enough in death duties to enable chancellor Winston Churchill to lower the basic rate of income tax.) In 1886 Guinness Breweries had become a public company and the multi-millionaire had set out to form an art collection, buying some 240 drawings and paintings in the space of four years. Some 60 of these are on display at Kenwood today – a mix of late-18th-century British portraits, 17th-century Dutch and Flemish old masters and French rococo art.

Adam regarded Kenwood as one of his most significant achievements and the brothers devoted the entire second part of their calling-card *Works in Architecture* to its design. In Mansfield he found a supportive client, who 'gave full scope to my ideas', and the house's relative modesty allowed him a freedom impossible at Syon (see page 261) or Osterley (see page 240). He transformed the nine-bay entrance or north front through the addition of a massive full-height portico spanning the central three bays, its pediment supported on four Ionic columns. At the time the Highgate-to-Hampstead road ran just outside, and the portico ensured that the house – no isolated country seat but a suburban villa designed to impress – would have a suitably imposing profile. It was only when the 2nd Earl commissioned landscape architect Humphry Repton to draw up plans for the grounds, with the result that Hampstead Lane was diverted to the other side of North Wood, that the approach to the house, as today, was via a picturesque serpentine drive, raising expectations of a romantic secluded residence rather than the neoclassical formality of Adam's frontage.

Adam used stucco on the south or garden façade to disguise the varying colours of the existing brick. This front was designed to be appreciated by family and friends from the terrace or lawn rather than to impress from a distance, so the architect topped a rusticated base with a delicate confectionery of swags, medallions, Greek-key patterns, honeysuckles and arabesques typical of his interiors. Adam described Kenwood's setting as 'magnificent, beautiful, and picturesque' and insisted that 'the decoration bestowed on this front of the house is suitable to such a scene'. But Kenwood's façade was also to be the perfect advertisement for stucco, for which Adam and his brother James had bought the patent from its Swiss clergyman inventor and even obtained an act of parliament giving them the exclusive right to manufacture the material. In 1778 they prosecuted a Mr Johnson who had obtained a patent for an improved version; the case came before Mansfield, who unsurprisingly found in favour of the brothers.

As Julius Bryant points out in his excellent guide to the house, Mansfield may have regretted his decision: Kenwood's façade deteriorated rapidly, and according to Repton, 'The Great Lord Mansfield often declared, that had the front of Kenwood been originally covered in Parian marble, he should have found it less expensive'. (The present façade is faced with fibreglass mouldings copied in 1975 from Adam's drawings.) Further evidence that Adam was more concerned with style than substance is found in a letter from Atkinson defending himself against the 3rd Earl's complaints about delays to the schedule of works. According to the architect, 'the ignorance or inattention of the former Architects to the House' had resulted in dry rot (from failing to give the walls time to dry before plastering), while the perishable timber they had built into the walls had to be replaced by new solid brickwork.

Adam's transformation of the south front also involved building a single-storey library extension to the east (an appropriate choice of 'grand room' for a bibliophile with no family portraits to display), mirroring the existing orangery to the west. And he added a third storey, roofing it before he took down the old roof so the house remained habitable throughout the alterations. The sprawling brick service wing to the east, which today houses a café and restaurant, was an addition by Saunders for the 2nd Earl to replace much less extensive facilities behind the orangery.

Adam's innovation was to introduce the ornamental vocabulary of Roman domestic architecture to his work (unlike the Palladians, who drew inspiration from public buildings), supplemented by

Antechamber to the dining-room wing, Kenwood House

elements from 16th-century Italy and from contemporary France. Certainly the scale and ornament of the entrance hall at Kenwood – decorated in blue and green with motifs that reflect its dual function as a dining room – are thoroughly domestic in comparison with the grandeur sought at Osterley or Syon. The relative modesty of the 'great stairs' is in part attributable to the layout of the house: because the main reception room (the new library) was on the ground floor, guests simply passed by the staircase – admiring the honeysuckle-motif balustrade (identical to that at Osterley) on the way – rather than ascending it to a *piano nobile*. The delicate oval lantern replaced a dramatic Adam ceiling when the landing window was filled in to accommodate Saunders' new wing.

The antechamber and library, built entirely by Adam, form an easterly extension to the south front. A basically unaltered realisation of a 1764 design by James Adam that typifies the brothers' early style, the antechamber consists of a screen of two marble Ionic columns opposite a Venetian window with a panoramic view over the lake and woods beyond. The unexpected sequence of spaces – the imposing portico, the domestic entrance hall, the lofty great stairs, the short passage cut through the exterior wall of the original house – is the embodiment of Adam's desire to introduce the movement found in nature into architecture: 'the rising and falling, advancing and receding have the same effect in architecture, that hill and dale, foreground and distance, swelling and sinking have in landscape.' The drama of the antechamber today is enhanced by the splendid vista through high double doors to the dining-room wing added by Saunders.

The library – regarded by aficionados as the finest example of Adam's late style – is a riot of pink, blue and gold confectionery that might just epitomise Adam at his worst. Like the antechamber, it uses screens of columns – set in front of semi-circular apses at each end of the double cube of the main room – to give drama to the space, but any plasticity of form is obscured by the marshmallow colours and elaborate piping that covers every surface. The style reaches its apogee in the mirrored recesses opposite the windows (sensibly Adam chose not to fenestrate the side facing the road

Music room, Kenwood House

but rather to reflect the romantic views from the tall windows overlooking the park). Here mirrors decorated with gilded urns and framed by uprights that seem to cobble together the range of Adam's decorative motifs are topped by arc upon arc of different patterns, with above them a gilded frieze of lions and heads of deer. The coved ceiling has panels painted by Venetian artist Antonio Zucchi, who was later to marry Angelica Kauffmann, two of whose paintings hangs in the antechamber. Above the chimney piece hangs a replica of a 1775 portrait of Mansfield decked out in full regalia beside a bust of Homer bequeathed to him by his friend and mentor Alexander Pope (who tried, unsuccessfully, to help his protégé lose his Scottish accent).

The change in scale from the original house and Adam's additions to Saunders' more imposing new wing is immediately apparent in the dining-room lobby, where the high coffered ceiling is topped by a balustraded lantern resting on four thin segmental arches. The sequence of two consecutive antechambers also gives the sense of a much larger house than Kenwood actually is. The dining room beyond – which contains two gems from the Iveagh bequest, a Rembrandt self-portrait of c. 1663 and Vermeer's *The Guitar Player* (c. 1672) – is impressive in scale but relatively free of decoration.

Running along the south front of the original house from the library and antechamber are Lord Mansfield's dressing room, the breakfast room, Lady Mansfield's dressing room, the housekeeper's room and the orangery. With the exception of the last, all are intimate and domestic in feel, with Adam's intervention restricted to designs for chimney pieces, cornices and architraves. Lord Mansfield's dressing room – a plain, squarish space – would have served as a study and reception room in which to see morning visitors. It was also the library until Adam added his new wing. The much larger breakfast room was until 1815 a separate drawing room and parlour or private dining room, both with direct access to the entrance hall. Lady Mansfield's dressing room is about half the size of her husband's; the similar-sized housekeeper's room is dominated by an incongruously large Venetian window placed to retain the symmetry of the façade rather than to correspond to any internal function. The light-filled orangery – originally a freestanding building which would have concealed the service wing from the terrace and lawn – was used like a traditional long gallery, for recreation in wet weather. Orangeries became a popular symbol of political affiliation (and wealth) after the accession of William of Orange in 1689.

The orangery provides a splendid vista through the length of Saunders' other wing, which consists of an antechamber framed by two screens of Ionic columns (echoing but not directly imitating Adam's antechamber), the green room and the music room. Though these lofty chambers are relatively unadorned, the most striking decorative motif being a frieze of gilded harps, the music room at least was to have had decorated panels by Julius Ibbetson, of which only the borders were completed. The walls today are hung with 18th-century portraits – mostly of such female icons as Emma Hamilton (depicted by George Romney as St Cecilia), courtesan Kitty Fisher (depicted by Joshua Reynolds as Cleopatra), and actress Mrs Jordan (depicted by John Hoppner as Viola in *Twelfth Night*). The house has continued to attract collections, and displays of Elizabethan portraits, miniatures, shoe buckles and jewellery are on show in the upstairs rooms.

More things to see & do

In 1793 the 2nd Earl (David, 7th Viscount Stormont) commissioned landscape architect Humphry Repton to prepare a book of proposals to remodel the grounds of Kenwood House as a unified landscape. The general effect was to create contrast and surprise, with highlights including the ivy arbour with its breathtaking opening on to the terrace, lawns and lake and the winding rhododendron walks. Today the grounds also contain sculptures by Henry Moore and Barbara Hepworth and the Brew House café garden, designed by landscape architect Arabella Lennox-Boyd. English Heritage also runs a series of Picnic Concerts each summer, see *www.picnicconcerts.com*.

Rear façade with Doric colonnade, Lauderdale House

Lauderdale House

Waterlow Park, Highgate Hill, London N6 5HG
Tel: 020 8348 8716
www.lauderdalehouse.org.uk
Nearest transport: Archway LU or Highgate LU
Open: Tues-Fri 11.00-16.00, Sat 13.00-17.00, Sun 12.00-17.00
Admission: free
Wheelchair access: limited

An unattractive pebbledash building with an uninspiring five-bay Georgian entrance front, a surprisingly unthought-out arrangement of windows on its long south-east side and a fine Doric colonnade at the back, Lauderdale House is nevertheless endowed with a history – both architectural and social – that's one of the most interesting in this book.

One of the few surviving large timber-framed London houses, Lauderdale was built in 1582 by Sir Richard Martin, warden and master-worker at the Royal Mint, for his younger son Richard, probably with a rich bounty of 'Spanish gold' earned from financing Sir Francis Drake's circumnavigation of 1577–80. The Martins' home was designed to a U-shaped plan around a central courtyard. The long south-east flank (the base of the U) was probably divided into three rooms with a traditional great chamber on the first floor; the present entrance hall in the north-east (right-hand) wing was probably a dining room. A single-storey building at the open end of the courtyard, connected by a corridor to the dining room, contained the kitchens. As at Whitehall (see page 285), the construction is timber frame infilled with wattle and daub, with the larger upper-floor frame resting on projecting joists, a method known as continuous jettying. The slight projection of the upper floor today and the asymmetrical fenestration on the long front are the clearest clues to the building's Tudor origins.

Subsequent owners include merchant Sir William Bond (in residence 1599–1625), who was the brother of the younger Martin's wife Anne, and lord chief justice Sir Henry Hobart (1625–35), who had built Blickling Hall in Norfolk. The house received its first makeover in the early 1640s, when wealthy widow Lady Home transformed it into a residence befitting an aristocrat by widening the single-room-deep long flank with the addition of a corridor on the courtyard side to provide independent access to the rooms in the two shorter wings, extending the entrance wing to the north to create a servants' hall in the empty corner between the dining room and kitchens, and adding a third storey to the opposite wing (which I will call the café wing in reference to its present function).

On Lady Home's death in 1645 the house passed to her younger daughter Anne, who just over a decade earlier had married John Maitland, 2nd Earl of Lauderdale. A staunch royalist, Maitland spent nine years in prison during the interregnum and from 1649 was forced to lease out his Highgate house to John Ireton, brother of Cromwell's son-in-law. After the restoration he was rewarded with the post of secretary of state for Scotland and from 1667 was one of the five members of Charles II's inner circle of advisors, the Cabal ministry. When Lauderdale's daughter Mary married at Highgate in 1666 it was the king who gave her away. It is perhaps unsurprising, then, that when Lauderdale separated from Anne to pursue Elizabeth, Countess of Dysart (see Ham House, page 205), a wife more suited to his enhanced status, the king should ask that Lauderdale House be let to his own mistress, actress Nell Gwynn. Though there is no direct evidence to support persistent claims that Gwynn lived at Lauderdale House – or the story that she held her infant Charles out of one of its windows and threatened to drop him unless the king made him an earl – an inventory of the house and its contents made in 1685 (see below) describes the first-floor rooms tucked away in the corner of the café wing, accessed by a separate staircase, as 'the kinges chamber and closett'.

Anne retired to a Calvinist community in Paris and died in 1671; shortly afterwards Lauderdale and Elizabeth married and the newly created duke and his wife embarked on the ambitious refurbishment of Ham. Some idea of the state of Lauderdale House, meanwhile, can be gained from a letter from the exiled Anne to her husband, in which she complains that the house 'is likely to fall down – particularly that part my mother built. I was already afraid that all that weight [of Lauderdale's books] at the top of the house would bring the old house on my head... Remember that it is only mine for my lifetime and then goes to your heirs; I have not the power to take it from them. So I look to you for the repairs.' (Quoted in its 'translated' form from Barber, Cox and Curwen's fascinating study of the house.)

In what must have been a contrast with the royal shenanigans of the previous years, the house was bought in 1677 by Quaker merchant William Mead, who married Sarah Fell, the step-daughter of Quaker founder George Fox. Among Mead's alterations were the reconstruction of the staircase and the installation of an elaborately carved recess in the dining room known by the improbable name of Nell Gwynn's Bath.

The next owner, John Hinde, was a property developer who with Sir Thomas Bond, grandson of previous owner Sir William, built up the area around Old Bond Street. In September 1685 Hinde was declared bankrupt with assets of no more than £10,000 and liabilities estimated at up to £200,000. The inventory of Lauderdale House made by his auditors gives us a clear picture of the building at that time. As in the Martins' dwelling, the entrance hall probably doubled as a dining room. The long flank was made up of two parlours: the white parlour adjoining the dining room, which contained an organ and therefore may also have served as a chapel, and the green parlour beyond (replacing two rooms of the original dwelling). In the café wing was a red parlour and brewhouse. The kitchen and servants' hall occupied the same positions as in previous schemes. Mrs Hinde's bedroom was above the dining room, with a nurse's room above the servants' hall. The tripartite arrangement of the long flank was retained on the first floor: the rooms are described as a matted gallery (or great chamber), best chamber (Mr Hinde's bedroom) linked to a dressing room in the corridor extension added by Lady Home, and beyond it in the café wing the 'kinges chamber and closett', with a separate staircase, and a further bedroom. The six attic rooms were empty.

In 1688 Lauderdale House was bought by its last owner-occupier, Tory MP and philanthropist Sir William Pritchard, and in the century that followed his heirs leased it out among others to Sir Thomas Burnet (c. 1752), son of the Earl of Lauderdale's arch-enemy Bishop Gilbert Burnet. In the 1760s Matthew Knapp transformed the exterior into the neoclassical-style building we see today, adding columns at the corners of the long front to give a more 'classical' profile to the overhanging upper storey, replacing the oriel windows with Georgian sashes and concealing the irregularities of the café front by extending the upper floors forward, capping them with a pediment and supporting the extension on wooden Doric columns. It is known from his diaries that John Wesley (see page 72) stayed here twice in the 1780s, describing it as 'one of the most elegant boarding houses in England'. From 1794 to 1837 it was leased as a school.

The colonnade on the café front was extended to the north in the first half of the 19th century and a billiards room, adjoining the kitchen wing and filling in the open side of the courtyard, was added behind it. It was probably at about this time that the façades received their pebbledash render. The dining room was extended internally by replacing the wall to the white parlour with the Ionic columns still in place today and the green and red parlours were combined into a single L-shaped room by means of a similar screen. The last private occupant was James Yates (in residence 1850–71), who in 1827 had helped establish University College London. Yates had no children and it's likely he transformed the bedrooms in the long flank into the long gallery we see today.

The last private owner of the house was Sir Sydney Waterlow, the wealthy head of a firm of banknote-printers. From 1872 to 1878 he let the house rent-free to St Bartholomew's Hospital and in 1889 gave it to the London County Council, which converted the upper floor into five flats for park-keepers and the ground floor into a refreshment room. In 1961 the council decided to bring the whole house into public use and embarked on an ambitious programme of restoration thwarted by a fire in 1963. The GLC then reroofed the house and inserted a steel carcass within the Tudor structure. After a public campaign to reopen the house it was let to the Lauderdale House Society in 1978 and the money from the fire insurance was used for a partial restoration of the ground floor. It is run as a community arts venue with rooms available for hire.

The illustrious history of Lauderdale House can barely be discerned in the building as it stands today. On the right of the entrance, Nell Gwynn's Bath – probably intended for displaying gold and silver plate – houses a plethora of leaflets about local activities. The entrance hall/dining room and adjacent reception room are now a single space devoted to exhibitions; the beams are original and part of the original doorway to the yard has been revealed. The Ionic columns installed in the early 19th century are still in situ here and in the café, located in the south-west wing behind the 1760s colonnade.

The staircase, installed by Mead, is lit by an octagonal lantern probably designed by royal serjeant painter James Thornhill in the early 18th century. Upstairs is another exhibition space and the 27-metre long gallery (which is not always open); though created post-1850, this space gives the best sense of the house's former glory.

All in all, a building that's perhaps more interesting to read about than to visit, unless you're inclined to participate in one of the admirable range of community activities or enjoy the terrace café.

More things to see & do

Lauderdale House runs a wonderful programme of exhibitions, poetry readings and concerts including old-time music hall, cabaret and jazz seasons and Sunday-morning family classical concerts. See *www.lauderdalehouse.org.uk*.

The pleasant terrace café has views over Waterlow Park, which covers 8 hectares and includes tree-lined walkways and three ponds.

North Outskirts

Forty Hall

Forty Hill, Enfield EN2 9HA
Tel: 020 8363 8196
Nearest transport: Enfield Town Rail, then bus 191 and short walk
Open: closed for refurbishment until early 2012
Admission: free
Wheelchair access: ground floor only

Forty Hall was built in 1629–32 for City merchant Nicholas Rainton, a fabric importer and a puritan (see the cheerless portrait) who had refused to lend money to Charles I and was imprisoned briefly in 1640 for failing to supply accounts to the crown. The house's architect was Edward Carter, who had worked with Inigo Jones, whom he succeeded as surveyor to the king's works. Rainton retired to Forty Hall at the outbreak of the Civil War in 1642; since his children and grandchildren had all predeceased him by the time of his death four years later, the property was inherited by a great-nephew. Purchased by what was to become the Parker-Bowles family in 1895, it was sold to the council in 1951.

Forty Hall is a well-proportioned three-storey red-brick Jacobean mansion that compresses the features of grander residences into a compact square plan. Three of its elegantly simple five-bay façades have been compromised by the addition of elaborate porches at the turn of the 18th century. The house was extended to the west in 1636 with further additions in c. 1800, 1898 and 1928 to augment the kitchens and service quarters. Though it was once thought the roof of Forty Hall was initially supported on gables, as at Boston Manor (see page 203), it is now believed to have been one of the first hipped roofs in the country.

The passage between the front and garden entrances divides the house into the grand rooms to the east – surprisingly small, though perfectly formed – and the more cramped service quarters to the west. The great hall in the north-east corner – a medieval concept writ tiny – would have been used for formal receptions and was originally divided from the passage only by a screen until the central arch was filled in by a door to transform the room into

East front and entrance (north) front, Forty Hall

a parlour in c. 1788. The plain panelling (originally unpainted), bold strapwork ceiling – prefabricated and laid out on the floor before being lifted and plastered into place – and asymmetrically positioned fireplace, its cherub heads and obelisks signifying prestige and power, fade into insignificance beside the elaboration of the 17th-century screen wall with its arcades, scallop shells and semi-grotesque busts. In the drawing room to the south is more panelling, a delicate plasterwork ceiling and an original fireplace and overmantel incorporating a series of paired Doric half-columns.

The Rainton room in the south-west corner was transformed in the mid 18th century by replacing the party wall with the adjacent corridor by a screen with a ceiling-high central arch supported on fluted Ionic columns. The cupboard to the right of the fireplace was probably once a privy with a chute down to the cesspit. The rooms between the Rainton room and the present reception area would originally have been the kitchen and pantry; the reception area was the steward's room (before the Civil War stewards were often the younger sons of gentlemen), conveniently located to supervise the running of the house, its plasterwork decoration of musical instruments and scores probably done c. 1750 when such motifs became fashionable. The staircase, last remodelled in 1897, has beautiful twisted balusters which may date from a rebuilding in c. 1700. Several of the upstairs rooms have 17th-century ceilings and early-18th-century panelling.

As at Gunnersbury Park (see page 176), the elegance of the family rooms at Forty Hall was maintained by a horde of servants living both in the house and in outbuildings located alongside the brewhouse, stables, mill-house and laundry around a spectacular colonnaded inner courtyard to the west of the house. From the end of 2010 the house has been undergoing a major refurbishment which promises new displays that will reveal the layers of its history.

Queen Elizabeth's Hunting Lodge

Ranger's Road, London E4 7QH
Tel: 020 8529 6681
Nearest transport: Chingford Rail
Open: Wed-Sun & bank hol Mondays 12.00-17.00 (April to Sept),
    Fri-Sun 10.00-15.00 (Oct to March)
Admission: free
Wheelchair access: ground floor only

'Well I remember as a boy my first acquaintance with a room hung with faded greenery at Queen Elizabeth's Lodge... and the impression of romance that it made upon me!... yes, that was more than upholstery, believe me.' William Morris, 'The Lesser Arts of Life', 1882

Sited at what feels like the start of the countryside and looked after by an enthusiastic team huddled around a fan heater so as not to disturb its venerable timbers with 21st-century central heating, Queen Elizabeth's Hunting Lodge retains something of the original magic that inspired William Morris, along with much of its original woodwork. The building was commissioned by Henry VIII, though it's unlikely he visited it as by the time of its completion in 1543, four years before his death, he was already in poor health.

Based on an L plan with an integral stair tower, the three-storey structure – made up of massive oak timbers which challenged the skills of Tudor carpenters – was originally a form of grandstand for viewing the hunt, its sides open to the elements. Elizabeth I may have used the lodge as she is known to have hunted in the forest on a number of occasions; in 1589 she ordered a survey as the structure was in a state of disrepair.

Hunting in Elizabethan times was very much a staged affair, popular as an entertainment for visiting dignitaries, with the deer driven by dogs via a series of corrals and ambushes towards the hunting party in the lodge and then slaughtered with a showy display of riding and archery. The queen would first approve the droppings presented to her by the head huntsman to determine whether the chosen stag was a suitable quarry and would slice through the dead animal at the end to assess the quality of the meat.

The lodge's most dramatic space is the top-floor room with its far-reaching views over the forest. From the 17th century, when the timber frame was covered in plaster and windows inserted, this was used for sessions of the manor court, where complaints about rent and land distribution would be brought before the lord of the manor. The middle floor would have been draped and highly decorated. The unplastered ground floor was for servants.

Though not strictly speaking a house, the lodge was lived in by a keeper from the 17th century and for several generations was the home of the Watkins family. It was acquired by the Corporation of London in 1878; while the top floor was used as a tea room and then to house the collection of Epping Forest Museum, the lower floors were lived in by the Butt family until 1926.

More things to see & do

Stretching over 2400 hectares, Epping Forest is the largest public open space in the London area. As well as being used for recreation, two-thirds of its land is a designated Site of Special Scientific Interest and Special Area of Conservation. The Epping Forest Visitor Centre adjacent to Queen Elizabeth Hunting Lodge is open daily and provides information about guided walks and cycle rides and horse riding, as well as the various festivals, exhibitions and open-air theatre events staged within the forest. For more information see *www.cityoflondon.gov.uk*.

Fulham Palace, see page 172

West

West

7 Hammersmith Terrace (Emery Walker House)

7 Hammersmith Terrace, London W6 9TS
Tel: 020 8741 4104
www.emerywalker.org.uk
Nearest transport: Stamford Brook LU
Open: Thurs-Sat tours at 11.00, 12.30 & 14.30 (April to Sept);
    advance booking essential
Admission: £10/£5
Wheelchair access: ground floor only

Like Linley Sambourne's house (see page 147), the former home of printer and publisher Emery Walker (1851–1933) is a time capsule, preserving the decor and possessions of its owner and his family untouched and unchanged. Walker, who lived at No. 3 and then No. 7 Hammersmith Terrace from 1879 until his death, was less wealthy and socially aspirational than *Punch* cartoonist Sambourne, with very different, if equally strong, ideas about the kind of art his home should promote and contain. But both houses offer an intriguing insight into family life in their time, as well as commemorating influential and popular figures who might otherwise have been forgotten.

Hammersmith Terrace, a row of 17 tall, narrow brick houses with gardens that back on to the Thames, was built in the 1750s. Unusually, all the staircases are at the entrance side and the larger rooms face the garden, so maximising the views of the river to the south. As a result, the two-bay street façades are quirkily irregular, with the small windows that light the staircases offset above the entrances, which have Doric porches. During the last quarter of the 18th century, Nos 7 and 8 belonged to Philip James de Loutherbourg, a designer of scenery and lighting effects for David Garrick at Drury Lane.

In 1877 Walker had married exotic beauty Mary Grace, but she soon retired to a cottage in the country because of ill-health. The couple had one daughter, Dorothy, who moved with Walker into No. 7 in 1903 and remained there after his death. In 1948 she was joined by her companion Elizabeth de Haas, recruited through an advert in *The Lady*. When Dorothy died in 1963 she left the house to Elizabeth, who lived here until her own death in 1999, spending her last years trying to secure its preservation.

Hammersmith in the last quarter of the 19th century was crowded with small industries such as breweries and timber wharves as well as being home to several artists. Walker first met his more affluent neighbour William Morris (see Kelmscott House, page 186) on a train returning from a Socialist rally in the East End, and when Morris founded the Socialist League in 1884 Walker became its secretary. Unlike the Oxford-educated Morris, Walker had left school at 13 to become an apprentice, first to a draper and then to a printer who pioneered new photo-gravure techniques for reproducing works of art. By the time he was in his late 20s he was co-director of his own very successful printing company, Bootall & Walker; photographs taken during an Art Workers Guild trip to Seville show him every inch the English gentleman, facing down the July heat in suit and homburg with furled umbrella in hand. Morris was apparently inspired to set up the Kelmscott Press in 1891 after hearing Walker's lecture on 15th-century type founder and printer Nicolas Jenson at the Art Workers Guild, and Walker acted as an unofficial advisor and sounding board for Morris' ideas.

Another Hammersmith neighbour was T J Cobden-Sanderson, an artist and bookbinder with whom Walker founded the Doves Press in 1900. The tension between Walker's understanding of commercial realities and Cobden-Sanderson's artistic idealism meant the relationship soured, with the latter eventually throwing the Doves type and punches into the Thames from Hammersmith Bridge to prevent what he feared would be their vulgar exploitation in Walker's hands. Elizabeth de Haas was to sell many of the Doves Press books to fund the trust that now conserves her former home; their simple beauty can be appreciated from a photocopy of the opening of the Doves Press bible, with its elegant type and initial 'I' (designed by calligrapher Edward Johnson, who moved into No. 3 after Walker left) descending the full depth of the page.

Conservatory, Emery Walker House

Drawing room, Emery Walker House

Visitors gather for the tour in the front room on the ground floor (the telephone room in Walker's day), which serves as a cramped shop and kitchen (the basement that once housed the kitchen is now a separate flat). The dining room at the back of the house, with a small round table at its centre, is a rare example of a London room still hung with a Morris textile, in this case Bird, which also covered the walls of the much grander drawing room at nearby Kelmscott. Walker was with Morris when he died and kept a drawer of relics including a lock of hair and pair of spectacles that can be seen here. There is also a well-worn chair given to Walker by Morris' widow Jane, its cushion, with its woven inscription 'MM to EW', a gift from Morris' daughter May, who from 1890 lived and ran her embroidery workshop at No. 8 Hammersmith Terrace.

Another close friend among the arts and crafts fellowship was Philip Webb, architect of Morris' Red House (see page 338), who made the sideboard and wall-mounted glazed bookcase on the back wall and left Walker many of his possessions including the octagonal mahogany and brass wine cooler that stands beside the door. There is also furniture by arts and crafts designers Ernest Gimson and Ernest and Sidney Barnsley, whom Walker knew well and visited frequently in their Cotswolds craftsmen's colony. In 1922 Walker bought Daneway, the manor at Sapperton in Gloucestershire where Gimson and the Barnsleys had their workshops. Photographs of the rambling medieval pile line the staircase, which seems almost too narrow a space for the strong presence of Morris' Willow wallpaper.

The shed-like conservatory that projects into the garden from the end bay of the dining room was probably designed by Cobden-Sanderson. It has a plaster frieze of grapes and shelves of pottery brought back from holidays in North Africa by Dorothy and Elizabeth de Haas. The first-floor drawing room, above the dining room, contains more examples of Barnsley and Gimson furniture as well as the plan chest from Webb's office and a set of the delicate glasses he designed for Morris' wedding in 1859. As in the room below, the atmosphere is homely and informal, yet with the sense that each of the many objects was carefully chosen and treasured.

Among the pictures are a delicate pencil sketch of May Morris by Edward Burne-Jones and small, life-filled portraits of Emery and Dorothy. The room on the street side of the house was transformed into a bathroom by Dorothy in the 1960s and today has been partially restored to its former function as a parlour.

Emery slept in the attic room, now offices, because it had the best view. The main bedroom on the first floor, papered in Morris' jolly Daisy print, was last occupied by Elizabeth de Haas. Among the relics of late-20th-century life are a number of Virago classics, including Radclyffe Hall's *The Unlit Lamp*. On the bed is a crewelwork bedspread of flowers garlanded in blue swirls made for Mary Grace Walker by May Morris.

William Morris is reported to have said he 'did not think the day complete without a sight [of Walker]'. And Philip Webb described him as 'the Universal Samaritan... to be laid on like water, only we don't pay rates for him.' A successful businessman, pioneer of print technology, committed and hardworking socialist and advisor to the foremost artists' presses of his day, he was knighted in 1930. This fascinating house, in which his own story fades into the background in comparison with those of his better-known contemporaries, is testament to his modesty and popularity as much as to his own achievements.

18 Stafford Terrace
(Linley Sambourne House)

18 Stafford Terrace, London W8 7BH

Tel: 020 7602 3316

www.rbkc.gov.uk/linleysambournehouse

Nearest transport: Kensington High Street LU

Open: guided tours (90 minutes) Wed 11.15, 14.15; Sat-Sun 11.15, 13.00, 14.15, 15.30; costumed tours Sat-Sun 13.00, 14.15, 15.30 (Sept to June); Victorian Christmas Encounters, see page 153

Admission: £6/£4/£1

Wheelchair access: none

18 Stafford Terrace is a time capsule: a Victorian/Edwardian home preserved almost unchanged since the death of *Punch* cartoonist Linley Sambourne in 1910. Unlike the houses of more famous figures, often acquired decades after their deaths and filled by curators with furniture and mementoes, here a home and its contents are displayed intact as used by the Sambourne family – even, allegedly, down to the contents of the drawers.

Stafford Terrace was built between 1868 and 1874 – the high point of Victorian domestic development in north Kensington – as the final phase of construction on the Phillimore estate, once attached to Campden House. The grey-brick house, three storeys plus attic and semi-basement, has a heavy stuccoed bay on the three lower floors and is distinguished from its neighbours only by its quirky glazed window boxes. According to the 1871 census, the estate's inhabitants included retired officers, senior civil servants, a barrister and several tradesmen.

'A little messenger boy, with pillbox hat, white gloves and bicycle, waited by the gate outside. His task was to be ever in attendance upon the whims of my grandpa – rushing all over London with last-minute drawings or messages.'
Anne Messel on her grandfather Linley Sambourne

The 30-year-old Linley and his wife Marion bought No. 18 in late 1874, shortly after their marriage, with financial help from Marion's father, stockbroker and engineer Spencer Herapath, who lived nearby. Mrs Bentley, the house's first occupant, had died 18 months after its completion. Maud Sambourne was born the following year and her brother Roy three years later. This comparatively small Victorian household was supplemented by Linley's mother Frances, who would stay for months at a time, and three or four live-in servants: a cook, parlourmaid, housemaid and nanny or governess. Linley, unlike most of his middle-class contemporaries, kept a horse and carriage in the mews and would ride daily; his coachman was also employed around the house and as a personal servant. Though by no means poor (Linley earned a regular £38 per month for drawing cartoons and caricatures for *Punch*, rising to £100 in 1883), the family was probably less well-off than most of their neighbours, and the gregarious Linley's socialising with Kensington's artistic elite perhaps had something of an aspirational quality.

Formerly run by the Victorian Society, which Maud's youngest daughter Anne founded in 1958, 18 Stafford Terrace is now controlled by the local council and is open only for guided tours. Though these are wonderfully informative, the brisk pace and volume of visitors crowding each room mean there is little opportunity to examine the many objects or soak up the atmosphere. The tour begins with an excellent introductory video in the basement pantry. Visitors are then ushered into the ground-floor entrance hall, which sets the tone for what is to come: Sambourne wanted to make his home a palace of art and almost every inch of wall space is covered in his own drawings, work by his contemporaries or reproductions of the Old Masters he studied as source material. Typical of the time-capsule effect, a range of walking sticks, including a sturdy staff topped by a carved owl, stands attendance by the door.

The dining room at the front of the house has an endearingly worn carpet, stamped gilt ceiling paper and William Morris Pomegranate wallpaper, again largely obscured by pictures. Here Victorian family scenes rub shoulders with bloody classical dramas,

Drawing room, Linley Sambourne House

all given an artificial, alienating effect by being rendered in sepia at approximately A4 size, as ordered by Linley as a means of obtaining art on a limited budget. A high shelf contains a fine collection of blue and white porcelain, most of it, we are told, slightly chipped and presumably bought at bargain prices but still good enough to impress visitors.

At the back of the house is the morning room, where Marion would attend to correspondence, brief her servants and entertain friends. The rectangular bay at the back, its windows glazed in coloured glass that lets in relatively little light, was added when the Sambournes bought the house. The room appears cramped and crowded, and the heavy curtains, dark wallpaper and mirrors reflecting the plethora of objects all contribute to the feeling of claustrophobia. The many photographs show the ever-genial Linley, a somewhat uptight Marion and the strikingly beautiful Maud with her daughter Anne (1902–92), mother by her first husband to Princess Margaret's first husband Lord Snowdon, whose son bears the name Viscount Linley.

The stairs are hung mainly with cartoons and drawings by Sambourne and his contemporaries. As well as his work for *Punch*, he illustrated children's books and took on freelance commissions such as the ambitious diploma for the 1883 International Fisheries Exhibition, which shows his meticulous draughtsmanship when freed from the constraints of time that govern magazine work. The half-landing is extended to house a water garden: a tank filled with shells and a tinkling fountain that bring light and music into an otherwise gloomy space.

The dramatic drawing room fills the whole of the first floor, and every surface is again loaded with objects: I counted eight cabinets and chests of drawers, three desks and eight occasional tables, all stacked with framed photographs and mementoes. Though a second door was installed by the developer and there are two fireplaces, it is believed the room was always a single space. The Sambournes put in the parquet floor and covered their original Morris wallpaper at a later date in a Spanish leather so expensive they didn't do behind the mirrors or large pictures. So much of it is obscured by prints, you wonder why they bothered. The door is decorated with Marion and Linley's family crests (Linley was very proud of his association with the composer Thomas Linley, whose daughter Elizabeth married Sheridan). These are also incorporated into the stained glass of the rear bay, designed by Linley himself as an eruption of blowsy sunflowers much less successful than the stock geometric patterns in the morning room below. At the front of the room are armchairs and Marion's mirrored writing desk; towards the rear, which with the bay extension served as Linley's workspace until he was able to take over the attic nursery, is her baby grand piano.

Roy inherited the house after Marion's death in 1914 and he kept its contents almost unchanged until his death in 1946. His bedroom at the back of the house, reserved largely for Linley's mother until her death in 1892, is a sad tribute to early-20th-century bacherlorhood: the stockbroker's only contributions to the décor appear to be a few books and several signed photographs of the actresses he courted in his youth, including 'Belle of New York' Edna May (who spurned him in favour of a series of millionaires).

The much lighter front bedroom was used by Anne and her second husband Lord Rosse as a London base from Maud's death in 1960 until the house was sold to the GLC in 1980. Though Anne installed the Morris wallpaper, the furniture – including a highly fashionable ebonised suite with white neo-grec decoration – was chosen by Linley and Marion. The fan in front of the fireplace is the equivalent of a visitors' book, with autographed drawings by the likes of artists Alma Tadema and Millais. On the walls are the more ambitious illustrations Sambourne provided for *Punch* annuals, photographs including Anne as a striking 1930s flapper dressed for George VI's coronation and a sketch of Maud by her younger son, the ballet, opera and film designer Oliver Messel.

In 1899 Linley took over one of the attic rooms as his studio, installing a skylight and fitted shelves at frieze height for his books and boxes of photographs. The weekly *Punch* editorial meeting was held over dinner on Wednesday and at the end each artist would be presented with a caption to work with. Sambourne would wake on Thursday mornings with an idea that he would act out and photograph in the garden, helped by his coachman, who would also be dispatched to the theatrical suppliers to borrow props. He would then develop and trace over the relevant photographs to give him the outline for his cartoon, which had to be completed by Friday afternoon. Anne remembers: 'It was a house of perpetual motion, sometimes guests and relations, but often models coming in and out from grandpa, and now and then the little figure of the artist himself in his black-and-white plaid suit bounced down – with great gold watch in hand, to make it tinkle for the children.'

Sambourne used the mezzanine bathroom as his darkroom, installing a coffin-shaped marble bath, its surface impervious to chemicals. On the wall hang surreal portraits and self-portraits staged for his cartoons: policemen arresting a mannequin, hunters engaged in ballet, the irrepressible artist snapped in the garden wearing a dress and holding a fan or striking silly poses in fancy hats. The biggest surprise, however, are the titillating pictures he took at the Camera Club of nude or near-nude females giggling provocatively, in softcore lesbian couplings, in black stockings, wrestling – a blatant assault on the seemingly genteel Victorian values that pervade the rest of the house.

More things to see & do
The year is 1899 and the Sambourne family's preparations for dinner are unsettled by revelations of a possible scandal from 'below stairs'. Suspend your disbelief and join costumed actors for a promenade through the house's interior based on Marion Sambourne's diary entries. Admission to the Victorian Christmas Encounters is £20 including mince pies and mulled wine. To book call 020 7602 3316 or email *museums@rbkc.gov.uk*.

Carlyle's House

24 (formerly 5) Cheyne Row, London SW3 5HL

Tel: 020 7352 7087

www.nationaltrust.org.uk/main/w-carlyleshouse

Nearest transport: South Kensington LU then bus 49
   or Sloane Square LU then bus 19

Open: Wed-Sun & bank hol Mondays 11.00-17.00 (March to Oct)

Admission: £5.10/£2.60/family ticket £12.80

Wheelchair access: not suitable for wheelchairs

'To see how they live and waste here... Flinging platefuls of what they are pleased to denominate "crusts" into the ashpits!... In Scotland we have no such thing as "crusts".' Jane Welsh Carlyle, quoted from Thea Holme's 'The Carlyles at Home'

Some four weeks after his marriage to Jane Welsh (1801–66), the 31-year-old Thomas Carlyle (1795–1881) patronisingly described his wife in a letter to his mother as 'a good little girl... asking, as it seems, nothing more whatever of her destiny, but that in any way she could make me happy.' Eight years later, Jane, a middle-class doctor's daughter who had married the poor if promising son of a stonemason, persuaded her husband to abandon the remote Scottish farm of Craigenputtock she had inherited from her father, and in which they had lived for the previous six years, for London. The couple moved into this house in Cheyne Row in June 1834 and were to stay here until they died.

And indeed much of those 32 years for Jane was spent trying to secure the conditions – chiefly absolute silence and food prepared to strict instructions – that would enable the fussy (or sensitive) historian Carlyle to write his masterworks *The French Revolution* (1837), *The Life and Letters of Oliver Cromwell* (1845) and *Frederick the Great* (1858–65). From an annual budget of £200, increased in 1855 to £230 after she presented her husband with an ingeniously argued parliamentary-style budget pleading her cause, she managed all their financial affairs, including the contracts with successive

Screen decorated by Jane Carlyle, drawing room, Carlyle's House

landlords and Carlyle's income tax, for which she appealed in person for reductions to the Inland Revenue commissioners. Quick-witted, cultured and determined, Jane entertained a circle of friends independently of her husband that included revolutionary-in-exile Mazzini, biographer John Forster and novelist Charles Dickens. Her vivid letters have a wit and elegance that outshine most of her contemporaries; she too could have been a writer, but instead she turned her considerable intelligence to running her home as efficiently and economically as possible in much the same way as the frustrated housewife at the heart of Marilyn French's 1970s feminist classic *The Women's Room* tackled the housework using the research tools of a PhD graduate.

The Carlyles chose Chelsea because, as Carlyle wrote to Jane during his initial house-hunting mission, it was then 'unfashionable; it was once the resort of the Court and great, however; hence numerous old houses in it, at once cheap and excellent'. Their red-brick three-storey Queen Anne house, a standard L in plan with a small projection at the rear, was built in 1708 on a site owned by Lord Cheyne and rented to the couple for £35 per annum. The ground-floor parlour – described accurately by Carlyle as 'unfashionable in the highest degree but in the highest degree serviceable' – is endearingly tatty and intimate. Here Jane fitted the drawing-room carpet from Craigenputtock, filling in the gaps with dyed blanket. The piano at which she would play and sing Scottish ballads was brought to London in 1842 after the death of her mother. The fireplace was installed in 1843, after Carlyle decided the existing grate could not be endured 'for another twenty-four hours'.

In 1865, after Carlyle finished *Frederick the Great* in his attic workroom, the parlour was repainted for him to use as a study. Since the freehold of the house was purchased by public subscription only 14 years after Carlyle's death, to be restored by arts-and-crafts designer C R Ashbee, much of the furniture here is original, including the small chaise, Jane's armchair, the central table from Craigenputtock and the dining chairs, which (like most of their possessions) had once belonged to Jane's parents. The degree to which the room still resembles the Carlyles' living space can be gauged from Robert Tait's 1857 *A Chelsea Interior*, of which Jane remarked: 'The dog is the only member of the family who has reason to be pleased with his likeness'. And indeed while Carlyle, standing writing in his floor-length dressing gown, cuts a handsome, improbably youthful figure, Jane looks bitter and pinched in comparison with the nearby miniature painted some 30 years earlier, which depicts her as a carefree Jane Austen heroine with bouncy ringlets.

In the smaller back dining room, separated from the parlour by big double doors, hangs a crude likeness of Frederick the Great bought for Carlyle by Jane for 6 shillings the day before her death. In the china closet behind, Mary Russell, a maid who had been with the household for about 18 months, gave birth in 1864 to an illegitimate child, who was smuggled out of the house wrapped in Jane's best table linen by the other servant, Helen. Incredibly, Jane didn't find out about the incident until some months later, and derived a certain degree of wry amusement from the idea that her husband was at the time entertaining novelist Geraldine Jewsbury in the dining room, with 'just a thin small door between!' Both Mary and Helen were summarily dismissed. A display case holds a number of valentines and keepsakes that belonged to Charlotte Southam, a maid from 1858 to 1860, whose aunt blew the whistle on Mary. In another case are Jane's much less frivolous mementoes, including a dying gift from her garrulous mother, whose visits to Cheyne Row inevitably ended in tears.

The 18th-century pine panelling in the entrance hall and stairwell was papered over by the Carlyles. Carlyle's trademark hat hangs by the door to the garden, for the ever-practical Jane a source of food as well as flowers. Carlyle transformed the plot from a jungle shortly after they moved in, digging after lunch as an antidote to writing. Here he used to walk, sit and smoke (as depicted in the etching in the parlour), keeping ready-filled clay pipes in niches in the walls.

The basement kitchen, home to a succession of 34 servants in 32 years, is a miserable place. The stone sink and dresser were installed when the house was built; in 1852, after Jane had secured a 31-year lease on the property with no increase in rent because of the substantial improvements the couple were planning, the Carlyles fitted a new range, water was laid on and gas lights arrived – one above the front door for visitors and one above the range so food wouldn't be burned and wasted. Initially the maid slept on the bottom shelf of the dresser and kept her belongings in the back scullery; later the spartan iron bedstead was provided. In the back kitchen was a bath lowered from the ceiling by a complex arrangement of ropes and pulleys in which Carlyle would stand every morning pouring buckets of cold water over himself. The bedrooms were furnished with chamber pots and there was an earth closet in the garden.

Outside the first-floor drawing room is a portrait of Carlyle's mother which bears a striking resemblance to Jane. (Some idea of Jane's romantic feelings towards her father can be gained from the engraving in her bedroom of the Roman soldier Belisarius, whom she thought he resembled.) Like the parlour downstairs, the drawing room is comfortable rather than imposing, the most expensive-looking item a green leather armchair given to Carlyle on his eightieth birthday by John Forster. The space was originally Carlyle's sparsely furnished workroom and library; in 1843, while her husband was away, it became the subject of the first of what Jane called her 'domestic earthquakes' or remodelling projects, during which it was enlarged by removing the closet to the left of the chimney breast to give the room a third window, redecorated, and refurbished with more bookcases and more elegant furnishings including legacies from Jane's mother and the sofa, which she persuaded a dealer to trade for £1 and some old curtains.

Jane was justifiably proud of the economy and efficiency with which she had created 'a really beautiful little drawing room' but Carlyle was tense about having to start on his biography of Cromwell and so embarked on what sounds like a series of displacement activities. After three days he was in a rage 'for want of a closet or some equivalent to fling one's confusion in' ('Best to accumulate no confusion' was Jane's reply). Then the Misses Lambert, who had moved next door in 1839 with what Jane called 'all the things to be guarded against in a London neighbourhood, viz., a pianoforte, a lap-dog, and a parrot', began to play the piano, in contravention of an agreement she had reached with their father some months earlier to make no music until 2pm so Carlyle could work undisturbed. Carlyle decided to move his study into his second-floor dressing room, where a fireplace was installed (at the same time as the removal of the offending fireplace in the parlour). This meant abandoning his adjacent bedroom for the spare room on the second-floor front, which also became unusable when the builder suggested enlarging it by removing a partition. Jane describes her husband as 'a sort of domestic wandering Jew' searching the house for places to work and sleep, all the while 'wringing his hands and tearing his hair, like the German wizard servant who has learnt magic enough to make a broomstick carry water for him, but had not the counter spell to stop it'. A letter to her cousin Jeannie Welsh bemoaning 'the inconvenience of having one's spare room as it were annihilated' reveals something of her attitude towards her husband: 'Could you for instance sleep in a double-bedded room with Carlyle?'

In 1852, Carlyle's increased means and status necessitating a more comfortable space for entertaining, the drawing room was enlarged by taking three feet from Jane's bedroom. At the same time the panelling was removed, a new fireplace and new windows were installed and the room was redecorated. Jane's description of the builders' behaviour strikes a familiar chord: 'Workmen spend three fourths of their time in consulting how the work should be done, and in going out and in after "beer"... The builder promised to have all done in six weeks, painting included; if he gets done in six months is as much as I hope.' However, with Carlyle safely removed to Germany to research Frederick and a pair of loaded pistols under her pillow, there was a certain satisfaction to be gained in 'superintending all these men. I... am infinitely more satisfied than

I was in talking "wits" in my white silk gown with feathers on my head.' And Jane didn't limit her efforts to supervising: during the first of her 'earthquakes' she wrote to Carlyle that when work was delayed she had fallen 'immediately to glazing and painting with my own hands not to ruin you altogether.'

Two years after Jane's death Carlyle's niece Mary Aitken came to stay, living at Cheyne Row until her uncle's death. One of the few changes she made was to redecorate the drawing room, and the present William Morris paper is similar to the one she chose. Mary married her cousin Alexander Carlyle in 1879, and since Carlyle now lived more-or-less full time on the first floor, the second-floor front room (now part of the custodian's flat) became a nursery for their children. The secretaire bookcase in the drawing room was a present to the pair from Erasmus Darwin; the screen, originally made for the dining room, was decorated over a period of several months in 1849 by the indefatigable Jane with a collage of pasted-on pictures of people, landscapes and especially horses. It's the kind of thing my grandmother, a couple of generations younger than Jane and never one to leave anything plain that could be made fancy, used to do, and a method we as teenagers turned on our bedroom walls. Jane was also probably responsible for the naive inlaid decoration on the box that stands on the table, which once contained Goethe's wedding presents to the pair. Three cards on the wall that accompanied subsequent gifts bear verses in his florid hand. The veneration in which Carlyle was held by the end of his life is apparent in the eightieth-birthday testimonial on the landing wall signed by the likes of Tennyson, Darwin, George Eliot, Thackeray, Trevelyan and Trollope.

The bedroom at the back of the first floor was probably the guest room in the early years, with the Carlyles occupying the second floor. Later it became Jane's bedroom, and it is extraordinary to realise that the bed on display here is actually the four-poster 'red bed' she was born in, which she used for most of her life and which Carlyle used at the end of his. (The hangings are those made for Carlyle's bed by Jane shortly before she died.) The family's straightened means can be guessed at by the fact that Jane didn't have a washstand until 1850, when her husband bought her the marble-topped mahogany one in the dressing room here, presented with a note (displayed upstairs in the study) saying: 'Prophecy of a Washstand to the neatest of all Women/Blessings on her bonny face, and be it ever blithe to me, as it is dear, blithe or not'. The other washstand and the hipbath would have stood in Carlyle's dressing room above.

In 1853, with Carlyle still irritated by noisy neighbours, the couple embarked on an ambitious plan to build a new study at the top of the house: 'silent as a tomb, lighted from above'. The room was to cost £169, and architect John Chorley, working with Cubbitts, promised it would be finished in six weeks from a start date of mid August, with the workmen using the outside of the house to minimise disruption to the interior. It didn't quite happen as planned – and after the fifth Irish labourer fell through the ceiling, the Carlyles felt compelled to move out to stay at a cottage belonging to their friend Lady Ashburton; the work was eventually finished towards Christmas. But all was not well. First, Carlyle found the quality of the workmanship and the proportions of the space disappointing. The stove wouldn't burn and the skylight let in the sounds of the outside world, which resonated to the extent that Jane declared: 'The silent room is the noisiest in the house'.

Nevertheless, Carlyle used his study for his 12 years' work on *Frederick the Great*, after which he moved down to the parlour and the study became a maid's bedroom. Today the ascetic, functional-looking space houses his desk – again made originally for Jane's father – and mementoes including crammed pages of manuscript, a walking stick, a shaving-soap box and the like. But it's worth planning to spend some time here, for on the table are not only copies of Carlyle's letters to various friends and relatives but Jane's too. Listen to the sounds of the outside world no architect could exclude and delight in a wit no hardship could blunt.

Chiswick House

Burlington Lane, London W4 2RP
Tel: 020 8995 0508
www.chgt.org.uk
Nearest transport: Chiswick Rail or Turnham Green LU
Open: daily 10.00-17.00 (April), Sun-Wed & bank hols 10.00-17.00
    (May to Oct)
Admission: £5/£4.30/£2.50/family ticket £12.50
Wheelchair access: ground floor only

Chiswick House

Most rueful biographical speculation follows the model: 'if only
(s)he had had more education/money/connections, how much
more could (s)he have achieved?' With Richard Boyle, 3rd Earl of
Burlington, the inverse applies: if only the privileged aristocrat had
had to earn a living from his architecture, how many more Palladian
masterpieces – or follies, depending on your viewpoint – might we
have to celebrate?

Burlington was born in 1694 into one of the richest Anglo-Irish dynasties. He was appointed lord treasurer of Ireland under George I, and his wife Lady Dorothy Savile, heir of the 2nd Marquess of Halifax, was lady-in-waiting to the Princess of Wales. Following the accession of George II, Burlington was made a privy councillor in 1729. Three years later he opposed Whig prime minister Robert Walpole's excise bill against smuggling and fraud; unlike Lord Chesterfield (see Ranger's House, page 310), who when ousted from office for the same offence defected to the opposition, Burlington resigned all his commissions and moved to Chiswick, which became his principal residence.

Like most contemporary nobility, Burlington had made a grand tour of Europe, spending almost a year in 1714–15 accumulating some 800 trunks of paintings and objects. In 1719 he embarked on a second tour, this time inspired by his studies of Giacomo Leoni's first English translation of Palladio's *Quattro Libri dell'architettura* and Colen Campbell's *Vitruvius Britannicus*, a survey of classical architecture in England. Campbell was the champion of the new Palladian movement associated with the Whigs and the Hanoverian succession. He was architect to the Prince of Wales, he prepared the initial designs for Marble Hill House (see page 234), home of the prince's mistress Henrietta Howard, and in 1722 Walpole commissioned him for his Norfolk house, Houghton Hall. Burlington had hired Campbell to rebuild his London residence, Burlington House in Piccadilly (now the much-altered home of the Royal Academy), as early as 1719. And from about the same time the architect was also involved with work on the original house at Chiswick, a mid-17th-century mansion bought by the 1st Earl of Burlington in 1682, for which the 3rd Earl later designed a new front elevation.

In 1725 the Chiswick house was badly damaged by fire; perhaps as a result, Burlington set about designing the annexe that today is regarded as a manifesto of the Palladian movement. In an era when architecture became the province of scholars, Burlington's new building was characterised by a single-minded adherence (whatever the inconvenience to the house's users) to geometrical

Gallery, Chiswick House

laws believed to govern the harmony of the universe. There was also a profusion of references to the architecture of antiquity, redeployed – albeit in a sometimes playfully rococo way – not just as ornament, but to confer meaning. While Burlington House was decorated to illustrate the virtues of chastity and marital fidelity, Chiswick incorporates an allegorical expression of the arts.

The precisely chiselled architectural gem that resulted is a variation on Palladio's Villa Rotonda transplanted to the north, its chimneys concealed in ranges of obelisks on the roof, a solution initially proposed by Campbell for Marble Hill. The absence of a kitchen (but inclusion of a copious wine cellar) has led to speculation that the villa was intended merely as a place for art and conversation, a cross between a gallery and a gentlemen's club. However, an inventory of 1770 shows that it contained most things a functioning household might need, and certainly the bedrooms were used: Lady Burlington died in her chamber in the south-east corner in 1758, five years after her husband and a year after Charlotte, the last survivor of their three daughters.

Burlington's two-storey villa, built between 1727 and 1729, has a square plan with an octagon at its centre from which is accessed the procession of square, rectangular, circular and octagonal rooms that surround it. The entrance in what for clarity will be called the south (actually south-east) front is via a modest door in the rusticated sub-basement. A flamboyant double staircase leads to the pedimented portico, supported by fluted Corinthian columns copied from the Temple of Jupiter Stator in Rome. This gives direct access, via a narrow passage, to the central first-floor saloon or tribunal, used for ceremonial occasions. The house is topped by a shallow stepped dome above the tribunal modelled on the Roman Pantheon, its semi-circular windows replicas of those in the Baths of Diocletian. At the sides of the entrance front stand statues of Burlington's mentors: Andrea Palladio (1508–80) and Inigo Jones (1573–1652), whose Queen's House at Greenwich of a century earlier (see page 306) is the London building Chiswick most closely resembles. The much plainer east and west façades are dominated by single Venetian windows; the north front has three Venetian windows and a staircase to the garden.

The visitor is most aware of the house's geometry on the ground floor, where the inward-looking rooms with their relatively low ceilings are obviously carved out of a larger envelope, with the leftover spaces sometimes awkwardly visible. The octagonal lower tribune, ringed with Tuscan columns, the order recommended by Palladio for hallways, is lit only by daylight from its four approach passages. Below it is the vaulted wine cellar, lined with barrels. Documents indicate that the plainer rooms to the east (not open to the public) were probably a linen room and butler's pantry; those to the west – a square room at the front of the house in which a video is screened and a larger rectangular room behind with information about the villa's history – are described in the inventory as bedchambers. The three rooms on the north front – a central rectangle with apses at each end leading to a small circular room (to the west) and octagon (to the east) – housed Burlington's library and are presumed to be the apartment from which he would emerge to receive guests waiting in the lower tribune. His portrait, dressed in a pale-blue silk suit, pink coat and turban, shows him every inch the handsome aesthete, from his delicate arched eyebrows to his tapering fingers.

As at Palladio's Villa Rotonda, vertical circulation is via circular stair-towers concealed behind the diagonals of the octagon. The largest and most dramatic room of the *piano nobile*, the central octagonal tribunal or saloon, is hung with most of the paintings known to have been here in about 1740: a mix of stuffy portraits of royalty such as Anne of Austria, Louis XIII and Charles I and voluptuous mythological female nudes as in Schoonjans' *Rape of Proserpine*. The outstanding feature is the intricate, lace-like coffering of the lofty ceiling.

Above the library are the three rooms of the gallery, probably intended as an enclosed loggia for dining or exercise. Their distinct geometries and interconnecting plan recall the sequence of spaces in Roman baths. Below the heavily gilded ceilings are relatively plain walls ornamented with a frieze of festoons of flowers and leaves emerging from woven baskets supported on female heads – perhaps an allegory of the creation of the Corinthian capital, described by Vitruvius as a female order derived from a basket placed inadvertently on top of an acanthus plant that unexpectedly breaks into leaf.

The main room to the west is the red velvet room, in which Burlington displayed the major paintings in his collection. The ceiling is an allegory of the arts painted by William Kent, whom Burlington met in Rome on his second grand tour. The adjacent square blue-velvet room on the entrance front, used as a study and hung in Burlington's day with Dutch landscapes, has an exotically rich ceiling supported on heavy brackets with a central allegory of architecture (also by Kent). The wealth of decoration involved in the gilded ceiling, deep-blue walls, ruched silk blinds and ornate gilded overmantel, squeezed into a tiny space, borders on camp. Opening off it – in a sequence reminiscent of Russian dolls – was the red closet, the smallest of the three rooms in the west range and the one that held the most, and most precious, paintings. Opposite the red velvet room in the eastern flank is the green velvet room, also primarily for the display of pictures that today include views of the gardens commissioned by Burlington himself. The bedchamber to the south was originally hung with tapestries; the closet beyond it probably functioned as Lady Burlington's study.

To the north-east is the link building, built in 1732–33 to connect the new annexe to the old house, perhaps as a result of Burlington's decision to make Chiswick his main home. No one knows whether this was to be a permanent arrangement or whether he intended eventually to extend the annexe and pull down the old house, as his ancestors were to do half a century later. Originally the link building consisted of a hall connected to a loggia at right-angles to it (now destroyed). The first-floor hall is subdivided by two Corinthian colonnades; the ground-floor room (now containing a sphinx and statues purloined from Hadrian's Villa outside Rome) has screens of Tuscan columns. The once lavishly furnished summer parlour beyond was described by Horace Walpole (see Strawberry Hill, page 254) as 'Lady Burlington's Dressing Room, built at her own Expence'. Today it has information about the history of the house.

After Burlington's death Chiswick was inherited by the 5th Duke of Devonshire (his grandson by his daughter Charlotte), who in 1788 demolished the old house and added heavy flanking wings to his grandfather's delicate design. The 5th Duke's wife Georgiana (daughter of the 1st Earl of Spencer; see Spencer House, page 66) was a leading political hostess for the Whig party; Whig leader Charles Fox died at Chiswick in 1806. The 6th ('bachelor') Duke entertained Tsars Alexander I and Nicholas I and Queen Victoria and Prince Albert here; prime minister George Canning died at Chiswick in 1827. From 1858 the house was let to tenants, including the Duchess of Sutherland – who received both Gladstone and Garibaldi here – the Prince of Wales (in the 1870s), and from 1892 to 1929 T S and C M Tuke, Quaker pioneers in the treatment of mental health. The Devonshires sold the house to the council in 1929 and the wings were demolished in 1956–57 to re-expose the purity of Burlington's concept. As Richard Hewlings points out in his excellent guidebook, at the time his reputation as an architect was riding high: he had recently been rehabilitated by Rudolf Wittkower and others and was revered as an important precursor to the modern movement.

In addition to his own pioneering work, Burlington fulfilled an important role as a patron, housing William Kent, musician George Frideric Handel (see page 35), poet John Gay and sculptor Guelfi in his Piccadilly home. Both before and after his resignation from politics, he had enough connections to obtain positions of importance for his protégés (Kent, for instance, worked on Kensington Palace, see page 190, and was made deputy surveyor of the king's works in 1735). And behind Burlington House in Piccadilly he laid out an estate of fashionable houses, two designed by himself, one by Kent, four by Campbell and two by Leoni, in streets whose names reflect the sources of his vast wealth: Cork Street for his paternal ancestors, Clifford Street for his maternal ancestors and Savile Row for his wife's family.

View of the Exedra taken from inside Chiswick House

'To build, to plant, whatever you intend,
To rear the column, or the arch to bend,
To swell the terrace, or to sink the grot;
In all, let Nature never be forgot.'
Alexander Pope, 'Epistle IV. To Richard
Boyle, Earl of Burlington', 1731

More things to see & do

Chiswick House Gardens were the birthplace of the English landscape movement and the inspiration for great gardens from Blenheim Palace to New York's Central Park. They are open from 7.00 to dusk daily and entry is free. The wonderfully understated and thoroughly modern café designed by Caruso St John is open daily from 8.30 to 18.00 (summer) and 8.30 to 16.00 (winter). The house also hosts an impressive programme of events. See *www.chgt.org.uk*.

Fulham Palace

Bishop's Avenue, London SW6 6EA
Tel: 020 7736 3233
www.fulhampalace.org
Nearest transport: Putney Bridge LU
Open: Sat-Wed 13.00-16.00, guided tours at 14.00 on 2nd & 4th Sun
   & 3rd Tues of every month
Admission: free, tours £5
Wheelchair access: call in advance

Fulham Palace – until recently the country retreat or sometimes main residence of the Bishops of London – is a case where the whole is less than the sum of its parts. Successive occupants – usually men of substantial means enriched by revenues from the diocese – added wings, half-heartedly remodelled rooms or ruthlessly butchered the work of their predecessors to conform with their own taste, their particular practical requirements or what they believed to be the fashion of the day. The building has been leased to the council since 1973 and its major rooms now house a museum, gallery and café, with offices on the upper floors.

Though the earliest part of the existing complex is the great hall, which dates from 1480, it's known there was a palace here as early as 1141. The plan of the present conglomeration consists of two courtyards – the large western (entrance) quadrangle and the smaller, purely internal eastern court – both surrounded by ranges of rooms. The great hall sits between the two.

Visitors enter via the picturesque western quadrangle, which largely dates from the late 15th and early 16th centuries. Three sides have original brickwork with a diaper pattern picked out using black, twice-baked bricks; their quality can be appreciated by comparison with the refacing of the southern range undertaken in the mid 19th century by Bishop Blomfield, whose machine-made bricks and painted diamonds lack the charm or durability of the rest. During Blomfield's time the quadrangle was a service area including a bakehouse, brewhouse, dairy and laundry (for washing sent from the bishop's townhouse in St James's Square). The doorway to

Western quadrangle, Fulham Palace

the palace, set below a charming early-16th-century oriel window, dates from the time of Bishop Howley (1813–28); the entrance to the quadrangle has massive gates that probably formed part of the medieval building.

Bishop Sherlock (1748–61) described Fulham Palace as 'a very bad old house'. He modernised the great hall and added a parlour to the north-east corner. Bishop Terrick (1764–77) was more ambitious. A former vicar of Twickenham and an admirer of Horace Walpole's Strawberry Hill (see page 254), he employed the surveyor of St Paul's, Stiff Leadbetter, to build him three single-storey ranges of rooms around the eastern quadrangle. Topped with battlements, the eastern, garden front featured chunky two-storey square corner towers and a central square porch; the northern elevation had gothic windows that can still be seen. Bishop Howley, who was later to make his mark on Addington Palace (see page 317) when he became Archbishop of Canterbury, was horrified by the 'gothicky nonsense' he inherited. He hired Samuel Pepys Cockerell to remodel the eastern range into a suite of grand rooms with a uniform flat seven-bay façade, add a second storey throughout and rid the building of its towers and crenellations.

The great hall is exceedingly modest, with none of the drama of its near-contemporary in the Old Palace at Croydon (see page 336). It originally had a large room on the ground floor and a great chamber or several smaller rooms above. Sherlock removed the first floor and installed the present coved ceiling; the mock-17th-century windows date from the time of Bishop Porteus (1787–1809). The hall was converted into a chapel by Howley, who was reportedly offended by the stench of beer from the cellar below the chapel then in use. Bishop Tait (1856–68) restored it to its original function of grand dining and reception room, adding the present late-17th-century screen and panelling and hiring William Butterfield to build a new chapel to the south of the complex.

Butterfield's chapel – its exterior red brick with true diaper patterning – was similarly messed about by Bishop Wand (1945–55). The original interior had the architect's trademark bold horizontal bands of polychrome brick on the lower walls, topped by elaborate tiled patterns and exposed rafters. Wand had the rafters replaced by a barrel vault and the walls painted over with a series of murals by Brian Thomas. The marble flooring, probably recycled from the great hall, remains.

The integrity of Sherlock's neo-Palladian parlour was destroyed when it was turned into a kitchen by Howley after he built his new suite of rooms. A century and a half later, when the room was converted into the home for a computer, a false ceiling was installed, obliterating the rococo plasterwork. Restored to their former glory, the fine proportions, delicate plaster panels and elaborate doorcases can now be appreciated.

Bishop Howley's impressive and beautifully proportioned panelled dining room now houses a museum with information about the palace's history. His elegant drawing room and light-filled breakfast room have been sympathetically converted into a café and Bishop Terrick's dining room and drawing room in the southern range are a gallery for contemporary art. The dining room has the palace's other fine plasterwork ceiling. Next to Howley's dining room is the comfortable library – originally part of Terrick's chapel – he had made for the books bequeathed by anti-slavery campaigner Bishop Porteus. Above each bookcase is a letter of the alphabet to aid classification and behind one of the cases is a secret door.

More things to see & do
The extensive gardens at Fulham Palace include rare trees and shrubs, woodland, meadows, lawns and an 18th-century walled garden. They are open daily from dawn to dusk, with occasional tours (see *www.fulhampalace.org* for times). The gallery (usually open daily, 10.00-17.00) hosts a changing programme of contemporary art linked to the palace. The Drawing Room Café is also open daily (10.00-17.00) and holds a BBQ on the lawn during summer weekends.

Gunnersbury Park Museum

Popes Lane, London W3 8LQ
Tel: 020 8992 1612
www.visithounslow.com/Gunnersbury_Park_Mansions
Nearest transport: Acton Town LU
Open: daily 11.00-16.00 (Nov to March) & 11.00-17.00 (April to Oct)
Admission: free

The core of the ugly neoclassical stuccoed Large Mansion that houses Gunnersbury Park Museum was built early in the 19th century by developer Alexander Copland, possibly with the involvement of Sydney Smirke, whose brother was one of Copland's executors. Though it's no longer possible to be certain which rooms were added at which point, it seems that the house as it stands today – in particular the over-extended south façade, 11 bays long with a central three-storey section with arched first-floor windows over a Doric loggia – is very much Smirke's creation, whether from before or after he was engaged as architect by financier Nathan Mayer Rothschild (1777–1836), who bought the house in 1835.

South façade, Gunnersbury Park Museum

Rothschild, whose clients included the British government, to whom he'd loaned money to fund the Napoleonic wars, had been advised to avoid ostentation because of the secret nature of the deals by which he had amassed his fortune. Following his death, his wife Hannah set aside such concerns, holding a house-warming 'breakfast' two years later at which she entertained 500 guests at a cost of £2000 – around one-seventh of the price Nathan paid for the house and its grounds.

Following Hannah's death, the property passed to her son Lionel (1808–79), a friend of Disraeli who in 1858 became Britain's first practising Jewish MP after an 11-year fight for his right to be admitted to parliament without having to swear a Christian oath. (In 1875 the Rothschilds loaned Disraeli's government the funds to secure the Suez Canal, earning themselves £100,000.) Lionel's third son Leopold was a racehorse enthusiast who established a stud at Gunnersbury. All three generations were known for their philanthropy, in particular their funding of education and healthcare. The house remained in the family until it was sold to the council in 1925.

Nathan hired Smirke to make improvements as soon as he bought the house, enlarging the kitchens and servants' quarters and building an orangery, but it was probably Hannah who commissioned the imposing French-inspired neoclassical interiors that can be glimpsed behind the museum's changing displays. The rooms to the east and west of the entrance hall were originally the parlour and library respectively. Behind the library, in the heart of the house, is a further hall or 'corridor', top lit with an oval gallery at first-floor level. Along the south elevation is a run of three grand rooms accessed via an anteroom. The central drawing room, flanked by the loggia, is an elegant space divided into three by two sets of Ionic marble columns. Its pretty ceiling features a trellis pattern and oval painting of the four seasons. The dining room to the west and drawing room to the east have higher, more heavily moulded ceilings, richer door surrounds and sturdier columns; the drawing room has a conservatory that echoes the curve of its eastern bay.

The council has laudably tried to increase the property's relevance to local people by concentrating resources on the servants' quarters – usually neglected in house restorations but here the only part set up as it was once occupied. The size of this wing brings home the amount of labour involved in catering to the whims of a wealthy family and its guests before modern services arrived. The 1881 census lists Lionel's widow Charlotte in residence along with 13 female and seven male servants – two cooks, a butler, three servants and a footman – plus 13 coachmen. The photograph of the 25 staff employed by Leopold in 1915 illustrates the last gasp of a social structure that was largely destroyed by the Great War.

More things to see & do

The Gunnersbury Park Museum grounds include ornamental gardens, woods and lakes as well as sports facilities. The museum hosts a range of exhibitions about the history of the borough.

Hogarth's House

Hogarth Lane, Great West Road, London W4 2QN
www.hounslow.info/arts/hogarthshouse
Open: closed for refurbishment until summer 2011 or beyond
Wheelchair access: ground floor only
Nearest transport: Chiswick Rail or Turnham Green LU

'He swerved between elation and anxiety, becoming more prone to anger or melancholy in times of stress... He won favours and commissions, then mocked himself and his patrons. He worked with his fellow artists, then turned on them again, feeling isolated and misunderstood. All the time he nervously assessed his achievement, judging it sometimes confidently by his own standards, sometimes miserably by the response of critics, sometimes resignedly, simply by the money that he made.'
Jenny Uglow on Hogarth at 60, from 'Hogarth A Life and a World' (1997)

William Hogarth bought the Chiswick house that now bears his name in 1749 and used it as his summer retreat for the remaining 15 years of his life. Then aged 53, he was famous thanks to the popular success of such print series as *A Harlot's Progress* (1732), *A Rake's Progress* (1735) and *Marriage A-la-Mode* (1745). The Engravers' Act of 1735, for which he had lobbied vigorously, protected him from pirate copyists, so assuring him a substantial income. He was co-proprietor of the academy in St Martin's Lane – the leading school for painting and the graphic arts – and was a governor of St Bartholomew's Hospital, the Foundling Hospital and Bedlam. He had an apparently affectionate relationship with his wife Jane – daughter of James Thornhill, serjeant painter to George I and II (responsible for decorations at Hampton Court and Kensington Palace, see pages 214 and 190) – with whom he had eloped in 1729. And he had a wide circle of acquaintances within the London club and drinking scenes as well as several close and loyal friends. Yet these were not happy years.

The Chiswick house, described by its new owner as 'the little country box by the Thames', was reached via a small track from Chiswick Lane and was surrounded by high walls similar to those that shield it from the heavy traffic today. Probably built in the first decade of the 18th century and first appearing in public records in 1718, it was a simple two-storey brick cottage, two rooms wide and one room deep. Hogarth doubled its size, adding a kitchen extension to the western end with a room above, and raising the roof to create a third storey. It's likely he also installed the grand bay with arched windows above the entrance, which dominates the front of the house. Though Hogarth may often have been unhappy, bitter and angry, the house feels as if it might have provided a comfortable and comforting escape from the pretensions and pressures of the London art world – a modest retreat where you could put up your feet, relax and be soothed by the simple and intimate pleasures of family life.

Chiswick at the time was little more than a village, though in the first half of the century a few grand houses had sprung up including the Palladian villa built by Lord Burlington (see page 162) and decorated by William Kent, who in 1722 had ousted Hogarth's future father-in-law from the commission for decorating Kensington Palace. Hogarth despised and derided both men. While most of Hogarth's life – in terms both of time and intellectual and emotional energy – still centred on London, where he retained a house in the fashionable Leicester Fields (now Leicester Square), he did find like-minded neighbours at Chiswick including Thomas Morell, one of Handel's librettists (see page 35). His house was often full of women – his wife Jane, her mother Lady Thornhill, Jane's young cousin and companion Mary Lewis, and Hogarth's sister Anne. Though Jane and William were childless, they supervised Chiswick wet-nurses for children left at the Foundling Hospital and invited foundlings and village children to their home.

The 1750s began well for Hogarth with the publication in 1751 of his prints *Beer Street* and *Gin Lane*. *Beer Street* is a traditional scene of comic revelry, whereas the disturbing *Gin Lane* depicts a city of wrecked humanity. (Gin had arrived from Holland with William and Mary and by the 1750s almost one in five houses in Holborn was licensed for its sale.) The *Four Stages of Cruelty* was published six days later. Hogarth declared his aim to be 'preventing in some degree that cruel treatment of poor Animals... the very describing of which gives pain'. But the moral of the series – whose anti-hero Tom Nero moves from torturing a dog and whipping a nag to the murder of a maidservant that results in his hanging – obviously goes further.

Hogarth was determined his prints should be cheap enough to be bought by the poor for whom he claimed they were chiefly intended and so eschewed the fine detail that would make engraving too expensive. His other successful series from his time in Chiswick was *Four Prints of an Election*, a satire on the antics leading up to the election of 1754, many of its details based on the corrupt practices in Oxfordshire revolving around local squire Sir James Dashwood. Not completed until 1758, the series shows the country teetering on the brink of anarchy. The paintings from which the prints were derived were eventually bought by John Soane in 1823 and now hang in the picture room of his museum (see page 58).

Whatever his success with the public, Hogarth found himself increasingly isolated within the art world. The son of a schoolteacher who had unwisely sunk his funds into a Latin-speaking coffeehouse and ended up in prison for debt, he had served his apprenticeship with a silver-plate engraver rather than on a grand tour. Pragmatically as well as idealistically, he championed the notion of a British school of art of equal value to the French and Italian traditions imitated by many of his fellow artists and lauded by such cognoscenti as Burlington. He had long been embroiled in a battle with his colleagues at St Martin's Lane about whether the school should be run on democratic principles, as he wished, or as a more formal, elite-led academy along the lines of those in Paris and Rome. It was a battle Hogarth was to lose posthumously with the establishment of the Royal Academy, with his arch-rival Joshua Reynolds as its first president, just four years after his death.

Despite the success of his satirical prints and moral dramas, Hogarth felt the need to prove himself a painter of the stature of his father-in-law and the equal of the French and Italian old masters. In 1751 he advertised the sale of the paintings for his popular 1745 *Marriage A-la-Mode* print series by auction at his London home. Just two bids were received, and the paintings were sold for only 120 guineas rather than the £500 Hogarth had been expecting. The public humiliation was a bitter blow. The following year he began the laborious task of writing and rewriting *The Analysis of Beauty*, a treatise setting out his theories on art and painting with which Morell helped in the later stages. The work was remarkably well received, though criticisms of Hogarth's pretension, dogmatism and lack of learning sent him into a fury. For much of 1755–56 he worked on a vast altarpiece for St Mary Redcliffe church in Bristol, but it led to no further commissions. Then in February 1757 he announced in the *London Evening Post* that he would thenceforth devote his time to portrait painting. Though he received a few commissions, he seemed more comfortable painting friends and family, whose portraits he was often loath to part with. (His 1757 portrait of his close friend, the actor David Garrick, and his wife Violette was not handed to its subjects until after Hogarth's death.)

In spring 1757 Hogarth was appointed serjeant painter to George II following the resignation of his brother-in-law John Thornhill. It was a highly lucrative post, which he had coveted since the death of his father-in-law, but he almost immediately began to belittle it, seeing it as a less illustrious role than Reynolds' job of painting the court beauties, not least because payment was made by the Board of Works, which also dealt with plumbers, bricklayers and masons. From now on Hogarth was responsible for all commissions for painting and gilding, including such high-profile commands as the decoration of the Chapel Royal for young George III's wedding in 1761 and of Westminster Hall for his coronation two weeks later.

Despite such public recognition, Hogarth remained determined to demonstrate his worth as a painter of serious subjects. His greatest folly was *Sigismunda*, undertaken in 1758 at the request of Richard Grosvenor, who commissioned a painting on a subject of Hogarth's choice at a price named by the artist. Grosvenor was expecting a comedy of manners like *The Lady's Last Stake*, commissioned by his friend the Earl of Charlemont and using the young Hester Thrale (a friend of Dr Johnson's, see page 46) as a model. Instead, Hogarth chose as his subject Boccaccio's story of a young woman who against the will of her father married his lower-class protégé, only for the father to kill his son-in-law and send his heart to his daughter in a jewelled cup which she fills with poison and drinks. The story had obvious resonances with Hogarth's past and he used sketches of Jane grieving at the recent death of her mother as a model for the stricken heroine. Hogarth named his price as 400 guineas – nearly the same as had been paid recently at auction for an Italian-school painting of the same subject. But Grosvenor wriggled out of the agreement and once more Hogarth was subject to public humiliation.

In the early 1760s Hogarth became close to a group of young satirists that included Charles Churchill, who from 1762 was deputy editor of *The North Briton*, an audacious opposition paper that derided prime minister John Bute (owner of Kenwood, see page 115) and supported the populist cause of opposition leader William Pitt, in particular his desire to continue the Seven Years War with France. In his 1762 print *The Times*, Plate I, Hogarth suggested the damage Pitt had done Britain and showed *The North Briton* as the fuel feeding the fire. The paper's editor John Wilkes retaliated by devoting an entire issue to a scabrous attack on Hogarth, mocking him as 'house-painter' to the court, doubting his authorship of the *Analysis*, deriding *Sigismunda* and criticising his vanity, envy and malevolence. Hogarth's response – a caricature of Wilkes – drew an even more vehement denunciation from Churchill.

Hogarth had been ill for almost a year after the rejection of *Sigismunda* and now his health deteriorated further. For some time he had been becoming increasingly vague (a story has him returning home via a hackney coach from Mansion House when his own carriage was parked outside) and the last two years of his life were largely devoted to making rambling notes for an autobiography and revising his prints, working much of the time in his studio in Chiswick. After his death in 1764 Jane lived on at Chiswick for a further 25 years with Mary Lewis and until 1771 with Hogarth's sister Anne. Lewis continued to live here until her death in 1808, when the house was let to various tenants. It was bought by Lt Col Robert Shipway in 1901 and opened to the public in 1904. Five years later it was gifted to the council.

At the time of writing, the house was closed for refurbishment, and precise details of the likely décor and arrangement of the rooms were unavailable. What follows is therefore limited to a description of the plan and the way the rooms were used when the Hogarths were in residence.

On the left of the present front door is the three-bay dining room, a space that before Hogarth's alterations was two tiny rooms divided by a central staircase; the present room's central window would have been the original front door. It is here that the Hogarths received visitors. To the right was the servants' hall, with a trapdoor to the cellar below, and the kitchen.

The narrow curved staircase leads to a landing. Above the dining room was Hogarth's small bedroom; on the other side of the landing was the parlour with its large three-bay window. The room beyond, above the kitchen extension, was a library. On the second floor and in the attic were bedrooms for relatives and rooms for servants. Hogarth's studio, above the stable block in the garden, collapsed in 1868.

Plans for the house promise new displays about Hogarth, his family and other inhabitants as well as a collection of his prints. It is to be hoped these include such pictures as the 1745 self-portrait that formerly hung in the bedroom, showing the artist with his beloved pug, one of many he owned in his lifetime. The image reveals a man of short stature, with a round face, full mouth and snub nose that seem refined versions of the features of many of his characters.

Kelmscott House
(William Morris Society)

26 Upper Mall, London W6 9TA
Tel: 020 8741 3735
www.morrissociety.org/Kelmscott_House.html
Nearest transport: Ravenscourt Park LU or Hammersmith LU
Open: Thurs & Sat 14.00-17.00
Admission: free
Wheelchair access: partial

'As I sit and work at home I hear the yells and shrieks... It was my good luck only of being born respectable and rich, that has put me on this side of the window among delightful books and lovely works of art, and not on the other side, in the empty street, the drink-steeped liquor-shops, the foul and degraded lodgings.' William Morris, lecture at Burslem town hall, 1881

Kelmscott House was the London home of William Morris (see also Water House, page 354 and Red House, page 338) from 1878 until his death in 1896. At the time, Hammersmith bordered a slum district known as Little Wapping, and Morris, whose study and bedroom were on the ground floor at the front of the house, would often be disturbed by urchins shouting in the street or swinging on his gate. During his time at Kelmscott, Morris became increasingly preoccupied by social injustice and committed to political activism, travelling round the country to preach revolutionary socialism. In 1884 he founded the Socialist League, working as its first treasurer and the editor of its mouthpiece *Commonweal*, and in 1890, as the organisation became dominated by anarchists, he set up the Hammersmith Socialist Society, a precursor of the Fabian Society. The Kelmscott coach house – simply decorated with matting on the whitewashed walls, a bare floor and a kitchen table on the platform at the north end – served as a venue for meetings. Morris then entertained speakers such as Annie Besant, George Bernard Shaw, Keir Hardie and Peter Kropotkin in his beautiful and spacious house.

Kelmscott House

Built in the late 1780s, Kelmscott is a fine example of Georgian architecture, three storeys high and five bays wide, its red-brick façade punctuated by simple mullioned sashes and a doorcase supported on Ionic pilasters. Unfortunately for visitors today, only the ground floor of the two-storey coach house and the basement of the house proper – now the headquarters of the William Morris Society – are open to the public. The rest has been leased to a private tenant since the society, which was bequeathed the house in 1970 but not the money to maintain it, lost a legal battle to retain it as a research centre and museum.

It was the painter Dante Gabriel Rossetti, on a house-hunting expedition, who came across Kelmscott (then called the Retreat) and suggested it to Morris. The Morris family changed the name to match Kelmscott Manor, the Oxfordshire home Morris had leased with Rossetti to give his wife Jane and the painter space to conduct a love affair. Previous residents in the Hammersmith home had included Sir Frances Ronalds, who in 1816 constructed the first electric telegraph in the garden. Morris took over the lease from novelist and poet George MacDonald, also an inventor of nostalgic fables, who had lived here since 1867.

This was a busy period in Morris' life. In addition to his political activities, he had taken over sole ownership of the design firm Morris, Marshall, Faulkner & Co in 1875 (renaming it Morris & Co) and the company was expanding rapidly as its textiles and wallpapers became standard issue for the artistic middle classes. Then in 1891, inspired by a lecture on typography at the Art Workers Guild by fellow socialist and neighbour Emery Walker (see page 141), he established the Kelmscott Press to produce books 'which it would be a pleasure to look upon as pieces of printing and arrangement of type'. Over the next seven years, with Walker as advisor, the press was to issue 52 books for which Morris designed three typefaces and more than 600 decorative initial letters, ornaments and borders.

Work may have provided a release from unhappiness at home. Though his younger daughter May (1862–1938) had taken over the embroidery department at Morris & Co, Jenny, a year her senior, had developed epilepsy, with each terrifying new seizure threatening further brain damage. Then in 1883 Jane, who had ended her relationship with Rossetti a couple of years before the move to Hammersmith, began a new affair with charismatic socialist poet, explorer and philanderer Wilfrid Scawen Blunt. This time Morris may have been kept in ignorance, especially as Jane's devotion seems to have been unrequited. Certainly Shaw, with whom May had an affair that was to wreck her own marriage, described William in the 1890s as still besotted: 'He could not sit in the same room without his arm round [Jane's] waist. His voice changed when he spoke to her as it changed to no one else.'

Visitors to Kelmscott today get little sense of Morris' life here. In the basement you can see one of the original Kelmscott printing presses, still fully operational, as well as mementoes of the printing house such as letters from compositors and Burne-Jones' cartoon of a plump Morris carving a woodblock. A pleasant room with steps to the garden contains a Philip Webb-designed fireplace and such drawings as Morris' reworking of his 1857 design for the ceiling of the debating hall at Oxford Union, during which project he met Jane. In the coach house is the original design for the Bird textile that once covered the walls of the drawing room and can still be seen in the dining room of Emery Walker's former home at 7 Hammersmith Terrace. Alongside it hangs a portrait of actress Athlene Seyler, who was born during Morris' time at Kelmscott and lived in the coach house for 50 years until her death in 1990 at the age of 101.

Kensington Palace

Kensington Gardens, London W8 4PX
Tel: 0844 482 7777
www.hrp.org.uk/kensingtonPalace
Nearest transport: Queensway LU or High Street Kensington LU
Open: daily 10.00-18.00 (March to Oct) & 10.00-17.00 (Nov to Feb)
Admission: £12.50/£11/£6.25/under-5s free/family ticket £34
Wheelchair access: limited

Until it was given a new lease of life as a tourist venue through its association with Britain's favourite princess, the late Diana, Princess of Wales, coupled with a £12 million refurbishment programme due for completion in 2012, Kensington Palace was very much a poor relation to Buckingham Palace (see page 15) and Hampton Court (see page 214). Much like many of its former inhabitants, in fact, since the palace functioned as a residence for the monarchy only for William III and Mary II, Queen Anne, and Georges I and II, thereafter housing a succession of undistinguished royalty including several of George III's children, whose upkeep was described by the Duke of Wellington as 'the damnedest millstone about the necks of any government that can be imagined'. Most persistent was George's fourth son Edward, Duke of Kent, who lived at Kensington from 1798 until he fled to Brussels in 1812 to escape his creditors. Five years later, following the death of Charlotte, the future George IV's only legitimate daughter, Edward returned to Kensington married to Charlotte's widower's sister, who some months later gave birth to the future Queen Victoria.

Victoria and her mother continued to live at Kensington until her accession in 1837 at the age of 19, alongside such minor royals as Edward's younger brother Augustus, Duke of Sussex (from 1805 to 1843), and the future George IV's estranged wife Princess Caroline of Brunswick (from 1808 to 1821), who also had a house at Blackheath (see Ranger's House, page 310). Victoria's sixth child Louise, a sculptor, took over Augustus' apartments following the death of his widow in 1867 (her statue of her mother stands outside the east front); from 1867 to 1883 the apartments formerly

Kensington Palace

occupied by Victoria and her mother were given to the Duke and Duchess of Teck, whose eldest daughter Mary was to marry the future George V; from 1901 to 1940 Victoria's youngest daughter Beatrice inhabited the rooms that today house the royal ceremonial dress collection. Diana was assigned rooms in the palace from 1981 until her death in 1997.

The original house was a Jacobean mansion built c. 1605 for Sir George Coppin, possibly by John Thorpe, who was also probably the architect of Charlton House (see page 291). In 1689 William and Mary bought it from secretary of state Lord Nottingham as an alternative to Whitehall Palace. In the 13 years of William's reign, his surveyor of the kings works Christopher Wren and clerk of the works Nicholas Hawksmoor added several new wings, including the queen's gallery extending to the north and the king's gallery flanking the south façade. These, together with the original mansion, comprehensively rebuilt in 1718–22, probably to the design of the future George II's architect Colen Campbell (see Marble Hill House,

191

King's gallery, Kensington Palace

page 234), constitute the state apartments whose restoration from the taxpayers' purse was reluctantly authorised by parliament in 1897 on condition they be opened to the public.

At the time of writing, the palace was embarking on a major refurbishment programme. Until June 2012 the state apartments are to house the temporary exhibition 'Enchanted Palace', for which theatre company Wildworks and a stellar cast of artists and designers including Vivienne Westwood, William Tempest and Stephen Jones have created installations that respond to the stories and characters who have peopled the various rooms. So the text that follows is a brief description of the permanent features of the spaces that will remain accessible to the public.

Most memorable of the great spaces of the *piano nobile* is the king's grand staircase, with *trompe l'oeil* murals painted in 1725–27 for George I by William Kent. The dramatic simplicity of the black marble staircase with its chequerboard landings and iron balustrade contrasts with Kent's illusionist painting, which transports the decidedly unglamorous British court to an Italianate setting that its creator would have regarded as the height of civilisation (Kent had been in Italy, where he had met Lord Burlington – see Chiswick House, page 162 – from 1714 to 1719). Among the recognisable characters are Kent and his mistress, surveying the scene from the ceiling; Kaspar Hauser-prototype Peter the 'wild boy', discovered outside Hanover and presented to the king as a curiosity; and one of the pages of Marble Hill House's Lady Henrietta Howard, who balances nonchalantly on the wrong side of the balcony balustrade.

The square presence chamber, part of one of the pavilions Wren added to the corners of the original house, has a ceiling decorated by Kent in an Etruscan/Pompeiian style that looks refreshingly modern – stylised figures and plant forms in startlingly bold reds and blues set with geometric regularity on a white ground. The less radical privy chamber, also with a ceiling painted by Kent, leads to the gloriously lofty cupola room, the principal state room of the palace. Here Kent's love of *trompe l'oeil* extends to the feigned coffering of the ceiling, the 'fluting' of the giant Ionic pilasters that dominate the decor and the 'moulding' of the bases of the columns supporting the massive marble doorway surrounds, as well as some armoury on the walls. The room was his first major commission for interior decoration, gained in 1722 after he undercut by almost 50 per cent the price quoted for the ceiling by the royal serjeant painter James Thornhill, an event that signalled the decline of the fashion for the baroque and the ascendancy of Palladianism. Thornhill never really recovered, and his future son-in-law William Hogarth (see page 179) satirised Kent in his engravings, commenting: 'Never was there a more wretched dauber that soonest got into palaces in this country'.

The king's drawing room is almost as lofty and imposing, with the added advantage of uninterrupted views over the park. Kent's ceiling boosted the royal ego with its depiction of the all-powerful Jupiter with the cowering Semele, the lover he inadvertently destroyed with his divine power. According to diarist and courtier Lord Hervey, Queen Caroline dispensed with some of the pictures – which include Vasari's *Venus and Cupid* and two voluptuous female nudes – while George II was away; on his return he insisted on having his 'fat Venus', as indeed she is, reinstated. The king's state bedchamber was converted for use by Princess Victoria and the Duchess of Kent in 1834–36.

The 30-metre-long king's gallery has been restored to the scheme Kent devised for George I, though the extraordinary wind-dial above the fireplace with its representations of the four known continents showing European elegance, Asians as Europeans with turbans, nude African 'savages' and a European traveller conversing with feathered 'Indians', was made for William III. The original picture hang was by Kent, though George II's predilection for plump female bottoms is again in evidence in many pictures, including Tintoretto's *The Muses*.

The queen's apartments, consisting of bedchamber, drawing room, dining room, closet and gallery, are on a noticeably smaller, more domestic scale.

Leighton House

12 Holland Park Road, London W14 8LZ
Tel: 020 7602 3316
www.rbkc.gov.uk/LeightonHouseMuseum
Nearest transport: High Street Kensington LU
Open: Wed-Mon 10.00-17.30
Admission: £5/£1 (unlimited return within a year)
Wheelchair access: none

Garden façade, Leighton House

Built just a decade before the nearby Linley Sambourne House (see page 147), Leighton House is as idiosyncratic as its neighbour is stereotypical. Both owners were artists who wished to transform their houses and workplaces into palaces of art, but the wealthy, unmarried Leighton had the means and opportunity to give full expression to his ideas of what such a palace might be.

From the outside, Leighton House seems to shut its face to the world, with its large north-facing studio window invisible from

Arab hall, Leighton House

the street and its red-brick façade giving little hint of the wondrous, fluid interior or the openness of its garden rooms to the light and views. Frederic Leighton (1830–96) started work on his house with architect George Aitchison, a personal friend, in 1864. The son of a doctor whose father had amassed a considerable fortune as physician to the Czarina in St Petersburg, Leighton had spent much of his teen years in Europe, where the family moved because of his mother's ill-health, studying art in Berlin, Frankfurt and Florence. After an independent European journey that involved some three years each in Rome and Paris, he returned to London in 1859.

Though he had met with early good fortune when his *Cimabue's Madonna Carried in Procession through Florence*, exhibited at the Royal Academy in 1855, was bought by Queen Victoria, Leighton had subsequently fallen from favour, his success deemed too easily gained. But the sale of *Dante in Exile* in 1864 to the dealer Gambert for 1000 guineas signalled a rise in his reputation and financial prospects. By 1878 he was elected president of the Royal Academy and at the end of his life he was created a peer, the only British artist so honoured. Handsome, cultivated and with a private income, he was much sought after in London society and was a firm favourite with the Prince and Princess of Wales. Leighton House provided a showcase for his art and ceramic collections, an exhibition space for his paintings in advance of their appearance at the Royal Academy and a place to entertain friends at dinner parties and musical evenings.

The house as originally conceived was an L-shape made up of the present entrance hall, staircase hall, dining room and drawing room, with the front door positioned at the western window of the current entrance hall. The only rooms upstairs were the studio, bedroom and bathroom: Leighton had no intention of disturbing his routines by accommodating visitors overnight. The ante-room or hall of Narcissus, Arab hall and library were built between 1877 and 1879 and the silk room above the library in 1895. In 1889 he added the glass, wood and iron winter studio to the east of the studio proper, originally supported on four cast-iron columns with a void below.

Nothing in the elegant façade or unimposing entrance hall prepares the visitor for the sensual magic of the staircase hall, hall of Narcissus and Arab hall, a continuous space with gilded ceilings and walls tiled in luminous blues and greens. At the foot of the stairs stands a stuffed peacock, symbol of the aesthetic movement, which sought to mitigate Victorian ugliness by introducing beauty from other cultures. Here the vivid blue tiles (designed by ceramicist William De Morgan) contrast effectively with the Japanese-inspired polished ebonised wood used for the staircase and the Roman-inspired black and white mosaic floor. The hall of Narcissus is named from the bronze statue that stands at its centre, with the blue tiles and shimmering ceiling suggesting water and reflections respectively.

Intended to evoke the world of the *Arabian Nights*, the Arab hall, with its tinkling fountain and golden dome, was created by Aitchison as a setting for the tiles Leighton and his friends had acquired from Rhodes, Damascus, Cairo and Tangier, which he first visited in 1852. All use a similar palette of blues and greens, but their content ranges from inscriptions and abstract patterns to leaves, birds and flowers. The jigsaw effect of fitting the various collections together adds to the appeal. Aitchison's design was inspired by the banqueting room at the Moorish palace of La Zisa at Palermo, where a black marble table with water running down a central channel for the diners to rinse their hands stood in place of Leighton House's black marble basin. Leighton commissioned his friend Walter Crane, best known as an illustrator of children's books, to design the glittering mosaic frieze of birds and deer, and Aitchison created the copper and wrought-iron chandelier, a modern-day crown of thorns.

It seems a shame to quibble about such a magical space. And if the theft involved in this Victorian temple to beauty had been purely intellectual, there would be no need. But the 16th- and 17th-century tiles here are cultural and religious artefacts – the large panel above the entrance, 'bought' by traveller and *Arabian Nights* translator Richard Burton from a hill temple at Sind (then in northern India), contains a passage from the creation myth in the Koran ('He has

Library, Leighton House

created man and taught him speech/[He hath set] the sun and the moon in a certain course...'); the brown 14th-century tiles in the west wall have had the faces erased, and the images of birds on the south wall their throats slit by chipping a line in the glaze, to conform with Islamic edicts against the representation of living things. And while the elaborate Ottoman-style grilles on the windows were an effective way of protecting Leighton's privacy, their connotations of the harem, where women were to be heard but not seen, introduce sinister overtones.

The library beside the entrance hall was used by Leighton as a study and the low bookcases are the original fittings. The desk is strewn with letters and sketches and among the many pictures are Leighton's portraits of his elder sister and father. The fireplace, positioned seemingly nonsensically beneath the window with its flue rising to the left of the glass, echoes that in the drawing room opposite.

Leighton's drawing room seems to have been designed around his art collection, in particular the four large panels of Corot's *Times of Day* (reproductions of which are on display), whose brown he sampled in choosing his wallpaper. In contrast with the richly decorated, inward-looking halls, the room is lit by full-height windows to the garden and an unusual semi-circular bay with a circular sketch by Delacroix (a copy of the original) inset into the ceiling. The effect of this and the positioning of the fireplace, its surround of wispy grasses designed by Leighton himself, is thoroughly unconventional, as if Leighton and Aitchison had reworked assumptions from scratch. The doors are made of the ebonised woodwork found throughout the house, with stylised plant forms picked out in gold; the chandelier is a fantasy of pink, blue and clear glass baubles and flowers.

Leighton had the large and pleasant dining room decorated in red to show off his collection of ceramics. He left few records of his private life, and rumours that he had a child with one of his models or the supposition that he was homosexual cannot be confirmed. But it's hard not to read his interpretation of the Orpheus myth displayed here, in which the songster appears to be pushing his wife Eurydice from him, as an expression of homosexual revulsion. The door to the right of the chimney piece led to the service stairs; a bedroom and butler's room have been recreated in the basement.

The spacious top-lit landing above the ante-room leads to a day-bed, also brought from the Middle East, which projects over the Arab hall. With its grille filtering views of the golden dome, and the sound of the fountain, it seems a stage set for erotic fantasies. Created to display his fine collections of 16th-century Venetian art and paintings by his contemporaries, the windowless silk room, top-lit by a dome that matches the one above the landing, extends that space to make it a usable and pleasant room rather than just a passage. Leighton's bedroom, above the entrance hall, is surprisingly modest, sparsely furnished and decorated with a swirling blue William Morris print.

The spacious studio is not as cluttered as photographs show it in Leighton's day but still contains many of the books, sketches, props and beautiful objects that served him as inspiration. The walls are painted a rich red, his preferred colour for displaying pictures; at the far end is a gallery that he would stand on to reach the top of his larger canvases. Behind it is the area where his models would prepare themselves, with a door leading to the service stairs. The winter studio beyond now houses temporary exhibitions.

Among the paintings in the studio proper is the overwrought *Clytie* (1895), a portrait of the nymph who fell in love with Apollo kneeling with her arms outstretched towards a flaming sky. The model was actress Dorothy Dene, whom Leighton befriended and encouraged towards the end of his life, their platonic relationship possibly the source for Shaw's *Pygmalion*. Opposite hangs the larger-than-lifesize *Death of Brunelleschi* (1852), its background of classical ruins reflecting the country and era the artist regarded as his spiritual home. His actual home, along with his art, displays the contradictions of this fantasy of a more glorious age filtered through Victorian constraints. In his home, at least, we should be grateful the fantasy won out.

West Outskirts

Boston Manor

Boston Manor Road, Brentford, Middlesex TW8 9JX
Tel: 0845 456 2800
www.hounslow.info/arts/bostonmanorhouse
Nearest transport: Boston Manor LU
Open: closed for structural repairs at time of going to press,
    please check website for details
Admission: free
Wheelchair access: limited

This charmless three-storey red-brick Jacobean mansion was constructed in 1623 for Lady Mary Reade, who wanted the work finished in a hurry in time for her wedding to her second husband, Sir Edward Spencer of Althorp. Modest in scale (the original house probably comprised only the four left-hand bays of the present building viewed from the front door, and was just one room wide), her home had none of the court-inspired grandeur of Charlton House (see page 291), completed a decade earlier, or the fine proportions of Forty Hall (see page 133), built a decade later. In 1670 the house was bought by merchant banker James Clitherow, who probably added the two right-hand bays and the heavy stone window surrounds and architraves. The council bought the house in 1923.

The Clitherows were bankers with royal connections. Though successive generations had large families for whom they made generous provision, there was still money to spare for local philanthropy. Another James (1766–1841) and his wife Jane became friendly through their good works with William IV and Queen Adelaide and in 1834 they were the first commoners to entertain the royal couple to dinner. According to James' sister Mary, Jane was appreciated because of her 'honest manner and sound judgement which she ventures to express to His Majesty'; Queen Adelaide – married to a man almost 30 years her senior who had spent 20 years living with an actress and had ten illegitimate children – described Jane as 'a friend who tells me true'.

The plain exterior of the house with its three gables and elaborate 19th-century stone porch gives way to a hall with an original plaster ceiling and 19th-century wood screen. The dining room at the front is light and pleasantly proportioned. Occasionally open to the public is the unatmospheric library at the rear – accessed from the hall or through an ante-room in the massive spine wall that holds the chimney stacks, allowing for flush fireplaces. The elaborate Grinling Gibbons-style frame above the fireplace, carved with cherubs and flowers, is 17th century; the Puginesque ceiling was probably installed by General John Clitherow in 1847.

The heavy oak staircase, part of the original house, has its balustrade echoed on the wall opposite in painted *trompe l'oeil* – an effective joke. But nothing prepares the visitor for the breathtaking space of the first-floor state drawing room, hung with gold damask and with a ceiling – probably by Edward Stanyon, who created those in the long galleries at Blickling Hall, Norfolk and Langleys, Essex – that fully merits its description as a high-water mark of Jacobean elaboration. On a pale-green background, overlaid with an intricate pattern of enriched double ribs with strapwork in lower relief, are roundels containing a remarkable series of emblematic high-relief figures, with faces like Hogarth caricatures, portraying the five senses, the elements, peace and plenty, war and peace, and faith, hope and charity. The equally elaborate overmantel has a central image of the angel stopping Abraham from sacrificing Isaac taken from a 1584 engraving by Abraham de Bruyn. The state bedroom at the rear has a similarly elaborate ceiling with nipple-like pendentives.

On the stairs to the second floor is a large stretch of 18th-century wallpaper showing Roman ruins – a folly, a sphinx, an obelisk – in greys and golds. Lightly protected but unrestored, it gives a magically romantic insight into how this everyday space must once have looked.

Ham House

Ham Street, Ham, Richmond-upon-Thames, Surrey TW10 7RS
Tel: 020 8940 1950
www.nationaltrust.org.uk/hamhouse
Nearest transport: Richmond Rail then bus 371 or ferry from
    Twickenham towpath (by Marble Hill House, see page 234)
Open: Mon-Thurs, Sat & Sun 12.00-16.00 (April to Oct);
    tours (40 minutes) 11.30-15.00 (March & Nov)
Admission: £9.90/£5.50/family ticket £25.30

Often referred to as 'Sleeping Beauty' or 'the house time forgot', Ham House was in fact seriously and serially meddled with during its first century, before the rot of poverty set in. Built between 1608 and 1610, like its exact contemporary Charlton (see page 291) it was designed on a regular Jacobean H plan, with the south front transformed in the 1670s by the addition of a grand suite of rooms filling the space between the H's two legs and spilling out at their sides.

Ham was built for former naval captain Sir Thomas Vavasour. By 1626, however, it had passed to the dashing William Murray (to judge by the portrait in the duchess' private closet), whose uncle (like Charlton's owner Sir Adam Newton) had been a personal tutor to one of the sons of James I, in this case the ill-fated Charles. William joined the royal establishment as a whipping boy who would be punished for the prince's misdemeanours. On Charles' accession he was appointed gentleman of the bedchamber, and with Inigo Jones – architect of the radical Palladian Queen's House designed less than a decade later (see page 306) – was a member of a select group of collectors, connoisseurs and arbiters of taste who advised the king. In 1637 he embarked on an ambitious programme of remodelling and refurbishment at Ham cut short by the outbreak of the Civil War in 1642. Following Charles' execution in 1649, he went into exile in Holland. His house was transferred to his wife, and following her death in the same year was willed to their four daughters, the three youngest of whom were hunchbacks.

Elizabeth, the eldest daughter, was to inherit the title bestowed on her father in 1643, becoming Countess of Dysart on his death in 1655. In 1648 she had married wealthy landowner Sir Lionel Tollemache; the couple lived mainly at his family seat of Helmingham Hall in Suffolk and their London home in Covent Garden. Highly educated and politically astute, Elizabeth cultivated Cromwell, with whom she is said to have had a liaison, while at the same time risking her life to work for the restoration of the monarchy through the Sealed Knot, a secret society that gathered information on behalf of the court in exile (her pseudonym was Mrs Legge). She was widowed in 1669 and in 1671, a decade after the restoration, she married John Maitland, 2nd Earl (and subsequently Duke) of Lauderdale, secretary of state for Scotland and a powerful member of Charles' inner cabinet, the Cabal. (She had probably had a long-standing affair with him; certainly she had persuaded Cromwell to save his head from the block during his nine-year imprisonment in the interregnum and entertained him openly at Ham after she was widowed.) The couple married soon after the death of Lauderdale's wife (see Lauderdale House, page 126) and almost immediately embarked on an ambitious programme to extend Ham with a suite of rooms designed by Elizabeth's cousin William Bruce.

Ham's north (entrance) front is spectacular – a three-storey red-brick structure with stone dressings, consisting of five bays between projecting wings with the junctions effected by rectangular cloistered blocks originally topped by turrets with ogee caps. The frontispiece above the door was removed in the 1740s; the Italianate busts in niches between the ground- and first-floor windows were moved from the garden wall c. 1800. The symmetry promised by the façade breaks down immediately inside, however, as the imposing great hall stretches off to the left with service spaces to the right, in accordance with Tudor tradition.

The great hall is enhanced by the decision of Elizabeth's son Lionel, 3rd Earl of Dysart, to take down much of the ceiling, creating a double-height well. The black-and-white marble floor probably dates from 1610; the full-height figures of Mars and Minerva on the chimney piece may have been modelled on William Murray and his wife Katherine. Among the portraits are the women two of the family eloped with: Henrietta Cavendish, who ran off with the 3rd Earl's son, and Charlotte Walpole (whose uncle, Horace, lived across the river at Strawberry Hill, see page 254), who secretly married the 5th Earl in 1760. The family living room at the front of the eastern wing was transformed into a chapel by Elizabeth and Lauderdale in the 1670s. The great staircase behind it was remodelled by William Murray in 1638–39 as a magnificent prelude to his state-of-the-art state apartments on the *piano nobile*. It succeeds in impressing: the robust balustrades are decorated with remarkably bold carvings of arms (originally highlighted with gilding); on the walls hang copies of paintings by Miguel de la Cruz, probably gifts from Charles I, who commissioned them when he and Murray were in Spain together in 1623 to search for a royal bride; the plaster ceiling is in the restrained style recently pioneered by Inigo Jones.

The museum room above the chapel was originally a bedroom. Among the paintings in the hall gallery (above the great hall and formerly the great dining room, the first of Murray's ambitious new suites) is a double portrait of the Duke and Duchess of Lauderdale, c. 1679, looking like two fleshy, well-fed villains – he smug, she wanton – living off the fat of the land, as indeed they were. A highly educated and intelligent man of coarse manners and passionate furies, the fiercely royalist Lauderdale used his iron rule of Scotland – where his task was to impose the absolute power of the crown on church and state – to line his own pockets. (According to his enemy, historian Bishop Gilbert Burnet: 'The sense of religion that a long imprisonment had impressed on his mind was soon erased by a course of luxury and sensuality, which ran him into a great expense, and which he stuck at nothing to support; and the fury of his behaviour heightened the severity of his ministry and made it more like the cruelty of an inquisition than the legality of justice.') The volatile Elizabeth was, if anything, worse. As Burnet put it: 'The Lady Dysart came to have so much power over the Lord Lauderdale that it lessened him much in the esteem of all the world... [She] was wanting in no methods that could bring her money, which she lavished out in a most profuse vanity.'

Green Closet, Ham House

The centrepiece of Murray's apartments, the north drawing room (which doubled as a state bedroom before the 1670 additions), was probably designed by Franz Cleyn, who also supplied the inset paintings of cavorting *putti*. The most prominent feature is the baroque fireplace surround with its distinctive twisted and spiral-fluted columns supporting Ionic capitals topped by an overmantel featuring more chubby *putti*. The sumptuous furniture includes an Indian carpet, a set of French chairs with gilded arms and legs in the shape of dolphins and an extremely costly and complex ivory cabinet, all probably purchased by Elizabeth in Paris in the 1670s. The long gallery that runs the depth of the west wing retains most of its original panelling. Among the portraits is one of Elizabeth at around the time of the birth of the second of the 11 children she bore between 1648 and 1661 (five of whom survived into adulthood) with a black servant, a status symbol at the time. Above the cloisters is the green closet, designed as a contrast to the scale of the long gallery to display miniatures in an intimate setting, its ceiling embellished by more Cleyn *putti*. The library closet and library in the south-west corner – with direct access from the duke's closet below – represent one of the first purpose-built facilities in the country, perhaps reflecting Lauderdale's unhappy experience at Lauderdale House, where the weight of his books threatened the building's structural safety.

Along the central flank of the south (garden) front run the antechamber to the queen's bedchamber, the bedchamber itself and the queen's closet. The antechamber still has what was probably the original 1672–74 swirling olivewood graining and 'blewe Damusk' hangings from about a decade later (now faded to a depressing brown). Though the queen's bedchamber, placed pivotally at the centre of the south front, is the most magnificent of the rooms added by the Lauderdales, its scale is unimpressive. The richly decorated closet beyond retains most of its original decor including the ceiling painting by Antonio Verrio, who had worked for Charles II, the parquet floor emblazoned with the Lauderdale ducal coronet, and crimson hangings.

The ground floor of the Lauderdale extension consists of enfilades of rooms for the duke and duchess on either side of the central marble dining room, its black-and-white floor replaced by the parquet installed along with the stamped-leather hangings by the 4th Earl of Dysart (Elizabeth's great-grandson) in the 1750s. The rooms to the east comprise a withdrawing room, the volury room (in the wing of the original house), which takes its name from the birdcages flanking the bay window, and the duchess' two private closets, where she would read, write and take tea with her close friends. Both have painted ceilings by Verrio, that of the inner private closet depicting the penitent Mary Magadalen (who looks not unlike the duchess herself) – perhaps suggesting secret Catholic leanings. Alongside various family portraits, including those of her parents and eldest son, is a startlingly erotic overmantel of Medea by William Gouw Ferguson.

To the west of the marble dining room are the duke's dressing room, a bedroom (in the wing) and the duke's closet. The bedroom – hung with almost Rothko-like modern reinterpretations of the original damask – was the nursery in which Elizabeth's many children were raised before the 1670s additions. It was subsequently occupied by the duchess; in 1673 she ceded it to her husband but she was back by 1677, at which point he moved to the volury room or napped in the 'sleeping chayre' in the closet. The arrangement of having to cross each other's bedrooms to reach the private closets seems bizarre – the only logic being that Elizabeth was understandably attached to her two inner sanctums but at the same time wanted easy access to the bathroom below her bedroom. The suite of two rooms – a smaller space for the bathtub, which would have been enveloped by curtains to create a steamy atmosphere like a Turkish bath, with a larger outer room with a bed for relaxing in afterwards – can be seen in the basement along with the kitchens.

At the front of the west wing are the steward's hall and back parlour, for the use of senior domestic staff, who also had their own bedrooms in the garret, where all the servants slept. The cosy wood-panelled rooms contain photographs of more recent family (the house was presented to the National Trust in 1948) as well as a portrait of Lauderdale's brother, whom Elizabeth tried to sue for repayment of her husband's £5000 funeral expenses following his death in 1682 and who in turn contested his brother's will, which left almost everything to his wife. In any case, the Lauderdales had run up so much debt with their lavish refurbishment of Ham and various Scottish properties that even the sale of most of their assets, the mortgaging of Ham and the pawning of pictures and jewellery failed to satisfy their creditors.

Elizabeth retreated to Ham, where she died in 1698 following several lonely years in which it would seem from a letter to one of her daughters that she repented at least the consequences of her ways:

'All my movable estate is sold (even to the disfurnishing of this my dwelling house)... And now what can I or what must I further do? But condemn my own mistaken measurs which have proved so fatal that should I be cutt in pieces to gratify owr Enemyes none of my children nor their children would be the better.'

More things to see & do

Ham House's 17th-century formal gardens include the cherry garden, where lavender parterres are flanked by vaulted trellises of pleached hornbeam with a statue of Bacchus at the centre. The south terrace border has been replanted with a similarly geometric arrangement of cones of yew and clipped flowering shrubs. Below the terrace are eight grass plats surrounded by gravel walks and beyond this can be found the wilderness, a formal maze-like planting of hedges of hornbeam, concealing compartments containing four circular summerhouses.

Beside the kitchen garden is one of the oldest freestanding orangeries in England, now used as a café serving produce supplied from the garden. Other outbuildings include an ice house, still house and dairy.

Cherry garden, Ham House

'It is so blocked up and barricaded with walls, vast trees, and gates, that you think of yourself an hundred miles off and an hundred years back. The old furniture is so magnificently ancient, dreary and decayed, that at every step one's spirits sink, and all my passion for antiquity could not keep them up... In this state of pomp and tatters my nephew intends [Ham] shall remain.' Horace Walpole, 1770

Hampton Court Palace

Hampton Court Road, East Molesey, Surrey KT8 9AU
Tel: 0844 482 7777
www.hrp.org.uk/hamptoncourtpalace
Nearest transport: Hampton Court Rail
Open: daily 10.00-18.00 (April to Oct) & 10.00-16.30 (Nov to March)
Admission: £14/£11.50/£7/family ticket £38

Gatehouse, west front, Hampton Court Palace

Hampton Court Palace makes it into this book by the skin of its teeth, its eastern end apparent on the fringes of just some editions of the *London A-Z*. That this eastern third can clearly be seen to be composed of ranges of buildings grouped around two courtyards – the larger one is Fountain Court – and that these courtyards are in fact modest in comparison with the grand scale of Base Court behind the main entrance are indications of the scope of the enterprise. Hampton Court is simply vast. This, coupled with its marginal geographical status, means the level of detail in this entry is necessarily curtailed.

The palace at the core of Hampton Court was built by Thomas Wolsey from 1515, the year he became a cardinal and was appointed lord chancellor to Henry VIII. The son of an Ipswich butcher, he had a meteoric rise to power, and by this stage was in receipt of a healthy income from his roles as Archbishop of York and administrator of the sees of Bath and Wells and the abbey of St Albans. His *parvenu* displays of wealth – including not only the creation of the palatial Hampton Court but also lavish entertainments (his household numbered 429) at the Westminster townhouse Henry later converted into Whitehall Palace – irked the 23-year-old king. His failure to procure papal consent for Henry's divorce from his first wife Catherine of Aragon eventually led to the forfeiture of all his property to the crown and his arrest for high treason. He died in 1530 on his way from York to London.

Wolsey's palace was unprecedented in scale and grandeur, but this didn't prevent Henry from spending a further £62,000 (about £18 million in today's terms) on rebuilding and refurbishing it. Designed to impress visiting dignitaries (in August 1546 the French ambassador and his retinue of 200 gentlemen, together with 1300 members of Henry's court, were entertained for six days), it also functioned as a vast holiday camp, with tennis courts, bowling alleys, pleasure gardens and hunting freely available. In the course of his reign, Henry was to spend only 811 days here (on average three weeks a year), though his queens were more frequent visitors and it was the venue for three of his six honeymoons.

Wolsey's house began as a relatively modest affair surrounding Clock Court (still the centrepiece of the complex), with a great hall to the north, a range of royal suites to the east, and private and service spaces to the south and west. It was later extended westwards by the creation of the considerably larger Base Court, surrounded by 40 guest suites, each consisting of two rooms and a garderobe. Base Court today is still largely as Wolsey intended, though the wings flanking the entrance gate were added by Henry VIII to house communal lavatories – grandly titled the Great House of Easement and seating up to 28 people at a time – and kitchens.

The palace has been divided into five separate tours to facilitate visitor orientation. 'Henry VIII at Hampton Court Palace' begins in the modestly scaled Wolsey Rooms, thought to have been part of the cardinal's private lodgings, two of them lined with superb 16th-century linenfold panelling. The journey through Henry VIII's state apartments, which extend north from Clock Court, begins with the magnificent great hall, built on the site of Wolsey's smaller hall and breathtaking in scale. The sweep and craftsmanship of the vast hammerbeam roof gives a clear impression of the king's ambitions. The adjacent horn room – lined with antlers dating back to the 17th century and a gory testament to the park's attractions as a hunting ground – was originally a waiting room for the servants attending the 600-strong banquets next door. The vast great watching chamber, originally the entrance to Henry's state apartments, housed his yeoman of the guard. The chapel royal still retains its elaborately modelled star-spangled Tudor ceiling; the delicately carved screen by Grinling Gibbons was installed by Queen Anne in the early 18th century. The second visitor tour leads through the vast complex of the Tudor kitchens, with information on the logistics of feeding and clearing up after the hundreds of guests.

Little was done to Hampton Court in the century between Henry's death and 1689, when William III and Mary II hired Christopher Wren to transform the palace into a Versailles that would provide an alternative to the disliked Whitehall Palace and at the same time reinforce their status as legitimate rulers ushering

Great hall, Hampton Court Palace

King's staircase, Hampton Court Palace

in a new Protestant age. Though Wren's original plan to demolish the entire complex except the great hall was dismissed, much of the Tudor royal apartments were pulled down, to be replaced by state apartments planned around the new Fountain Court. Cost-cutting and hasty construction led to the collapse of the south range, killing two workmen, and only the shell of the new buildings was complete when Mary died in 1694. Work stopped, but four years later, after Whitehall Palace had burned down, William began the decoration of the interiors. Only the king's apartments, in whose design he was intimately involved, were completed by his death in 1702.

These make up the third visitor tour, accessed via Wren's operatic colonnade on the south elevation of Clock Court, which makes this a fittingly transitional space linking literally and stylistically the imposing Tudor Base Court to the west and the fussy William and Mary Fountain Court to the east. The change in tone is immediately apparent in the spectacular king's staircase, its walls and ceilings painted by Antonio Verrio. The mural features an allegory that glorifies William as Alexander the Great, triumphing over the Stuarts as his predecessor did over the Caesars, and shows him being commended to the gods by Hercules. It is intended to leave the visitor in no doubt as to William's divine and politically sanctioned right to take the throne from his Catholic uncle, James II. This is backed by a display of military might in the stark guard chamber beyond, where some 3000 weapons are arranged in grand geometric designs. The procession along the *piano nobile* of the new south front overlooking the privy garden continues through the presence chamber, eating room, privy chamber, withdrawing room, great bedchamber, little bedchamber and closet. Each has a more or less grand red throne which courtiers were supposed to bow to even when empty.

The presence chamber is dominated by a painting by Godfrey Kneller of William's arrival in England to claim the throne. The eating room, where the king would occasionally dine in public, has picture frames and doorcases exquisitely carved with fruit and flower motifs by Gibbons, who was responsible for most of the woodwork in these rooms. The culmination of William's grand design comes in the great bedchamber – in which he was dressed in the morning in front of privileged courtiers – where the baroque ceiling decorations by Verrio, tapestries, gilded furniture and red-draped bed, topped with ridiculous plumes, conspire to give the impression of no expense spared. The little bedroom is where William actually slept and the adjacent king's closet was his private study, from which two jib doors lead to the back staircase and the stool-room, equipped with a lavatory probably made for Charles II.

On the ground floor are the king's more intimate private apartments, beginning with three simple oak-panelled rooms with overmantels carved by Gibbons, the walls hung with paintings from the king's collection including one of him as King Solomon. The scale of the orangery, which stretches almost the full length of the state apartments above, reflects the new fashion for orange trees following the accession of the House of Orange, and is a further symbolic marker of William's status. The private drawing room, closet and dining room beyond were first opened to the public in 1992 following an ambitious restoration programme to repair the damage wrought by a fire of 1986.

Despite William and Mary's equal status as rulers, the queen's state apartments, left unfinished at Mary's death, are a much less grand affair. The fourth recommended tour on the visitor itinerary, they run along the north side of Fountain Court and make up the palace's new east front facing Long Water, created by Charles II, and the home park, where William's horse famously made a mountain of a molehill, fatally injuring its rider. Queen Anne commissioned Verrio to decorate the drawing room, but most of the refurbishment was the work of George II, who fitted out several rooms while still Prince of Wales and lived here with his wife Caroline from 1714 until he quarrelled with his father in 1717. He completed the work after he acceded to the throne in 1727 and Queen Caroline used the apartments extensively.

The modest queen's staircase was redecorated in 1734 with reliefs by William Kent, whom George and his father had employed at Kensington Palace (see page 190). The guard chamber and presence chamber to the north of Fountain Court, the former with a coved ceiling supported by bold brackets and a marble chimney piece featuring life-size sculptures of the yeomen of the guard, were designed by John Vanbrugh in 1717–18. Their austerity is a thoroughly modern contrast with the baroque richness of the king's apartments. The public dining room, originally intended as a music room, is the entry point to the suite of state apartments along the palace's east front. The queen's audience chamber – still with its original red throne-canopy – leads to the central drawing room, where Verrio's paintings for Queen Anne constitute an allegory of British naval power that includes images of Cupid drawn by seahorses and a camp portrait of her feckless husband George before the fleet. The paintings were disliked by George II, who had them covered in wallpaper.

The queen's state bedchamber is decorated in red with a baroque ceiling by James Thornhill, the royal serjeant painter to George I, who had preceded Kent at Kensington. The impressive queen's gallery was hung by William III with Andrea Mantegna's *Triumph of Caesar*, now in the lower orangery but lit at such low levels its beauty is hard to decipher. George II installed the tapestries that line the walls today. The queen's closet was interconnected by a door to William III's closet; beyond it is the room of the ladies of the bedchamber, who in George and Caroline's time included his mistress Henrietta Howard (see Marble Hill House, page 234). According to the vice-chamberlain Lord Hervey, Caroline delighted in assigning Henrietta the most menial duties.

George II was the last king to occupy Hampton Court, making his final visit in 1737, shortly before Caroline's death. Under George III, much of the palace was divided into rent-free grace-and-favour apartments, a system that lasted until the 1970s. It was first opened to the public by Queen Victoria in 1838.

The final tour is through the Georgian Rooms, which form part of the eastern range of Clock Court and surround three sides of Fountain Court. The Cumberland Suite in the Tudor range on the eastern side of Clock Court was designed in 1731 by Kent for George II's second son the Duke of Cumberland. The presence chamber has a neo-Tudor ceiling with pendants but the bedchamber boasts sumptuous classical cornices and a bed recess screened with paired Ionic columns. The oak-panelled communication gallery running the length of the western range of Fountain Court is hung with portraits by Peter Lely commemorating the unlovely ladies of the court of Charles II. The cartoon gallery along the court's southern flank was designed by Wren for William III to house Raphael's *Acts of the Apostles*.

The queen's private apartments, which run parallel to the state apartments along the east side of Fountain Court, were also built by Wren for Mary II but lay empty until 1716, when they were refurbished for the Prince and Princess of Wales. The sequence runs

South front, Hampton Court Palace

from the drawing room, set up for a game of quadrille, through the bedchamber, which has locks on the door so its occupants could spend the night undisturbed, the dressing room and bathroom, closet (and garderobe) to the dining room. The private oratory boasts a fine octagonal dome and skylight.

A walk round the exterior of Hampton Court – built almost entirely of red brick with stone dressings – clearly reveals the two main stages of its creation. The symmetrical west (entrance) front with its turrets and battlements is largely as it was in Tudor times (some of it thanks to Victorian restoration), though the two-storey entrance gate was originally higher. The north front housing the service areas makes no pretence at unifying its collection of Tudor buildings behind a regular façade. Wren's 23-bay east front facing Long Water, by contrast, is a model of symmetry: three storeys

high with a row of small round windows above those of the *piano nobile* and topped by a balustrade, it has a seven-bay ashlar-faced projection at the centre, with the middle three bays projecting further and crowned by a pediment supported by elaborate fluted columns. Though it attempts the grandeur of Versailles, it lacks the necessary scale. The south front is made up of a similar regular Wren façade flanked by the exterior of Wolsey's Base Court, which is largely hidden by Wren's lower orangery.

More things to see & do

The Hampton Court Palace park covers 300 hectares including the vast deer park and some 26 hectares of formal gardens. Features include the lower orangery exotics garden, recreated from records of the 2000 exotic species collected by William and Mary, and the formal privy garden, dotted with marble sculptures and based on a design of 1702. At 580 metres, the broad walk herbaceous border is the longest in Britain.

Begun in 1690 as a form of courtly entertainment for William III, the maze consists of a kilometre of winding paths lined by yew-tree walls. The great vine – planted in 1768 by 'Capability' Brown – still produces an annual crop of black, sweet grapes that are sold in the palace shops in early September.

For an architectural gem on a smaller scale it's also worth visiting William III's banqueting house, where the lushly erotic paintings by Verrio compete with fine river views.

You can eat at the Tiltyard café, the Privy Kitchen coffee shop or take a picnic and find a secluded spot to enjoy it.

Headstone Manor

Pinner View, Harrow, Middlesex HA2 6PX

Tel: 020 8861 2626

Nearest transport: Harrow-on the Hill LU/Rail then bus H14,
  Harrow North LU then 15-minute walk or bus H10,
  Harrow and Wealdstone LU/Rail then 15-minute walk or bus H9

Open: Sat & Sun, tours at 15.00 (April to Oct)

Admission: £3/children free

Approached via a bridge over Middlesex's only water-filled moat, Headstone Manor looks like nothing more than an old farmhouse in the middle of a field. Yet behind this unremarkable exterior lies the oldest timber-framed house known to have survived in the county, while the remains of the aisled hall and two small rooms to the right of the house viewed from the bridge constitute the oldest surviving structure in this book.

Headstone takes its name from a corruption of de la Hegge, the family who from 1233 owned the land on which it stands. The oldest part of the present house has recently been dated to 1310; excavations indicate that the moated enclosure may have been full of buildings in medieval times. The manor was acquired as a local residence for the archbishops of Canterbury by John Stratford in 1344 and was leased to tenants from 1382 – including the Redynge family, who lived here for more than 100 years from 1397. Tenants were bound by an agreement that specified the proportion of produce and the accommodation due the archbishops on their visits.

In 1545 the house was surrendered to Henry VIII, who sold it to one of his court favourites, Sir Edward North. In 1631 it passed to the Rewse family (Simon Rewse was receiver-general to Lord North), who added a tower, porch and small room at the rear. In 1649, the Rewses having incurred debts during their support for the king in the Civil War, it was sold to William Williams. He added a substantial new wing, including a cellar, pantry, kitchen and bedroom, which almost doubled the house's size. The massive chimney stack with its diamond-shaped shafts dates from this time.

The wing at the rear was added in the 1770s when the front of the house was given a fashionable brick façade.

In 1925 the house was sold to Hendon Rural District Council and in 1986 it became part of the Harrow Museum. The house is currently sparsely furnished with items from the museum collection to suggest how the rooms may have been used.

More things to see & do

The grounds of Headstone Manor contain three other remarkable buildings that make up the Harrow Museum. The late-18th-century granary, three storeys high with a surprising number of windows on its upper floors, was moved here from nearby Pinner Park in 1991. It now contains a permanent exhibition about the agricultural history of Harrow and collections from the area's industrial past. The small barn has information about the site.

Most impressive, though, is the tithe barn – an uninterrupted space 43 metres long and 9 metres high dating from 1506. Despite housing a café, shop and temporary exhibition space as well as children's workshops and a series of Tuesday Talks, its glory is undiminished.

The Harrow Museum is open daily except Tuesday (12.00-17.00 in summer, 12.00-16.00 in winter). Admission is free. See *www.harrow.gov.uk*.

Kew Palace

Royal Botanic Gardens, Kew, Richmond, Surrey TW9 3AB

Tel: 0844 482 7777

www.hrp.org.uk/kewpalace

Nearest transport: Kew Gardens LU/Rail

Open: Mon 11.00-17.00, Tues-Sun 10.00-17.00 (April to Sept);
   Queen Charlotte's Cottage Sat & Sun 11.00-16.00 (June to Sept)

Admission: visitors to the palace must buy tickets to Kew Gardens
   (£13.50/£11.50/children free), which include entry to Queen
   Charlotte's Cottage, plus tickets to the palace £5/£4.50/children free

Garden façade, Kew Palace

The owners of Britain's smallest royal palace never quite determined how best to use it. Nursery, overflow accommodation for unwanted teenagers, asylum, hospice and holiday home: Kew Palace served all these functions during the 175 years of its royal occupation. Despite its jolly appearance, its story is largely a sad one, dominated by the illness of George III (1738–1820), the death of his wife Queen Charlotte and the perhaps unfulfilled lives of their several unmarried daughters. Even today, curators seem uncertain about how the palace might best function, with room settings, mementoes, recorded voices and projections jostling uncomfortably for visitors' attention.

Kew Palace was built by merchant Samuel Fortrey in 1631. A grander contemporary of Forty Hall (see page 133), it was made entirely in brick by master masons who drew their eclectic motifs from pattern books and timber-frame traditions. The three central bays of the seven-bay façade are framed by shallow two-bay projections, with each section topped by a pedimented gable pierced by a dormer window. The arched openings of the central bay are framed by sets of columns, the three storeys are divided by horizontal bands and all the windows are surrounded by rustication. At the garden side the central three bays are recessed to accommodate a stuccoed neo-classical loggia at ground-floor level. The overall effect, intensified by the colourwash that stains the façade a vibrant ochre, is friendly rather than formal, welcoming rather than imposing.

After Fortrey's death in 1643 the house had several owners before being acquired in 1728 by Queen Caroline, wife of the newly crowned George II, as an annexe for her three teenage daughters – Anne, Amelia and Caroline – while the court was at nearby Richmond Lodge. For the past decade the girls had been separated from their parents and brought up by their grandfather George I, who had quarrelled with his son and banished him from the royal palaces. Caroline ordered a major refurbishment of her daughters' new home, replacing the windows, panelling and staircase and adding a service wing to the west. But their occupancy proved short-lived: Anne married in 1734 and moved to Holland after a brief honeymoon probably spent at Kew; Caroline stayed close to her mother and retired to St James's after the latter's death in 1737; Amelia spent less and less time at Kew and finally abandoned it in 1751 after she was made ranger of Richmond Park and given White Lodge as her home.

Following the death of George II's eldest son Frederick in 1751, Kew was once more refurbished for the use of teenage royals, this time for Frederick's two elder sons George and Edward and their personal tutors. George III succeeded his grandfather in 1760, at the age of 22; in 1764, during a family holiday at Richmond Lodge, his two young sons caught whooping cough and were isolated in the now empty Kew Palace. Perhaps this gave the king and queen the idea of using Kew as a nursery, for soon afterwards the various houses they owned in the area were transformed into quarters for their growing band of children (15 in total).

Like their father and uncle, the future George IV and his younger brother Frederick were installed with their own household and governors in Kew Palace itself, though this time before George had reached his tenth birthday. Soon a routine developed where the king and queen would spend Sunday to Tuesday at Windsor, Wednesday and Thursday in London and the remaining two days with their children at Kew. Once the children grew up, however, Kew Palace was once more left empty.

In 1788 George III suffered the first bout of the illness – probably the metabolic disorder porphyria, whose symptoms included periods of mental derangement and loss of control – that was to blight the rest of his reign. Windsor offered little privacy so he was moved to the White House, a remodelled Tudor mansion that stood directly opposite Kew Palace. The palace itself was furnished to provide overflow accommodation and lodgings for the groom of the king's bedchamber. During a second bout of illness a decade later, Kew provided a refuge for Queen Charlotte and her five unmarried daughters – Augusta, Elizabeth, Sophia, Amelia and Mary, by now in their 20s and 30s – and the king joined them as his health improved. A further bout of illness in 1804 saw him isolated in the service wing while his family occupied the main rooms.

King's dining room, Kew Palace

In June 1818 Queen Charlotte, by now in her 60s, went to Kew for a few days of convalescence. The royal succession seemed secure: the future George IV, who had been made Prince Regent in 1811 as his father sank further into ill health and mental incapacity, had been persuaded to end his liaison with the Catholic Mrs Fitzherbert (later a tenant of Marble Hill House, see page 234) in 1795 and marry his cousin Caroline of Bruswick, who had borne him a daughter, Charlotte. But in 1817 Charlotte died giving birth to a stillborn child and the race to find a legitimate heir resumed. George's younger brother William (later William IV) duly abandoned his mistress, the actress Dorothy Jordan, with whom he had ten children, for the more suitable Princess Adelaide of Saxe-Coburg; his younger brother Edward left his French mistress to wed Princess Victoria of Saxe-Coburg, eventually the mother of Queen Victoria. As Queen Charlotte was deemed too ill to travel, a double wedding was organised in the drawing room at Kew with a reception in the dining room below. Some six months later, the queen died in her bedroom in the palace and Kew was once more largely abandoned until Queen Victoria agreed its transfer to Kew Gardens in 1898.

Apart from periodic closures for refurbishment, it has been open to the public ever since.

Like Forty Hall, Kew Palace is two rooms deep, bisected by a central passage running from entrance to garden. The grandest space on each floor is the three-bay room to the east of the entrance, with a slightly smaller room and the staircase behind it; on the west side, each of the two-bay rooms is preceded by a small ante-room. The restoration and displays focus on the reign of George III, with recorded voices in most rooms drawing attention to aspects of his family's story.

Visitors enter the panelled anteroom to the west and then proceed into the king's library, probably a parlour in Fortrey's time. Some of the panelling, the plasterwork above the fireplace and the 'green man' masks above the arched niches that frame the fireplace are probably from when the house was built. The off-white decoration here and in the other ground-floor rooms dates from Queen Caroline's scheme of 1728, though a fragment of a female figure that formed part of the 17th-century black, white and grey paintwork has been discovered and exposed. Among the displays are a letter from the young George III to his grandfather and mementoes of Queen Charlotte. The pages' waiting room behind would previously have led to the now demolished west wing, where the king was incarcerated during his illness of 1804.

In Fortrey's time the king's dining room to the east would have been the great hall, divided from the entrance passage only by a screen. Still the grandest room on the ground floor, the space is nonetheless remarkably simple and domestic in scale compared to state dining rooms designed for entertainment such as that at Apsley House (see page 9), with the table set for an intimate party of eight. The strapwork above the fireplace and elaborate plasterwork above the door at the back are Jacobean; the organ that fills one of the walls dates from the 1740s. The smaller king's breakfast room behind may also have served as a schoolroom for both George III and George IV.

The queen's boudoir on the first floor, decorated in the bold colours and patterns popular at the turn of the 19th century and set out with games, cards and sewing, contains the palace's only surviving plasterwork ceiling, a delicate geometric lattice broken by medallions depicting the five senses. Here the recorded voices evoke Queen Charlotte's daughters, who bemoan her ill-health. The drawing room at the front of the house has a George III harpsichord and would also have served as a music room for the royal princesses of the previous generation, in particular Anne, who was a pupil of Handel (see page 35). Given the scale of today's royal weddings, it is hard to believe that almost 200 years ago a temporary altar was installed and two of George III's sons were married here.

On the other side of the house are Queen Charlotte's and Princess Elizabeth's bedrooms, both with adjacent anterooms. Elizabeth was an accomplished painter and her bedroom was decorated in the latest fashion, with alcoves with arched ceilings, green wallpaper with a flock border and a Grecian couch with red and yellow drapes. The queen's room, at the back of the house, is larger and more neutral; it is here that she died, pleading (according to the recorded voice) to go back to Windsor to see her husband once more.

The second floor of the palace contained bedrooms for Princess Augusta and Princess Amelia, whose death of consumption in her late 20s perhaps precipitated the king's final bout of illness in 1810. These rooms are unrestored, and while they lack the bright colours and rich fabrics of the bedrooms below, their very emptiness and a more imaginative use of soundtrack and projection convey something of the sadness of the lives of George III's daughters, closeted in Kew and unable to escape the influence of their sick father and distraught mother.

Kew Gardens also contains Queen Charlotte's Cottage, built c.1771 as a picturesque *cottage orné* where the family could have tea and take picnics. Though the heavy thatched roof, poor-quality bricks and battened rustic doors were meant to give the impression of rural austerity and organic growth, the house is in fact symmetrical in plan and its interiors elegantly proportioned, with one ground-floor room lined with Hogarth prints and the upper chamber decorated with a trellis design probably painted by Princess Elizabeth.

Queen Charlotte's Cottage

More things to see & do

The Royal Botanic Gardens at Kew cover some 120 hectares and contain the world's largest collection of living plants. The revolutionary Palm House, designed by Decimus Burton in 1844 using technology developed for shipbuilding, still impresses with its beauty and transparency. The Temperate House is the largest surviving Victorian glasshouse and the 1986 Princess of Wales Conservatory contains ten separate climatic zones. Also popular is the 18-metre high treetop walkway, designed by Marks Barfield Architects, creators of the London Eye. A less well known treasure is the Marianne North Gallery, lined with 832 small oil paintings of flowers and plants from Australia, Africa, Japan and South America that this remarkable Victorian painted on her travels.

You can be transported round the gardens on the Kew Explorer and there are several cafés and restaurants. For more information, visit *www.kew.org*.

Marble Hill House

Richmond Road, London TW1 2NL

Tel: 020 8892 5115

www.english-heritage.org.uk/marblehill

Nearest transport: St Margarets Rail or Richmond LU

Open: Sat 10.00-14.00, Sun & bank hol Mondays 10.00-17.00
   (April to Oct)

Admission: £5/£4.30/£2.50/family ticket £12.50

Wheelchair access: ground floor only

Marble Hill House

Contemporary with Lord Burlington's Chiswick House (see page 162), Marble Hill was initially planned by Colen Campbell (1676–1729), author in 1715 of the influential survey of classical architecture in England *Vitruvius Britannicus*, architect to the Prince of Wales (the future George II) and with Burlington the foremost champion of the new Palladian movement. Whereas the baroque style forged by Christopher Wren, who remained surveyor of works until 1718, was associated with the Tory party and the Stuarts, Palladianism was favoured by the Whigs (Whig prime minister Robert Walpole chose Campbell as architect for Houghton Hall) and the Hanoverian succession. It is therefore no coincidence that one of London's finest Palladian villas should have been commissioned by Henrietta Howard (1689–1767), woman of the bedchamber to the Princess of Wales and the mistress with whom, according to vice-chamberlain Lord Hervey, the future George II would spend 'every evening of his life, three or four hours in [her] company'.

The first 43 years of Henrietta's life were dogged by financial dependency, from the age of 17 on her first husband Charles Howard, the improvident youngest son of the 5th Earl of Suffolk, into whose household she had probably moved after she was orphaned at 13. (The household was based partly at Audley End, a Jacobean mansion of the type Marble Hill was to supersede, designed by the architect of Charlton House, see page 291.) After a spell living under assumed names in London to avoid angry creditors, Henrietta and Charles moved to Hanover in 1713 to 'ingratiate themselves with the future Sovereign of England', as her future friend and neighbour, Walpole's son Horace (see Strawberry Hill, page 254), remarked. Returning to England in the retinue of George I, Henrietta was given a post in the household of the Princess of Wales, while Charles was made groom of the bedchamber to the king. When George I and his son quarrelled, Henrietta followed her royal mistress, leading her husband to dismiss her as his wife.

Her loyalty was rewarded in 1723 when the Prince of Wales awarded her a settlement of £11,500. Her friend Lord Ilay bought her some land near his own home of Whitton Place near Twickenham, and champion of Palladianism Lord Herbert reduced Campbell's plans to a more affordable scale. In June 1724 builder Roger Morris set to work, though soon construction was interrupted, perhaps because Henrietta's husband was demanding money or because she was uncertain if her pension would be discontinued once George II became king. The house was finally finished in summer 1729 and in 1731 Henrietta was made more secure by a legacy from her brother-in-law, on whose death her husband became 9th Earl of Suffolk and Henrietta the Countess of Suffolk. Her troublesome spouse died two years later. In 1735 she married the Hon. George Berkeley, and the decade until his death, spent largely at Marble Hill, was perhaps the happiest time of her life, marred only by the death in 1744 of her only son Henry at the age of 37.

A near-cube, three storeys high and five bays wide, Marble Hill may be heavier and more solid than Chiswick but is still a Palladian gem of startling simplicity. The road front has a projecting pedimented centrepiece with a rusticated base topped by four double-height Ionic pilasters. The centrepiece of the plainer river façade to the south is unadorned, though the proportions of both fronts are enhanced by a slightly projecting plat-band between the ground floor and *piano nobile* and the banded entablature beneath the eaves.

There are in effect two central halls: a lobby to the north containing the staircase, and a grander space to the river, which at the time provided the safest and most comfortable means of transport. The low ceiling of the riverside hall is supported by four Ionic columns in imitation of the arrangement of the central court of a Roman house. In the south-east corner of the plan is the breakfast parlour, small but well proportioned with an elaborate arched screen designed by Herbert. The geometrical patterned wallpaper is a reproduction of samples found in the room that probably date from the tenancy at the end of the century of Mrs Fitzherbert, ill-treated mistress of the future George IV (see Kew Palace, page 227). On the walls hang prints and drawings: Campbell's design for the house, published in the third volume of the *Vitruvius Britannicus* as 'A house in Twittenham [sic]', has no pilasters or pediment on the north-front centrepiece but a double staircase leading to the *piano nobile*, as at Chiswick. Among the likenesses of Henrietta's friends is a series of sketches of neighbour Alexander Pope (1688–1744), who helped her design the grounds and kept an eye on the property while she was at court. In the south-west corner is the dining parlour, hung with a recreation of the Chinese wallpaper Henrietta chose for the room; in the 'paper room' in the north-east corner visitors can watch one of the better stately-home videos.

The grand mahogany staircase is a translation into timber of a balustraded stone stair. The story of how the boards, some of which are over half a metre wide, were procured illustrates the arrogant plunder that's still having an environmental impact today: George II simply instructed an English captain in the bay of Honduras to sail into harbour and cut down some trees, incidentally nearly provoking a war with Spain when he failed to seek permission from the Spanish governor. The 'great room' above the riverside hall is an 8-metre cube with a deeply coved ceiling that projects into the attic storey. Symmetry is retained by the introduction of two sham doors mirroring those leading to Henrietta's bedchamber and dressing room. The elaborately carved mouldings and frieze featuring sungod Apollo are by James Richards, successor to Grinling Gibbons as master carver in wood to the king. The views of Roman ruins by G P Panini above the fireplace and doors were commissioned for the room in 1738.

Henrietta's bedroom, hung with striking green-silk damask, follows the Palladian model, with a bed alcove screened by fluted Ionic columns that echo the screen in the breakfast parlour below. Adjoining it is a smaller and simpler bedroom named after Miss Hotham, Henrietta's great-niece and companion in her later years. Mirroring Henrietta's room to the west is the dressing room, probably used to receive guests informally in the mornings as well as to get dressed, to judge by a 1767 inventory that lists it as containing seven chairs covered in green damask. The 1724 portrait of an impressively young-looking Henrietta, reclining against a classical backdrop in an attitude usually reserved for men of letters, originally belonged to Pope; she bought it in the sale following his

Great room, Marble Hill House

death and gave it to Walpole to hang at Strawberry Hill. Mirroring Miss Hotham's bedchamber is the damask bedchamber, which presumably took its name from a bed hung with red damask curtains listed in the inventory.

Though the grand staircase stops at the *piano nobile*, a door on the landing opens on to an elegantly simple stone staircase leading to two further storeys used to entertain intimates and as quarters for domestic staff. The staircase could also be accessed via the jib door in Henrietta's bedroom and originally led down to a service wing to the east of the house that was demolished in 1909. This was built in stages from 1741 after Henrietta's niece and nephew Dorothy and John Hobart moved in and Henrietta and her husband entertained more frequently at Marble Hill. Arranged around the upper part of the great room, this floor contains a Jacobean-style long gallery and three bedrooms used by Dorothy, John and guests.

Following Henrietta's death, Marble Hill was lived in by her nephew John, after whose death it passed to her great-niece Henrietta Hotham, who rented it out to Mrs Fitzherbert and others. In 1825 it was sold to Jonathan Peel, brother of Robert, and it was occupied by his family until 1887. After standing empty for many years, it was sold to property developer William Cunard; building materials had already been moved on to the site and sewers dug when a public outcry led to the house being bought by the London County Council and others to be opened as a tea room in 1903. In 1966 it was restored and opened as the historic house we see today; since 1986 it has been run by English Heritage.

More things to see & do
Marble Hill House is set in 25 hectares of lawn, meadow and woodland designed by poet Alexander Pope in collaboration with Charles Bridgeman, landscape gardener to George I and George II. Among the surviving buildings are the ice house and Lady Suffolk's Grotto, a cave-like garden retreat built to Pope's design.

Osterley House

Jersey Road, Isleworth, Middlesex TW7 4RB
Tel: 020 8232 5050
www.nationaltrust.org.uk/osterley
Nearest transport: Osterley LU
Open: Wed-Sun 12.00-16.30 (April to Oct),
    Sat & Sun 12.00-15.30 (Nov to Dec)
Admission: £8.25/£4.15/family ticket £20.70

Osterley has for most of its history been associated with bankers.
It was built in the late 1570s by Sir Thomas Gresham, founder of
the Royal Exchange; in 1683 Nicholas Barbon, an unscrupulous
financier, building speculator and pioneer of fire insurance, bought
it with the idea of emulating the 'mercantile magnificence' of his

Osterley House

honourable predecessor. Barbon raised a mortgage of £12,000 on the property (which he had acquired for only £9500); one of the guarantors was Sir Francis Child, the son of a Wiltshire clothier, who had been sent to London, Dick Whittington-style, to serve an apprenticeship as a goldsmith. Like Whittington, he married the boss' daughter, in this case his sole heir; like Whittington, he became an alderman, lord mayor and MP and amassed a considerable fortune. By the end of the century, Child's banking and jewellery business was one of the largest in London. He was knighted in 1689 and appointed jeweller in ordinary to William III in 1698, but it wasn't until•1713, a few months before his death, that he was able to claim Osterley, which had been empty and the subject of legal wrangling since Barbon's debt-ridden death in 1698.

Francis was succeeded at Osterley by three of his sons: Robert, who survived his father by only seven years; Francis, who as head of the bank and director of the East India Company for 17 years built on his father's prestige and fortune; and Samuel, the only one of the 11 brothers to have married.

Gresham's red-brick two-storey house was approximately square, built around a central courtyard surrounded by a loggia, from which opened a single range of rooms. Four stair turrets were positioned in the internal angles. When Queen Elizabeth visited she complained that the courtyard would be better divided by a wall, which Gresham built overnight to please her.

It's likely that Barbon took down the stair turrets and replaced them with towers, topped by gothic ogee cupolas, at the corners of what for clarity will be called the west (actually south-west) front, as part of alterations which he claimed made the house uninhabitable to put off his creditors from moving in. It's probable that the second Francis Child first raised the height of the house to create a proper third storey and then raised the entrance and inner courtyard to first-floor level, as now, so this floor could become a *piano nobile* and the ground level a semi-basement for services. The entrance hall was placed in the east front with a library above. All the fronts had pediments and Samuel added two turrets to the entrance side to match Barbon's west front.

Samuel's son Francis was the first of the family to have been educated along with the nobility at Westminster and Oxford. On coming into his inheritance in 1756 he purchased a fittingly grand collection of books and embarked on a series of improvements to Osterley. He refurbished the library above the entrance hall and inserted Venetian windows at both ends of the gallery that runs along the west front. But like his predecessors, Francis made his alterations piecemeal, working from the inside out with little concern for the overall composition. It was left to Robert Adam to transform the house into what Horace Walpole (see Strawberry Hill, page 254) described as 'the palace of palaces... so improved and enriched, that all the Percies and Seymours of Sion must die of envy.'

Adam may have been recommended to Francis by the 1st Duke of Northumberland, his neighbour at Syon (see page 261), but another possible candidate is Sir Francis Dashwood, whose brother-in-law and nephew John and Charles Walcot were in debt to Child's Bank to the tune of £16,500. The Walcots had arranged Francis' uncontested return as MP for Bishop's Castle in March 1761; Dashwood commissioned Adam to produce designs for his own houses at Hanover Square and West Wycombe Park. Francis wanted to give Osterley a modern image and to reduce its size, but Adam's first plan – which involved the demolition of the entire east front and part of the north and south wings and refacing the exterior in stone or stucco – was dismissed as too ambitious. Francis then died, on the eve of his wedding, and work on the scheme as built began in 1764 under the eye of his brother Robert, who spared no expense in having Adam remodel his family home, which his wife Sarah then filled with porcelain, pictures and drawings.

If Osterley today is very much as Adam left it, it's perhaps thanks to Robert and Sarah's only daughter Sarah Anne, who at the age of 17 eloped with John Fane, 10th Earl of Westmorland. Robert, who died two months later, left his fortune to his daughter's second child to prevent it from going to the main line of the Westmorland family; when his widow Sarah died in 1793, her heir Sarah Sophia Fane was only eight years old. Sarah Sophia married George Villiers, 5th Earl of Jersey, and the couple made their home at Middleton Park in Oxfordshire. (A society wit, she inspired the character of Zenobia in Disraeli's novel *Endymion*.) So Osterley was let until 1883, after which George's grandson Victor and his wife Margaret used it to host a series of Saturday-to-Monday parties, attended by politicians, princes and writers. (Visitor Henry James made Osterley the backdrop for his novella *The Lesson of the Master*.) Victor and Margaret's son George died in 1923, only eight years after his father, to be succeeded by the 9th Earl, George Francis, who opened the house to the public in 1939 and gave it to the National Trust a decade later. Much of the Adam-period furniture, which was purchased by the nation and placed in the care of the V&A and subsequently the National Trust, is still in situ.

Though Adam transformed the exterior of the Childs' messy Elizabethan mansion by regularising the fenestration (which entailed the removal of the Venetian windows inserted only two years earlier), removing the floating pediments on the north and south fronts, and so on, Francis' refusal to have the red-brick walls refaced adds immeasurably to Osterley's charm: it's the combination of the turrets topped by gothic ogee cupolas, the warm brick and Adam's frozen neoclassical formality that makes such a romantic impression. Adam's masterstroke, however, came with his second response to his client's request that he reduce the house's size: by demolishing the centre of the east wing and bridging the gap with a massive transparent double-height portico, he provided an entrance whose drama could hardly be bettered.

Unfortunately visitor access today is by a much less awe-inspiring route. But even in Adam's time, the proportions of the long, low entrance hall must have come as a disappointment, despite the architect's trademark apses at each end and mix of trophy panels like those made for Syon and Cipriani reliefs of Bacchus and Ceres (reflecting the room's doubling as a dining room, as at Kenwood, see page 115). Vestibules at each inner corner lead to the north and south passages, which run along the courtyard sides of these flanks, with rooms opening off them.

The west front beyond the entrance hall is taken up entirely by a long gallery. The library – which opens off the north passage – has pedimented bookcases designed around the collection Francis had bought some ten years earlier. Painted white to allow the books to dominate and decorated with a wealth of delicate small-scale low-relief, it has a restraint and elegance reminiscent of the entrance hall at Syon. The breakfast room beyond (adjoining the portico) was largely untouched by Adam.

The eating room at the other end of the north passage, flanking the entrance hall, is decorated in pink and pale green with an appropriate array of vines, wine jugs and panels depicting eating and drinking. The largely unadorned long gallery beyond, off which opens a turret room fitted with a wooden commode, had been refurbished

Garden house, Osterley Park

in the mid 1760s, so Adam's intervention was limited mainly to the replacement of the Venetian windows, the choice of wallpaper and the design of the mirrors. The unassuming drawing room at the south side of the entrance hall has a ceiling modelled on the Temple of the Sun in Palmyra, a motif also used for the hall at West Wycombe Park.

Described by Walpole as 'the most superb and beautiful [room] that can be imagined', the tapestry room – next in line along the south passage and the first space of Adam's state apartment – is a stunning contrast. Probably at Adam's suggestion, its walls are completely lined by tapestries from the Gobelins factory in Paris, with medallions depicting the loves of the gods set against a red backdrop of stylised flowers dotted with darting, surprisingly lifelike birds. The chimneyboard, firescreen and furniture are covered in matching fabric.

The state bedchamber next door has a delicate green-painted ceiling on the theme of love, its central medallion inspired by Angelica Kauffmann's painting of one of the three graces being enslaved by love. The smaller surrounding medallions are by her future husband Antonio Zucchi. But it is the monstrous state bed that dominates the room – a temple to love decorated with nymphs, garlands, dolphins, sphinxes and *putti*, topped by a dome garlanded with silk flowers. It was too much even for Walpole: 'What would Vitruvius think of a dome decorated by a milliner?' The adjoining Etruscan dressing room has roundels depicting joyful nymphs and *putti* making music and dancing set within a stylised geometric framework.

The great stair off the north passage is screened by two sets of columns (Corinthian below, Ionic above) that echo the portico. The baluster is identical to that at Kenwood. The simple decorative scheme allows the central ceiling painting by Rubens to dominate. In an uncanny throwback to Barbon's career in fire insurance, the original, along with several other paintings from the house, was mysteriously destroyed in a blaze soon after it was moved to Jersey following Osterley's acquisition by the National Trust.

On the upper floor are the yellow taffeta bedroom and the Childs' private apartment: Mr Child's dressing room, Mr Child's bedroom and Mrs Child's dressing room. Refreshingly simple, spacious and light, they are largely as refurbished for Francis Child by Matthew Hillyard in 1759.

Below stairs are a substantial kitchen, operational until the 1930s, the steward's room, still room, wine cellar and housekeeper's room. And, as befits a banking dynasty, a strongroom installed by the 9th Earl of Jersey in 1929 to display the family silver.

More things to see & do

Osterley House is sited at the heart of 150 hectares of parkland that include three lakes created in the late 18th century from a series of natural ponds and streams. The pleasure grounds contain an oriental plane tree planted in 1755 and an Adam-designed garden house that once served as an orangery. The Stables Café and farm shop are supplied by the Sutton family, who have been tenant farmers on the land for several generations.

Pitzhanger Manor

Mattock Lane, London W5 5EQ
Tel: 020 8567 1227
www.ealing.gov.uk/pmgalleryandhouse
Nearest transport: Ealing Broadway LU/Rail
Open: Tues-Fri 13.00-17.00, Sat 11.00-17.00, some Sundays
   in summer 13.00-17.00
Admission: free

Pitzhanger Manor

'My object in purchasing these premises was to have a residence for myself and family, and afterward for my eldest son, who... had also shown a decided passion for... Architecture, which he wished to pursue as a profession. I wished to make Pitzhanger Manor-house as complete as possible for the future residence of the young Architect.' John Soane

Pitzhanger Manor is the house bought by John Soane (1753–1837) in 1800 as a weekend retreat, a place for entertaining friends and clients that would reflect and enhance his status as an architect, and as a future residence for his elder son John, then aged 14, whom he hoped would follow him in his beloved profession. Ten years later the house was on the market: Soane's roles as surveyor to the Bank of England (he succeeded Robert Taylor, architect of Danson House, see page 319, in 1788), professor of architecture at the Royal Academy (from 1806) and clerk of works at the Royal Hospital in Chelsea (from 1807) were becoming increasingly demanding and his son's debt-ridden behaviour at Cambridge (where much of the money was used to buy medical treatment) was seen by his self-made and self-educated father as feckless and extravagant. In fairness to Soane, he regarded his own impoverished upbringing and lack of connections as his greatest professional disadvantage and wanted to give his children a better start. But his overweening attempts to dominate them led to a lifelong feud with the younger son, George, while he never overcame his disappointment with John; a diary entry following a visit to Pitzhanger in 1820 reads: 'Walked round poor Ealing. O John, John: what has idleness cost you.'

Soane was attracted to Pitzhanger in part because its southern extension had been the first job he worked on after he left the Oxfordshire home of his bricklayer father to become an apprentice to George Dance the Younger in London in 1768. Dance got the commission from Thomas Gurnell, whose daughter Mary he was to marry four years later. The Gurnell family's association with the house – which was probably built in the mid 17th century – goes back to the start of the 18th century. In 1685 John Wilmer, a wealthy silk merchant closely linked with the nonconformist movement, bought Pitzhanger from nonconformist clergyman Dr John Owen. In 1711 Wilmer's eldest daughter Grizell married Quaker Johnathan Gurnell, also a merchant who later established a bank (in a fitting link with Soane, three of their descendants were governors of the Bank of England). Johnathan and Grizell lived at Pitzhanger from 1721 until it passed to Thomas on his mother's death in 1756.

Faced at last with no client to please, an unconfined site and a substantial budget (Soane's income for 1800 was the equivalent of about £350,000 in modern terms; Pitzhanger cost the equivalent of about £150,000 to buy), Soane took his time in deciding what to do (more than 100 drawings for various schemes survive in the Sir John Soane's Museum, see page 58). Eventually, he knocked down the whole of the Gurnells' house – 'an incongruous mass of buildings deficient in symmetry and character' – except the Dance extension. The three-bay entrance (east) front of the building he created in its place, immeasurably grander than the adjacent Dance wing, was an indication of how far he had come. The extension on the other side, which replaces a colonnade leading to the servants' wing, is a Victorian addition and a building designed as a lending library in 1940.

The three bays of Soane's façade, with windows on the ground floor only and medallions above, are framed by four Ionic columns supporting a projecting entablature surmounted by statues of female figures. The composition is a variation on the entrance to the Bullion Court in the Bank of England's Lothbury Court, itself an adaptation of the Triumphal Arch of Constantine in Rome. (The statues were taken from the Temple of Pandrosus at Athens and bought by Soane for £62 in 1801 as part of a job lot that included the 73 balusters and six vases that make up the Pitzhanger parapet.) Soane's aspirations embraced the notion of himself as the founder of an architectural dynasty along the lines of the Dances and Wyatts, and the various classical motifs of his new façade placed its creator firmly in a line of great architects stretching back to antiquity. Inside, as a precursor to the museum he was to establish in Lincoln's Inn Fields, he displayed his collection of paintings and

Staircase looking towards the eating room, Pitzhanger Manor

transformed a room in the basement into a mock-gothic 'monks' dining room' to accommodate the antique architectural fragments he was gradually amassing.

Pitzhanger, as much as Soane's London house, functioned as a calling card. In addition to using it as a showcase for his architectural ideas, he spent a fortune furnishing and equipping it, with his wife Eliza busily engaged in buying suitable items at auction. The family moved in first in 1804 and the house became the location for a series of summer parties guaranteed to make it a talking point among the potential clients Soane was concerned to impress. But the organisation and constant entertaining took its toll on Eliza, who felt isolated during her husband's frequent absences to oversee his work commitments. John and George were at school in Margate from 1802 and went up to Cambridge in 1805 and 1806 respectively and she and the boys much preferred to spend holidays in London, Margate or with Soane's family in Chertsey. Pitzhanger succeeded as a salon but never became a family home.

The visitor enters into a narrow vestibule, its lofty ceiling and upper walls decorated with low-reliefs. To the left is a dressing room probably intended for Soane's own use and now containing information about the house. The small space, with its neat fireplace and curved wall, is extravagantly lit by one of the two large arched windows of the entrance front. Behind it is the small drawing room, whose full-length arched windows originally opened on to a conservatory that ran the length of the rear of the house. Hogarth's *A Rake's Progress* – which Eliza bought at auction at Christie's for 570 guineas in 1802 – once hung here (now replaced by copies). Double doorways lead to the library, a beautiful, typically Soanean space with a big central French window that would also have opened on to the conservatory. The trellis-pattern decoration of the groin-vaulted ceiling echoes the breakfast parlour of 12 Lincoln's Inn Fields; the walls on either side of the window, the overmantel and the niches that flank the fireplace are typically furnished with mirrors to enhance the sense of space. The breakfast room opposite the dressing room has a more sombre colour scheme, its

Greek-key patterns and linear tracery chosen to complement the funerary urns, vases and sculptures on display. The shallow dome of the ceiling – its centre painted with cloud effects – is supported by four attenuated Egyptian caryatids painted to resemble bronze.

The vast eating room on the ground floor of the Dance extension is where Soane would entertain such friends as J M W Turner and John Flaxman, his colleagues at the Royal Academy and influential figures within the government and Bank of England, attracted presumably as much by Eliza's intelligent and pleasant company as by that of her hypersensitive, irascible husband. In the centre of the north wall is a semi-circular niche designed for a serving table; Dance's compartmentalised ceiling decoration with its lacy arabesques and rosettes survives. The room's drama is enhanced by a mirroring extension to the rear added in 1901 at the same time as the entrance-front porch. The monks' dining room in the basement has a typically Soanean plethora of arches and pedimented niches for the display of objects purloined from Greek, Roman and Egyptian sites. The tearoom next door was formerly a laundry.

The balusters of the elegant stone staircase, top lit by an oval lantern, are similarly recycled, this time more prosaically from the Gurnells' original house. The present municipal grey replaces a rich colour scheme that included 'black Marble & gold veins' for the basement, 'Porphyr' for the ground level and 'French rouge' for the first floor. The bust of Minerva was installed by Soane.

The first-floor drawing room above the eating room was also intended for use on formal occasions. The large, pleasant space has an elaborate plaster ceiling designed by Dance and much admired by Soane. The east wall originally had three windows (the central one was bricked up c. 1832 and the single window opposite enlarged); the pilasters that frame them are echoed on the west wall. The rest of the first floor consisted of four modestly sized bedrooms, one of which (above the small drawing room) is open to the public. The combination of a cross- and barrel-vaulted ceiling echoes the arrangement in the library.

Breakfast room, Pitzhanger Manor

Some 30 years after the Soanes left Ealing, the house was bought by Spencer Walpole and became the home of his four unmarried sisters-in-law, Frances, Maria, Louisa and Frederika Perceval, whose father was assassinated while he was prime minister in 1812. (His bust can be seen in the stairwell.) The family extended the house to the north and Frederika continued to live here until 1900, after which her nephew sold the house to the council, which turned it into a library. The extension beyond the Victorian wing, now an art gallery, was built in 1940. The library moved out in 1984 and the house was restored as a museum and arts venue.

Strawberry Hill

268 Waldegrave Road, London TW1 4ST
www.strawberryhillhouse.org.uk
Nearest transport: Strawberry Hill Rail or Richmond Rail then bus 33
Open: Mon–Wed, Sat & Sun 12.00-16.20 (April to Oct)
Admission: £7.25/£6.30/£4.45/family ticket £18.10

Strawberry Hill

When England's first prime minister Robert Walpole died in 1745, his youngest son Horace (1717–97) decided to use part of his inheritance to buy a country house. He was lucky to find one of the last undeveloped plots of land at Twickenham, at the time only two hours' coach-ride from London and highly fashionable. (Walpole described it to a friend as having 'dowagers as plentiful as flounders'.) The house he bought in 1749 for £776 10s was a relatively modest cottage, built in 1698 and known as Chopp'd Straw Hall because locals assumed its coachman owner had been able to afford it only by giving his employer's horses chopped straw and illicitly selling off the more valuable hay for his own profit. Within 50 years, Walpole – perhaps in an act of Oedipal rebellion against Houghton Hall, the house commissioned in 1722 by his father from England's leading Palladian architect Colen Campbell (see Marble Hill House, page 234) – was to use a style previously reserved largely for follies to transform his 'little plaything house' into a sprawling gothic mansion that initiated a new architectural fashion and turned the tide against classicism.

Walpole is largely remembered as a letter-writer whose first-hand accounts of politics and society are one of our most valuable sources of information on 18th-century life. The flamboyance and aestheticism he brought to Strawberry Hill applied to the man himself: he was described by his friend Laetitia Hawkins as 'always enter[ing] a room in that style of affected delicacy, which fashion had then made almost natural... knees bent, and feet on tip-toe, as if afraid of a wet floor.' His celebrated collection of books, pictures, furniture and antiquities, plus such curiosities as Cardinal Wolsey's red hat and Charles I's death warrant, aroused the interest of many would-be visitors; the auction at which it was sold off by his descendants in 1842 took 32 days and was so hyped that spoof catalogues appeared including such entries as a mouse that had run over Queen Adelaide's foot. Walpole staged lavish entertainments, at one of which – for French, Spanish and Portuguese dignitaries – he dressed in a 'cravat of Gibbons' carving, and a pair of gloves embroidered up to the elbows that had belonged to James I'. Among his close friends were poet Thomas Gray (who accompanied him on a grand tour of Europe in 1739–41), actress Kitty Clive, and the Countess of Suffolk at nearby Marble Hill, whose reminiscences contributed greatly to his *Memoirs of the Reigns of George I and George II*.

The house Walpole bought – an inelegant L-shaped structure at the eastern corner of the present building – could most kindly be described as having potential. His first job was to stamp its unpromising exterior with his personality by adding new façades and bays incorporating gothic elements drawn from the architecture of medieval castles and abbeys: battlements, finials and gothic ogee and quatrefoil windows. His attitude to borrowing, inside and out, had an air of 'make-believe' – designs for tombs were re-used as fireplaces and rood screens as bookcases, with no respect for the integrity of the original. Unlike in the work of 19th-century gothicists such as A W N Pugin, these embellishments were pure confectionery, done for theatrical effect with no structural rationale and using insubstantial materials (outside lath and plaster enclosed by brick, inside wood or plasterwork) to mimic stone monumentality. Walpole and the friends who joined him in a Committee of Taste to debate and design the new work – most importantly illustrator Richard Bentley, art connoisseur John Chute, and William Robinson of the Board of Works – wanted to do away with classical symmetry and rationality. (Walpole himself coined the term serendipity.) The effect is something like a fairytale castle stretched sideways with the expected elements rearranged at random.

In 1753–54 Walpole added a two-storey wing to the north to house the great parlour and library and in 1759 tacked the Holbein chamber on to the north-west corner. In the early 1760s he more than doubled the length of the south façade by adding an open cloister, above which was the long gallery. The round tower that terminates the gallery was built in 1763 and the thinner Beauclerk Tower in 1776. Further rooms were added to the northern side of the gallery, including the great north bedchamber (1770). Most of the façades of the 1750s and 1760s were designed by Chute, but the plainer, more linear offices to the south were conceived by James Essex and erected by James Wyatt in 1790. You could say Walpole had the builders in for 50 years.

Following Walpole's death, Strawberry Hill passed eventually to Lady Frances Waldegrave (1821–79), whose first husband John was a descendant of Horace's brother Edward. He died a year later and she married his brother George, who took a dislike to Strawberry Hill after being imprisoned by Twickenham magistrates for 'riotous behaviour' (an event that led Frances to miscarry her only pregnancy). George decided to sell Walpole's collection and let

Round room, Strawberry Hill

the house rot (Frances, unbeknown to her husband, bought back various Reynolds paintings of her inlaws and some of the original Flanders glass from the sale). Following George's death – like his brother from syphilis – she made a third marriage, at the age of 27, to the much older George Granvill Harcourt. In 1856 she decided to restore and expand her derelict inheritance: after spending £100,000, she stopped counting.

Frances' major change was the addition of a building linking Walpole's round tower and the Wyatt offices, containing a banqueting or drawing room, dining room, billiards room and accommodation for guests and servants. She was sensitive to Walpole's intentions, and to achieve the greater ceiling height of her grand new rooms she lowered the lawn, as well as adding a floor to each of Walpole's towers and some tall, highly decorated 'Tudor' chimney pots. She also filled in the cloisters to provide staff accommodation and linked the Holbein chamber and great north bedchamber.

Harcourt died in 1861 and two years later Frances married Chichester Fortescue, a Whig minister and secretary for Ireland. Strawberry Hill became the Liberal salon of the day, with guests including Palmerston, Gladstone and the Prince and Princess of Wales. Frances, whose fame eclipsed her husband's, was known as the Queen of Dublin.

In 1923 the house was bought for St Mary's Catholic Teacher Training College, and Sebastian Pugin Powell, grand-nephew of A W N, designed a chapel and various accommodation. Extensive restoration was undertaken by Albert Richardson after World War II. Since 2002 the house has been leased to the Strawberry Hill Trust, which almost immediately embarked on an eight-year restoration programme led by architects Inskip and Jenkins.

The main entrance to Strawberry Hill following Walpole's additions was from the London road, which the influential Lady Waldegrave had diverted to afford more privacy. Outside the front door is a colonnaded 'oratory' with a basin for 'holy water' and a niche in which Walpole placed a bronze saint. In this cloister (designed by Chute) was a Chinese bowl in which Walpole's cat drowned trying to catch goldfish, inspiring Gray's poem 'Ode on the Death of a Favourite Cat' with the lines: 'Not all that tempts your wand'ring eyes/And heedless hearts, is lawful prize;/Nor all, that glistens, gold.' Here both the earnest playfulness of Walpole's vision and the flimsiness of the structure supporting it are apparent: the cloister is vaulted with papier-mâché and the rust from the nails holding the laths in place can be glimpsed through the mock-stone rendering.

Walpole's hall – grey ceiling, grey floor, grey walls – was decorated to evoke the atmosphere of 'gloomth' that pervades his pioneering gothic novel *The Castle of Otranto* (1764). The idea was to create a scaled-down version of a medieval great hall, just as Bentley's rococo staircase is an uncomfortably cramped replica of a stair from Rouen cathedral. For Walpole, this hall was 'the most particular and chief beauty of the Castle'. The adjacent great parlour or dining room – the first of Walpole's extensions beyond the confines of Chopp'd Straw Hall – is at the opposite end of the house from the kitchen in the round tower, with no possible indoor route between them. The extravagant chimney piece, like many others in the house, was designed by Bentley, often based on drawings of details from medieval cathedrals. In 1750 Walpole bought 450 pieces of Flanders glass depicting peasants at work, stories from the scriptures, birds, flowers and coats of arms. Scattered throughout the house and sometimes arranged in seemingly random order, as here, the collection is one of the unexpected delights of Strawberry Hill.

The library is one of the most nonsensically decorated of Walpole's rooms, its book-lined walls fronted by an unevenly proportioned, cloister-like series of gothic arches (designed by Chute after yet more ecclesiastical precedents) that swing open to give access to the books. The Holbein chamber, designed by Bentley to house Walpole's collection of 20 original and 34 copied Holbeins, reflects the royal nature of the portraiture with purple walls and an elaborate papier-mâché ceiling based on that of a bedchamber at Windsor Castle. Though the room borrows the

Palladian device of a screened bed alcove (its screen modelled from Rouen cathedral), the plan locates the entrance at the alcove rather than the main part of the room, so visitors are obliged to squeeze past the bed.

Walpole's wedding-cake elaboration reaches its peak in the gallery, his main space for entertaining. Opposite the windows are recesses lined with mirrors edged in fretwork in a Moorish style that reflects the taste of new committee member Thomas Pitt, who had travelled to Iberia. The ceiling (designed by Chute) is a series of elaborate gilded papier-mâché swirls up to 2 metres deep that appear to spin out of the recesses like icing from a cake-decorator's nozzle. (Their origin is less fanciful – papier-mâché was made by barefoot women and children who risked their lives by treading down rags in lead solution.) Lady Waldegrave spent £20,000 (Walpole's total budget for the house, including the purchase price) on shipping the floor from a Viennese villa she had visited on one of her honeymoons. At the end of the gallery is the round room of the tower, with a ceiling based on the rose window of St Paul's Cathedral.

Walpole's 'tribune' – a small, once crammed treasure chest for the display of his coins, medals, miniatures and enamels – has a quatrefoil plan and domed ceiling. He referred playfully to this room of worldly goods as 'the chapel' – which is ironically what it became after the arrival of St Mary's. The great north bedchamber, like the gallery, is hung with crimson Norwich damask. Designed to impress but largely unused, it housed a grand bed decorated with ostrich feathers.

The 'Beauty Room' in the original Chopp'd Straw Hill has been restored so as to reveal the many layers of the house's existence, including panelling from the 17th-century cottage Walpole inherited, some exotic 19th-century wallpaper and some William Morris wallpaper chosen by the priests in the 20th century. There is also a museum room giving information about the house's colourful inhabitants and a café.

Syon House

Syon Park, Brentford, Middlesex TW8 8JF
Tel: 020 8560 0882
www.syonpark.co.uk
Nearest transport: Gunnersbury LU/Rail then bus 237 or 267
Open: Wed, Thurs, Sun & bank hol Mondays 11.00-17.00 (April to Oct)
Admission: £9/£8/£4/family ticket £20
Wheelchair access: none

Syon House

Syon House is the only major London mansion still in private hands, and though the guidebook may be coy about its present owner's finances, the *Sunday Times* 'rich list' of 2009 places the 12th Duke of Northumberland at number 178 in the UK, some 30 places above the Queen. Notable recent predecessors in the family line include the 10th Duke, Hugh (title-bearer from 1940 to 1988), who led the 1968 government investigation into bovine foot-and-mouth disease; Helen, 8th Duchess and mistress of the robes to the

Entrance hall, Syon House

late Queen Mother; the 6th Duke, Algernon (1867–99), who with his wife Louisa was a prominent member of the Catholic apostolic movement; and the 3rd Duke (another Hugh, 1817–47), whose receipts from coal and rent made him the richest commoner in Britain and whose wife was governess to the future Queen Victoria. The family today lives at Alnwick Castle, recently refurbished and given a new lease of life as a tourist venue by the *Harry Potter* films.

Syon was originally an annexe to an abbey for the Order of St Bridget that was established at Twickenham in 1415 by Henry V. Following the reformation, it became crown property and was eventually secured by Edward Seymour, Duke of Somerset and protector to the young Edward VI. It was he who began the house that forms the shell of the present building. After Seymour's execution in 1552 for plotting against the crown, Syon had various owners until in 1597 it was granted to Henry Percy, 9th Earl of Northumberland, who added the battlements and corner towers. During the previous 60 years it had housed Catherine Howard as she awaited execution and the coffin of Henry VIII on its way from Westminster to Windsor and was the place where the ill-fated Lady Jane Grey reluctantly accepted the offer of the crown made by her father-in-law John Dudley, who owned the house until he in turn was executed.

Henry Percy was a favourite of James I until his cousin Thomas was suspected of involvement in the gunpowder plot, at which point he was imprisoned in the Tower of London for 17 years. His son Algernon rose to the rank of lord high admiral and following Charles I's imprisonment was appointed governor to the royal children, who lived at Syon from 1646 to 1649. Algernon's son, the 11th Earl, died only two years after his father, leaving an infant daughter, Elizabeth, as his sole heir. She eventually married Charles Seymour, Duke of Somerset, and the couple were mistress of the stole and master of the horse to Queen Anne. (After Elizabeth's death in 1722 Charles married Charlotte Finch, whose younger sister Elizabeth was the wife of the Earl of Mansfield at Kenwood, see page 115.) Charles' son Algernon was succeeded by his daughter Elizabeth, wife of Sir Hugh Smithson, who in 1766 was created 1st Duke of

Northumberland. An associate of the 3rd Earl of Bute (the previous owner of Kenwood) and at one time considered a likely successor to him as prime minister under George III, Smithson engaged Bute's protégé Robert Adam to work on his homes of Northumberland House in London, Alnwick Castle and Syon (1762–73).

The exterior of Syon is plain to the point of austerity, its unadorned stone façades relieved only by battlements. The house is approximately square, built around a courtyard, with square turrets at the outer corners. Each flank is two storeys high with a sub-basement. On the ground floor (here the *piano nobile*) the west and south flanks are one room deep, the east wing has a long gallery (transformed by Adam into a library) on the outside and a suite of smaller rooms on the courtyard side and the north wing was extended by the 3rd Duke, who added the oak passage (which functions as a long gallery) to the outside. The 3rd Duke also faced the house in Bath stone, installed the battlemented porch on the west front and built a magnificent freestanding conservatory in the grounds. The east front (best appreciated from Kew Gardens) is topped dramatically by a statue of the straight-tailed Percy lion.

Adam's plans for Syon proposed a grand suite of rooms taking up the whole of the *piano nobile*, connected via four ovals to a circular saloon that almost filled the courtyard. In the event only five main rooms on the west, south and east sides were realised, though these are among his finest. The plain west front gives way to a stunning entrance hall that fully realises the architect's brief 'to create a palace of Graeco-Roman splendour'. A double cube just over 20 metres long, it cleverly accommodates the uneven levels of the Jacobean house by placing the stairs up to the adjacent rooms in a coffered apse at one end and a vaulted recess at the other, screened by Doric columns. The original decorative scheme was pure white, relieved only by the black and white chequerboard floor. (Sadly, the hall was repainted in 1974 to a colour scheme devised by John Fowler which picks out the wonderfully delicate plasterwork in muted greys and creams.) Among the imposing copies of antique sculpture is a bust of the 1st Duke, a balding Englishman got up in a toga.

The richly decorated anteroom in the south-west corner provides a startling contrast. Again Adam manipulates the space, here positioning the 12 Ionic columns – 'obtained' by his brother James in Rome and veneered in verd-antique scagliola – to create the impression of a square space further defined by the brightly coloured scagliola floor. The heavy ceiling is gilded, as are the statues in various states of undress that top the columns and the trophy panels that flank the entrance, which to modern eyes appear almost cubist in their deconstructed effect. Though Syon's grounds were transformed by 'Capability' Brown into a wonderfully informal landscape at the same time as Adam was introducing neoclassical formality to the house's interiors, the woodland and lake are barely visible through the windows, and Adam's rooms are decidedly inward-looking, never attaining the harmony of nature and architecture he achieved at Kenwood.

The dining room in the south wing is almost a triple cube with the doorways at each end positioned in apses screened by Corinthian columns. The colour scheme is refreshingly subtle after the excesses of the anteroom, though for the ceiling decoration Adam eschewed the delicacy of the entrance hall in favour of a vigorous pattern of fans and palmettes. The adjacent red drawing room – hung with crimson silk and with a remarkable coved ceiling inset with 239 medallions painted by Cipriani with lifelike figures in classical poses – is again a colourful and more sumptuous contrast. Apparently the 1st Duke, whose careful accounting led him to query Cipriani's demand to be paid more for medallions containing two figures, was caught trying to avoid import duty on the large French mirrors by smuggling them into the country in a diplomatic bag. Peter Lely's portrait of Charles I and his son James, Duke of York, is thought to have been painted at Syon when the 10th Earl had charge of the royal children. A jib door allows a glimpse into a 'private' study on the courtyard side of the building, left as furnished by the 10th Duke with a worn leather chair, a desk stacked with family photographs and a prominent crucifix.

The stunning long gallery/library – its length almost ten times its width – takes up the whole of the east front. Unlike at nearby

Osterley (see page 240), where the library is plainly decorated to allow the books to dominate, here Adam transformed a traditional panelled Jacobean gallery into a room 'finished in a style to afford variety and amusement' to the ladies of the house. Virtually every surface is covered in a palette of pink, blue and gold that echoes the glittering tooling on the many books. A false bookcase conceals a door that allowed the ladies to walk out on to the lawn. Above the books are portrait medallions tracing the lineage of the Percys via Harry Hotspur back to Charlemagne – a bald statement by the 1st Duke of the credentials of the family into which he had married. The tables below have informal snapshots of the family today. One of the two turret rooms is decorated with oriental wallpaper; the other is a richly stuccoed pink, blue and gold boudoir.

The print room in north-east corner, hung with family portraits, was enlarged by the 3rd Duke at the same time as he provided Syon with a traditional-style long gallery in the form of the oak passage that runs the length of the north front, half-panelled with timber rescued from the Jacobean house. From the print room visitors can look into the duchess' sitting room on the courtyard side of the east wing and the green drawing room on the courtyard side of the north wing. The small sitting room – more like a display of family life than a room that's lived in – contains furniture of various styles including two armchairs with covers embroidered by the 8th Duchess Helen and her sister in the 1930s. The much larger drawing room, still occasionally used by the family, has a preponderance of roomy sofas and some sweet snapshots of little girls practising flamenco dancing that soften the gloom cast by the grim family portraits. The only modern item is the telephone – none of the Northumberlands' wealth, it seems, is squandered on contemporary design. Next to the drawing room are the private dining room and a surprisingly functional kitchen adjoining the entrance hall. Upstairs, visitors can access a series of unremarkable, overfurnished bedrooms.

Anteroom, Syon House

More things to see & do

Syon House is set in 80 hectares of parkland on the banks of the Thames with splendid views across the river to Kew. Its grounds include tidal water meadows, a wilderness and some 16 hectares of gardens.

Syon Park was landscaped by 'Capability' Brown for the 1st Duke of Northumberland in the mid 18th century. Foreign trees and exotic shrubs were introduced, the river was transformed into a sinuous ornamental lake and the sweeping lawn was adorned with a 16-metre Doric column bearing a statue of Flora, the goddess of flowers. The grounds are still home to some 200 species of tree.

Great conservatory, Syon House

The great conservatory was designed between 1820 and 1830 for the 3rd Duke by Charles Fowler, who was also responsible for the old flower market at Covent Garden. The small room to the east, with a tiled floor from the Wedgwood factory, was originally the dairy. There is also an ice house, which would be filled with ice from the lake in winter to make sorbets and chill wine and champagne.

The family-friendly Syon Park also includes an indoor adventure playground, garden centre, aquarium, fly-fishing facilites and a restaurant. The park is open daily from 10.30 to 17.00 (March to Oct) and at weekends only from 10.30 to 16.00 (Nov to Feb). See *www.syonpark.co.uk*.

South-west

Library and study, Southside House, see page 273

South-west

Southside House

3-4 Woodhayes Road, London SW19 4RJ
Tel: 020 8946 7643
www.southsidehouse.com
Nearest transport: Wimbledon LU/Rail then bus 93 to Rose & Crown
Open: Wed, Sat, Sun & bank hol Mondays, guided tours only
    at 14.00, 15.00 and 16.00 (April to Sept)
Admission: £6/£3/family ticket £12
Wheelchair access: phone in advance

Malcolm Munthe MC (1910–1995), who lived for much of his adult
life at Southside and created the house visitors see today, returned
from the Second World War a modest hero and an injured and
tortured man. Just before war began he had been assigned the
safe Conservative seat of East Ham South and his future seemed
assured. During the war, as part of the Special Operations Executive,
he had worked as a spy and saboteur in Nazi-occupied Scandinavia
and participated in the covert preparations for the Allied landings
at Anzio in Southern Italy. By the time he came back to England, he
was haunted by visions of death and destruction and the country
he had hoped to lead into the second half of the 20th century was
changed beyond recognition. It is hardly surprising that he turned
to the past, creating at Southside and at the family's other home of
Hellens in Herefordshire a romantic version of family history as he
would have liked it to have been, spinning threads of truth into a
fantastic web presented with a wonderful sense of showmanship.

Though Malcolm Munthe liked to claim that Southside had
been acquired by his ancestors in 1685 as a country retreat from
the plague, it was in fact bought by his mother, Hilda Pennington-
Mellor, in the 1930s. Hilda had been brought up in the chateau of
Françon near Biarritz by parents who had made their fortune in
shipping and Egyptian cotton. Her neighbours included members
of Europe's royal families and she was briefly promised to the crown
prince of Serbia, but in her late teens, against her parents' wishes,
she married charismatic Swedish writer, physician and psychiatrist
Axel Munthe, a man some 30 years her senior. The marriage was

Dining room, South Side House

a difficult one: Axel's home of San Michele on Capri, his work as a physician and his intimate involvement with the Swedish royal family took him away constantly and his absences became longer and more frequent.

Hidden behind high brick walls, Southside gives the impression of wishing to keep the world away. The two-storey house has a ten-bay, William and Mary-style red-brick façade with two shallow pedimented projections – each three bays wide and set with central niches containing statues – framing the two middle bays. The entrance door is off centre, next to a large, ungainly Georgian bay. Though Malcolm Munthe added two wings – one merely a façade – and the clocktower in the 1960s to give his would-be stately home a greater semblance of symmetry, the overall composition only makes sense when you realise that the building was once two houses, with doors positioned where the niches are.

Visitors are led through the garden room at the back to what was once the entrance hall of the westernmost house, now containing a staircase but no front door. Alongside a quantity of Sèvres porcelain and a sketch of the family's lost chateau of Françon by Malcolm's elder brother Peter, who trained as a painter, is a remarkable series of miniature copies by Theodore Rouselle of Van Dyck's portraits of 17th-century aristocracy. Originally part of the collection of Philip, 4th Baron Wharton (1613–96), they were inherited along with some of Southside's other wonderful paintings by Malcolm, who was a friend of one of Wharton's heirs.

The breakfast room, also in the westernmost house, is lit by the Georgian bay, one of whose three windows was covered by a full-length portrait when Hilda became irritated by the postman's habit of knocking on the glass to gain her attention. The gilded leather frieze is cracked and flaking and the rose brocade looks tired and grey, but the room nonetheless retains a certain charm. The glorious Charles I sideboard is set with drinks and glasses and the mantelpiece is cluttered with photographs, toys and party invitations. Among the family portraits is a lifesize painting of the handsome Peter with sword and cape done by Malcolm when he was 17, perhaps an early indication of the Gothic romanticism that was to dominate his later retreat from the world.

The dining room behind, more than doubled in size by a Victorian projection built over what was probably once a courtyard, nevertheless appears too small and inelegant for the impressive family furniture. The flamboyant fireplace surround was cobbled together by Malcolm as an elaborate pastiche of imagined former grandeur. Almost every inch of wall space is hung with paintings ranging from the Stuart period to the early 20th century.

A monumental doorway from the breakfast room leads into the easternmost house, in whose double-height entrance hallway Malcolm gave his theatrical fantasies full rein. Into a relatively small space is squeezed a fireplace with an enormous baroque surround, a gallery supported by oversized Doric columns made of plywood to imitate stone, and two elaborate doorways. The bust of Charles I set into the pediment of the internal door was modelled by Wimbledon art students and the ceiling paintings are by Peter. Side by side with these restorations and inventions are such genuine treasures as Italian marble busts and paintings inherited from Axel Munthe and Jacobean furniture saved from Françon.

Upstairs, overlooking the garden, is Malcolm's very much lived-in library and study, though he himself liked to claim it was the room where his father wrote his bestselling memoir *The Story of San Michele*. Malcolm's own books of autobiography and translation are notable only by their absence. The battered leather furniture with leaking stuffing is testament to his son Adam's determination to retain the house's idiosyncratic character as well as to Malcolm's menagerie of unruly pets, including dogs and a tawny owl.

The Prince of Wales bedroom perhaps epitomises the way the myths surrounding Southside are grown from grains of fact. It is true that George II and his heir apparent Prince Frederick used to review the troops on Wimbledon Common; their difficult relationship meant they stayed in separate accommodation, with Frederick billeted in a less grand house than his father, possibly a house on the scale of Southside. It is also true that Axel Munthe treated the future Edward VII, though the monarch died long before Hilda bought her Wimbledon home. So why not elaborate on what may have been by furnishing the room with gold hangings and a bed with a crimson headboard decorated with a crest of ostrich plumes rising through a gold coronet? The room's cabinet of curiosities contains a bizarre mix of coronation trivia, figurines made by Malcolm and Peter when they were children, a Fabergé ring probably given to Hilda by her Biarritz Romanoff neighbours, cufflinks presented to Axel by Edward VII and a string of pearls alleged to have fallen from Marie-Antoinette's neck at her execution and to have been given to a Pennington ancestor by Josephine Bonaparte. Each item is carefully labelled, accurately or not, in Malcolm's spidery hand.

One of Malcolm's final projects was the tiny chapel above the dining room. A mix of bare concrete walls, a Swedish-style wood ceiling, old carpets and unmatched scraps of silk, its windows are still faced with Malcolm's own cartoons for the stained glass he hoped to install. Among the family photographs and cheap candlesticks sits a 13th-century pearwood Madonna and Child.

The original hallway of the easternmost house has painted hessian wallhangings that may have been decorated by Handel's scene painter. The light-filled music room looking on to the garden is Southside's grandest space – and the only one that's heated, to preserve the early Pleyel grand piano imported from Françon. Created from two smaller rooms, it has a screen of Ionic columns across the former division, a dozen or so elaborate wall-mounted chandeliers, niches with statues, some glorious 18th- and 19th-century paintings and a fine collection of French furniture in varying states of repair.

Southside today is run by a family trust headed by Adam Munthe. According to the curators for whom the house provides a much loved if at times chilly home, it is likely that it still holds many secrets. A recent discovery is a cache of more than 50 Worth gowns from the turn of the 20th century made for Hilda and her mother and found in a trunk in the basement. They deliver an insight into the privilege and glamour of Hilda's life before Southside, and a picture of the lost childhood that helped to shape Malcolm's imagination.

South-west Outskirts

Carew Manor

Church Road, Beddington, Surrey SM6 7NH
Tel: 020 8770 4781
www.sutton.gov.uk/index.aspx?articleid=1301
Nearest transport: Sutton Rail
Open: occasional tours on Sun 14.00 and 15.30 (booking required)
Admission: £4

More than most stately homes, Carew Manor has been successively rebuilt in line with contemporary fashion – a point made most clearly at the end of the guided tour, which takes visitors (wearing hard hats) to the cellar, where you can see walls layered like an onion. Originally a moated fortified house built by Sir Nicholas Carew in the mid 14th century, the manor was inherited in 1520 by another Sir Nicholas Carew. A one-time favourite of Henry VIII, he fell from grace in 1537 and was executed; his house and estate were forfeit to the king. The house was restored to the family by Mary I and in the 1570s Nicholas' son Francis engaged in a substantial bout of rebuilding and landscaping. Rebuilt again with a classical façade by another Nicholas in the early 18th century, the house was occupied by the Carews until gambler Charles Hallowell Carew was forced to sell in 1859 to pay off his debts. The Lambeth Female Orphan Asylum gave it its final facelift, adding the present Victorian-gothic red-brick façades, the clocktower and the cross passage at the front that closes off the courtyard. The building has been a school since 1954.

The great hall, the only part of the house open to the public, was probably built by Sir Richard Carew between 1493 and 1520. Though looking like similar ceilings elsewhere, the roof is in fact a fake – made of small pieces of wood covered with mouldings to give a false impression of thickness, perhaps as a cost-cutting exercise.

Honeywood

Honeywood Walk, Carshalton, Surrey, SM5 3NX
Tel: 020 8770 4297
www.friendsofhoneywood.co.uk
Nearest transport: Carshalton Rail
Open: closed for refurbishment until summer 2011,
    please check website for details
Admission: £1.60/80p
Wheelchair access: ground floor only

Honeywood

Honeywood was originally Wandle Cottage, a modest dwelling two rooms wide and one room deep in an attractive position overlooking one of Carshalton's many ponds. It is one of the few remaining examples of chalk and flint chequerwork construction, and the expanses of original exterior wall exposed in the two 19th-century extensions alone make Honeywood worth a visit.

The 17th-century cottage comprised what are now the shop and tea rooms on the ground floor and two rooms on the first floor, the smaller fitted out as an Edwardian dining room and the larger as an exhibition space for displays about the area's history. Their irregular shapes and alarmingly sagging low ceilings make both feel extremely old. The front room of the boxy north extension of 1896 is set up as a nursery; more elegant is the two-room mid-19th-century extension at the rear.

Around 1903 a top-lit billiards room and garden room were added to the south and the house took the name Honeywood after a house on the site of the extension. The billiards room has remained intact. The wood-panelled space contains the original table, placed under a skylight, surrounded by purpose-made leather sofas and fittings. The garden room is a light-filled, delicately detailed space with a mullioned bay and stained-glass side windows with a pattern of hearts and stylised leaves. Don't miss the Edwardian bathroom behind the dining room, which has the 'mayor's loo' from Sutton municipal offices – a fine affair decorated inside and out with blue flowers.

At the time of writing Honeywood was due to close for refurbishment, so displays may have changed when it reopens.

Little Holland House

40 Beeches Avenue, Carshalton, Surrey SM5 3LW
Tel: 020 8770 4781
www.friendsofhoneywood.co.uk/Little_Holland_House_2.htm
Nearest transport: Carshalton Beeches Rail
Open: first Sunday of the month 13.30-17.30
Admission: free
Wheelchair access: limited

'I built my Ideal House and all it contained... with only a small weekly wage of forty-five shillings;... with no practical experience of building, and without the aid of either a builder or an architect; which undertaking appeared to my friends to be a very ill-advised business indeed.'
Frank R Dickinson, *'A Novice Builds His Own Ideal House'*

When Frank Reginald Dickinson (1874–1961) began in October 1902 to build the home he was to occupy for 57 years, his aim was to create a house that 'stood up by itself, without the help of its neighbour; a house with beautiful things inside... a house and home that its like does not exist anywhere in these isles'. Inspired by the ideals and aesthetics championed by William Morris' arts-and-crafts movement and John Ruskin (who knew and liked the area), he bought a plot of land and subscribed to a mutual building society which awarded each £300 collected to one of its members selected by ballot. Frank had previously lived in a London basement, and while the money would have bought him a ready-built home, he was determined to go it alone. Unfortunately the cheapest builder's quote came in at £600, so he took his annual leave from his job at the Doulton factory in Lambeth and with the help of a brother on leave from the navy and another unemployed brother to act as foreman, plus a hired labourer, he began to lay the foundations ('I found... digging trenches was a much more strenuous labour than drawing plans on paper').

Within three months a shell was constructed to the plans he and his fiancée Florence had been poring over (his attitude to

Florence is a mix of reverence and condescension: 'I do not know if she understood a plan', he remarks in his memoir). They had also been working together on the essentials of furniture in his parents' cellar for the previous year or so. Then came some 12 months of weekends and holidays spent fitting the kitchen and bedroom before he and his bride moved in on 28 March 1904, their wedding night. Florence, meanwhile, had paid for the coveted green Cumbrian roof slates with the money saved for her trousseau: 'Could any woman make greater sacrifice?' asks Frank.

The house as built is charming and refreshingly free of pattern-book preconceptions, though layered with all that self-sufficiency are streaks of sentimentality and moralising. Frank anthropomorphises his creation shamelessly – 'there is also just another shy little window which has slipped round the front corner...' – while a quote accompanying a portrait of his 'good Master' Ruskin inset into the pine panelling in the dining room strikes terror in the heart: 'We will try to make some small piece of English ground beautiful peaceful & fruitful. We will have... none idle but the dead. We will have no liberty upon it; but instant obedience to known law & appointed person; no equality upon it; but recognition of every betterness that we can find & reprobation of every worseness.'

The simple pebbledash exterior with its ribbon windows – 'no fanciful sham Tudor work, but just plain brick' – gives way to a small lobby with doors to the comfortable kitchen in which the family would breakfast and a roomy living/dining space that runs from front to back of the house. In the front is the dining area; the rear is a sitting room with built-in settles on either side of the fireplace. All the furniture was designed and made by Frank in a mix of arts-and-crafts aesthetics – the attenuation of Mackintosh here, the tapering legs and square profiles favoured by Liberty and Mackmurdo there (he was an avid reader of The Studio). There are few non-essentials – a gramophone, an Italian walnut cakestand, some decorative pottery – yet the space is far from austere and the atmosphere bespeaks a confident sensuality, the hand of someone who has been prepared to rethink his family's needs from scratch and cater to them using the materials and forms of his choice rather than bowing to fashion and convention. In short, it is very modern, both in its conception and the stripped-down minimalism that has resulted – especially in comparison with the Victorian/Edwardian clutter of a home such as Linley Sambourne's (see page 147).

The beams between the two living areas are carved with crude stylised representations of plants and animals, but the major decoration is centred on the two fireplaces. The one in the dining room is topped by watercolour copies by Frank of paintings by two of his favourite artists: a Turner flanked by Victorian artist G F Watts' buxom *Eve Triumphant* and *Eve Repentant*. (Frank named his home Little Holland House in homage to Watts, who had lived in a house of that name for more than 20 years.) The sitting-room fireplace has dancing nymphs and Pans, above which Frank's oil triptych *Give to us each our daily bread* expresses his world view: in the middle is the working man, earning his wage by the sweat of his brow, while in the side panels science and industry, the monarchy, the church and the law wait with their hands outstretched for his money. Despite Frank's description of the house as 'a centre for gatherings and festivities, country dancing, play acting, musical evenings and discussion groups' along the lines of Morris' Red House (see page 338), the family portraits inset in the dado panelling are joyless: daughter Isabel is depicted as a severe and modern young woman while son Gerard looks positively cross; only Florence is softened by a smile.

The staircase that leads up from the dining room is itself a thing of beauty. The decoration in the master bedroom – accessed like the other rooms by an unusually large, roughly finished door with simple fittings ('a narrow door suggests meanness') – is in blues and greens: a dreamlike frieze of stylised trees and lakes and a blue-tiled fireplace above which is a copy of part of Burne-Jones' *The Sleeping Beauty* given to the couple as a wedding present by an art-student friend. Gerard's room contains a carved wedding chest made by father and son and a dressing table in which the son successfully translates his father's principles into a 1930s' aesthetic.

Whitehall

1 Malden Road, Cheam, Surrey SM3 8QD
Tel: 020 8643 1236
www.friendsofwhitehallcheam.co.uk
Nearest transport: Cheam Rail
Open: Wed-Fri, Sun & bank hol Mondays 14.00-17.00;
    Sat 10.00-17.00
Admission: £1.60/80p
Wheelchair access: ground floor only

Whitehall

Built probably for a yeoman farmer around 1500, Whitehall's
sparsely furnished, rickety rooms strongly evoke times gone by,
while the core of the building, helpfully exposed and elucidated for
the visitor, gives an insight into Tudor construction techniques.

The original house was two storeys high, three rooms long
and one room deep. The foundations are chalk blocks (exposed
below one of the original exterior walls in the Victorian kitchen
extension); the timber frame – of unseasoned and untreated local
elm and oak, probably felled only months before – was made up
in the carpenter's yard, marked to facilitate reassembly (some

marks are visible in one of the attic rooms), dismantled and re-erected on site. The ease with which this could be achieved was proved as late as 1922 when a similarly constructed house just south of Whitehall was dismantled and moved to allow the road to be widened.

The slightly larger, overhanging frame for the upper storey is supported on the upper-floor joists, which were cut to project beyond the lower-floor frame – a method called continuous jettying. The frames were then infilled with wattle covered with daub or rye dough (a mix of straw and clay), which was in turn coated with lime plaster. The roof is a crown-post construction originally covered in thatch or tiles (the post, beam and rafters are exposed in the attic). The windows – wooden mullions set in the gaps between the timbers – would have been unglazed and shuttered.

Visitors enter through the porch, added c. 1550, to the hall, which takes up about half the ground area of the original house. To the right is the service room, probably used to store food; to the left is the parlour, a pleasant square space with a large inglenook fireplace furnished as a kitchen/dining room (the fussy leaded windows here and in the hall are Georgian). Behind the hall and service room is the refreshment room, added along with the rooms above in about 1650. The new kitchen behind the parlour and the mezzanine bathroom were added around 1800, soon after the frame was weatherboarded. The exhibition room – a lean-to flanking the parlour – was probably built as a wash-house in the mid 19th century.

The staircase tower was added at about the same time as the porch, giving access not only to the first floor, formerly reached by ladder, but also to the newly created attic rooms. The mezzanine room allows a clear view of the original exterior wall and the external jettying of the upper storey. The bedroom above the parlour has a 17th-century door, found in one of the attic rooms, carved with Charles I's last word – 'Remember' – and 'D.O.M.' (*Deo optimo maximo*, 'To God most high'). This royalist graffiti suggests Whitehall may have been the home of the Reverend George Aldrich, who in 1645 founded Cheam School. Information about the school – including its famous

18th-century headmaster William Gilpin and former pupil Prince Philip – can be found in one of the spacious attic rooms.

In the dramatically sloping room above the porch is a display about the Killicks, who occupied Whitehall for over 200 years. John Killick first leased the house in the mid 18th century and in 1785 it was purchased by his son James. From 1853 – the start of more than a century of female ownership and occupancy – it was the home of James' grand-daughters Harriet and Charlotte, whose parents, William and Lucy, had lived at Whitehall with their 11 children. Harriet was a governess to the rector's children, Charlotte a governess to the headmaster's daughters and a music teacher at the school. We know that in 1881 three schoolmasters lodged in Whitehall with the sisters and their servant Ann Baker, and one of the attic rooms recreates the homely living quarters of a late-19th-century teacher, complete with a table set for tea, books and magazines, pictures and prints. Following Harriet's death in 1914, the house passed to her great-nieces Susan Mary and Harriet Maud – a formidable-looking pair, if a photograph taken in the garden with a circle of women friends is typical. After Harriet Maud's death in 1959, the house was bought by the council, which opened it as a museum in 1978.

It is in the unfurnished part of the attic, however, that you have the strongest sense of having gone back in time – to the extent that it's a shock to look out of the window and see 21st-century traffic.

More things to see & do

Run by the Friends of Whitehall, the house hosts temporary exhibitions, community events and a tearoom

Queen's House, see page 306

South-east

South-east

Charlton House

Hornfair Road, London SE7 8RE
Tel: 020 8856 3951
www.greenwich-guide.org.uk/charhse.htm
Nearest transport: Charlton Rail
Open: café and library only, Mon-Fri 8.30-18.00; Sat 9.30-17.00
Admission: free

Charlton House

Charlton House looks built to impress. Designed in 1607, less than ten years before Inigo Jones' radical neo-Palladian Queen's House (see page 306), it is one of London's most significant and last Jacobean mansions. Sturdy and unwieldy in comparison with Jones' beautifully proportioned gem, it was built for Sir Adam Newton, tutor to Henry Prince of Wales, son of James I, and is attributed to John Thorpe, architect of Audley End in Essex and probably of the core of Kensington Palace (see page 190).

In 1647 the house was sold to Sir William Ducie, a tradesman who spent his considerable fortune on repairing and redecorating his home and on entertaining. After his death it was bought by East India merchant Sir William Longhorne, who owned it until 1715. From 1767 until it was bought by Greenwich Borough Council in 1925, Charlton belonged to the Maryon-Wilson family. It is now run as a community centre, with access limited to the café and library.

Built on an H plan, Charlton has a massive three-storey, seven-bay red-brick façade with stone dressings, its elaborate central bay reminiscent of a solid brown fruit cake decorated with white icing. The twin towers at the sides of the two wings are topped by ogee roofs; the northern wing was bombed during the blitz and rebuilt with modern brick. The side extension was added in the late 19th century by Norman Shaw for the house's last private owner, Sir Spencer Maryon-Wilson.

Visitors enter into a double-height hall that stretches the depth of the central section of the house – an impractical arrangement since until the minstrels' gallery was added by moderniser Sir Thomas Maryon-Wilson in the 1830s (along with bathrooms, and wolves and bears for the park) there was no connection between the two sides of the first floor. Today the entrance hall is used as a café and the wood-panelled former chapel and adjacent Wilson room as a library. It's worth stopping to examine the library doors, carved with animals and probably original, and the oak staircase, its balustrades carved in the shape of plants with strings of plaster fruit and leaves decorating the walls behind, becoming more and more elaborate as it reaches the grand upper storey.

Eltham Palace

Court Yard, London SE9 5QE
Tel: 020 8294 2548
www.english-heritage.org.uk/elthampalace
Nearest transport: Eltham Rail
Open: Mon-Wed & Sun 11.00-17.00 (April to Oct),
    Mon-Wed & Sun 11.00-16.00 (Nov, Dec, Feb & March)
Admission: £8.70/£7.40/£4.40/family ticket £21.80

Eltham Palace

Eltham Palace is one of the ugliest stately homes I've seen. Indeed, from the outside you might be excused for mistaking it for a pretentious provincial town hall. Tacked on to a 15th-century great hall surviving from the royal palace that formerly occupied the site, this 1930s playhouse built for millionaire socialites Stephen and Ginie Courtauld is a triumph of ambition over taste and of decoration over architecture. But don't let that stop you from visiting: seeing how the other half lived, imagining yourself a guest at the party and planning how you might have done it all better make for a visit with particular pleasures.

Eltham manor first fell into royal hands in 1305, when Anthony Bek, Bishop of Durham, presented it to the future Edward II. For a quarter of a millennium, until the death of Henry VIII, it was one of the most used royal residences and one of only six palaces large enough to accommodate the 800-strong court. Edward III spent much of his youth here; Henry IV occupied Eltham for ten of his 13 Christmases as king; Henry VI and Henry VIII lived here for a large part of their boyhoods (in 1499 the palace was the site of a meeting between the latter, a nine-year-old prince, and Erasmus). However, Elizabeth I preferred the more convenient Greenwich, and Eltham was let out to tenants connected with the court. During the 17th century the buildings fell into decay; by the 19th – with the exception of a few structures such as the delightfully simple Tudor house, once occupied by Elizabeth I's chancellor, still standing beside the 1470s stone entrance bridge – the palace had deteriorated into a picturesque ruin.

The choice of Eltham as the site for a thoroughly modern country house was a romantic and visionary one; the Courtaulds' mistake was to hire inexperienced architects distinguished by their social connections rather than their portfolio. John Seely, the creative arm of Seely and Paget, professed himself inspired by Christopher Wren's work at Hampton Court (see page 214), which he mistakenly read as an attempt to restore the medieval palace rather than to create a Renaissance masterpiece. And indeed you only have to look at Seely's entrance façade – the elegantly curved neoclassical arcaded stone porch; the squat red-brick blocks of the wings with their windowpanes painted municipal British racing green; the twin towers (over the stairwells) with pagoda-style roofs; a roofscape that marries a concrete and glass-brick dome with three Tudor gables rescued from the ruins – to realise that eclecticism has its limits and rationality its place. It's a shame so much money didn't stretch to generous proportions or ceiling heights and that the courageous championing of modernity visible in the ocean-liner sleekness and technological innovation of the interior didn't translate into a modernist exterior.

The most striking space is the entrance hall, which seems to have functioned like a hotel lobby (male and female toilets and a pay-phone are positioned just off it; ashtrays and cocktail glasses are set out ready and waiting). Like much of the rest of the house, it is panelled in glorious (and no doubt costly) wood veneer, in this case Australian black bean. Designed by Rolf Engströmer, this was reportedly the first Swedish-style interior in Britain, inspired by Stockholm Town Hall, which the Courtaulds had visited in 1928. The lofty room is well lit by a clerestory and dome and Engströmer's furniture has a pleasing simplicity. But the initial sense of splendour crumbles on closer inspection: the circularity of the dome and the Marion Dorn carpet belies the triangular plan (give or take a few curved edges); the entrance wall is decorated with bizarrely vulgar marquetry scenes of Sweden and Italy (with the Courtaulds' yacht moored in Venice's lagoon), guarded by a larger-than-life Viking and a Roman soldier.

The drawing room, designed by Italian playboy aristocrat Peter Malacrida, is a mish-mash of styles: a monumental marble fireplace; false beams on the low ceiling painted to imitate Hungarian folk art (Ginie was of Hungarian and Italian parentage); faux-medieval wrought-iron grilles over the French windows; low-relief panels inspired by Egypt, Greece and Rome. As with many of the rooms in this inward-looking house, there is no attempt to exploit the lovely setting, with the heavy mullions spoiling the views of the garden outside. Malacrida also designed the boudoir and library –

surprisingly small-scale rooms again lined with wood, which makes the concealed lighting in the ceilings necessary even on a bright day. Ginie's boudoir is dominated by a six-seater sofa surrounded by shelving for books, lamps and telephones (the house was fitted with a state-of-the-art private exchange). In this 1930s semi writ large, Stephen's library has the feel of the office of a provincial bank manager. The books take up less wall space than the many pictures, for whose protection he designed an ingenious system of wood panels that could be pulled down from above and were themselves hung with woodcuts and engravings in an arrangement perhaps suggested by the picture room in Sir John Soane's Museum (see page 58). The art includes Turner watercolours and a miniature version of a memorial designed by his World War I comrade-in-arms Charles Sergeant Jagger. Among the books is a section on English schools, perhaps inspired by his friendship with Board of Education president Rab Butler, who drafted the reforming 1944 Education Act at Eltham.

The light-filled grandeur of the great hall – built by Edward IV from 1475 to 1480 – drives home the paucity of Seely's efforts elsewhere. Comparable in size with the great hall at Hampton Court, which it predates by half a century, the space was 'restored' by the Courtaulds in a manner influenced by the contemporary film industry's visions of medieval England (from 1931 Stephen was on the board of Ealing Studios). Among the additions are the minstrels' gallery, a quantity of 17th-century furniture, some angular art-deco lanterns topped by crowns, and hangings made of the 'art silk' (rayon) on which the family fortune was based – presumably the hefty budget didn't run to tapestries. Tacked on to the far end is an orangery and squash court (Ginie was a keen player) which is pleasant enough from the inside, if you ignore the overscaled Ionic pilasters, but from the outside couldn't have shown less sensitivity to its glorious neighbour.

The dismal twin stairwells, accessed from the entrance hall, rise to a ridiculous height, presumably in a bid to enliven the exterior with a couple of towers. Upstairs, the plan disintegrates

Dining room, Eltham Palace

into a series of chunky corridors and awkward landings with views over the ugly roofscape. On one landing hangs a portrait of the Courtaulds, upstaged by their lemur Mah-Jongg, bought at Harrods in 1923. Built into one of the corridors is the animal's cage, decorated with tropical murals and furnished with a bamboo ladder that leads down to the flower-arranging room off the entrance hall.

In Ginie's bedroom, the attempt at a circular plan is compromised by the leftover corners needed to accommodate the windows. Her ensuite bathroom gives the impression that the designer (Malacrida again) has unravelled the art-deco style into its parts – onyx walls; a gold mosaic-clad niche containing a statue of Psyche above a curved bath; an aggressively angular mirrored dressing table with a shiny black top – and failed to stitch them together again. Stephen's bedroom (designed by Seely) is more successful, and at least looks as if its owner might have tried to stamp it with his personal taste. The wood panelling is relieved by monochrome wallpaper depicting Kew Gardens, which forms a panorama covering the upper part of two of the walls, including the door leading to a blue-tiled bathroom that strives for a hamam effect. The guest rooms have numbered doors as in a hotel, except for the one labelled 'Batmen'. Seely's small but beautiful pear bedroom (named after the wood used for the panelling and fittings) demonstrates his skill at manipulating fine materials at a reduced scale.

The Venetian suite, one of only two double guest bedrooms, was designed by Malacrida, perhaps with Ginie's Italian mother in mind. It includes such nonsense as a 17th-century model tabernacle utilised as a cupboard, mirrored pastiches of some fine old panelling from the Courtauld's house in Grosvenor Square and a door faced with false books to match the real bookshelves opposite. The ensuite bathroom (probably by Seely) is simple and modern in contrast, lined in plain yellow Vitrolite (a new easy-to-clean surface) and with a bidet, the height of European chic. A reel of home movies of exotic holidays, pets and orchids gives an idea of couple's interests.

The most successfully decorated room is the dining room, which strives for drama through coherence and simplicity. It has a dramatic art-deco fireplace in ribbed aluminium and black marble inlaid with a mother-of-pearl Greek-key pattern; black doors with the same pattern in silver and applied lacquer animals, perhaps inspired by the delicate 18th- or early-19th-century Chinese screen at the entrance to the great hall; an aluminium-leaf ceiling; pale wood walls and an elegant dining suite. The moderne style was underwritten by state-of-the-art technology – central-heating coils concealed in the ceiling; a centralised vacuum-cleaning system; synchronous inbuilt clocks; a network of loudspeakers throughout the ground floor.

The Courtaulds vacated Eltham Palace in 1944 and moved to South Rhodesia (now Zimbabwe) seven years later. They left their home to the Army Educational Corps, which occupied it until 1995, when English Heritage took over the site. Eight years is not long to occupy a house you've commissioned and to some extent designed yourself. But perhaps its fundamental failings became all too apparent once wartime austerity put paid to the glamorous showmanship its interiors project so well.

More things to see & do

A rare and very fine example of 1930s landscape design incorporating intriguing elements of the medieval palace and a moat filled with water lilies and carp, Eltham Palace's gardens boast dramatic views over London. The Courtaulds were keen horticulturists: Stephen had a passion for orchids, which he raised in the glasshouses, and Virginia for roses. Their dream garden includes a sunken rose garden, a spring bulb meadow, a rockery with pools and cascades, a pergola whose Ionic columns were salvaged from the Bank of England and a woodland.

Eltham Palace, view from the south

Flamsteed House

Royal Observatory, Greenwich, London SE10 9NF

Tel: 020 8858 4422

www.nmm.ac.uk/places/royal-observatory/flamsteed-house

Nearest transport: Maze Hill Rail or Cutty Sark DLR

Open: daily 10.00–17.00

Admission: free

For all the importance of Greenwich as the place by which the world sets its clocks, the first astronomer royal John Flamsteed (1646–1719) lived in modest style. And his house, built by Christopher Wren for a mere £520 19s 1d from materials recycled from the Tower of London and Tilbury Fort, is a simple and elegant piece of architecture by contrast with the same architect's ornate Royal Naval College down the hill, completed some 30 years later. The idea of an observatory was suggested to Charles II by a French protégé of his mistress Louise de Kéroualle. Wren proposed Greenwich as a site and in 1675 the clergyman and mathematician Flamsteed was appointed at a salary of £100 per annum, from which he was expected to buy his own instruments. In 1692 he married Margaret Cooke, who helped him with his observations alongside two assistants. In order to make ends meet, he had to take on private pupils.

Wren's original house-cum-observatory was a square, two-storey red-brick building with elaborate wood dressings made to look like stone and two high square turrets at the ends of the three-bay front. The small pavilions to the sides were added in 1772–73 and the extension at the back that now functions as a museum was built between 1790 and 1835 to give more space to subsequent astronomer royals. The red time ball on the roof, which still operates at 13.00, dates from 1833 and was one of the world's earliest public time signals. Flamsteed was succeeded after his death by Edmund Halley of comet fame and his house was home to subsequent astronomer royals until 1948. Flamsteed House is now part of the National Maritime Museum.

Flamsteed's living quarters on the ground floor – a series of modest wood-panelled rooms – have been recreated with furniture

Octagon room, Flamsteed House

loaned by the V&A. There is no ostentation here, whether in the dining room set with a simple meal, the bedroom with its narrow bed (presumably he and Margaret, busily stargazing, didn't spend much time there), the study with its floor piled with books, or the sparsely furnished sitting room. A portrait of the bewigged astronomer, with his generous nose and heavy brows, has him looking suitably serious; engravings of the house soon after completion show how little the shell has changed.

The breathtaking moment comes with the light-filled double-height octagonal observatory that takes up the whole of the first floor. The tall narrow windows were designed to accommodate long telescopes and the view from the balcony of the Queen's House (see page 306), Royal Naval College and river beyond is one of London's finest. The lofty ceiling has a delicate plasterwork frieze of flowers and berries; patrons Charles II and James II, toes pointed as if to curtsey, stand above painted wood panelling inset with copies of the ornate Thomas Tompion wall clocks whose accuracy allowed Flamsteed to determine that the earth rotated at a constant speed and therefore to begin to map the stars (Margaret sold the originals after her husband's death). On the stairs is an etching of the room in use soon after it was built; in fact, because none of the walls are aligned with the meridian, positional observations were difficult, so Flamsteed set up his telescopes in a shed in the garden, with the observatory used to impress important visitors with its views of the night sky.

The ultimate purpose of Flamsteed's work was to produce a map of the stars that would aid navigation by enabling sailors to calculate longitude at sea. The problem was so acute that in 1714, stunned by such accidents as the drowning of almost 2000 men off the Scilly Isles, parliament offered £20,000 for a solution. This was eventually claimed by clock-maker John Harrison in the 1770s, after 20 years of wrangling to have his chronometer – the forerunner of all precision watches – validated. But Flamsteed's 45 years at the Royal Observatory and 30,000 observations did produce *Historia Coelestis Britannica*, a catalogue of some 3000 fixed stars and another example of a great British achievement built on low pay and miserable working conditions.

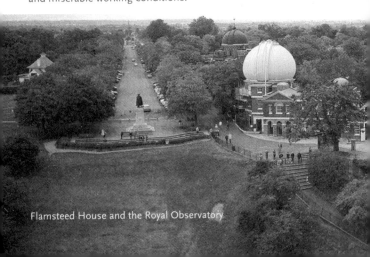

Flamsteed House and the Royal Observatory

More things to see & do

Flamsteed House is part of the Royal Observatory, which includes exhibition galleries devoted to astronomy and time, the largest refracting telescope in the UK, a planetarium with shows throughout the day, and the famous Prime Meridian line (Longitude 0), which divides the world's eastern and western hemispheres just as the equator marks the division between north and south. The red Time Ball on the roof has been raised and dropped at 13.00 since 1833 to give a daily signal. A camera obscura in a summerhouse uses a lens and rotating mirror to project a real-time panorama of Greenwich and the Thames.

Along with the Queen's House (see page 306), the Royal Observatory is part of the National Maritime Museum, whose galleries explore Britain's encounters with the world at sea from the 16th to the early 20th centuries. The Queen's House has changing displays of the museum's vast fine art collection as well as exhibitions by contemporary artists. See *www.nmm.ac.uk*.

Queen's House

National Maritime Museum, Greenwich, London SE10 9NF
Tel: 020 8858 4422
www.nmm.ac.uk/places/queens-house
Nearest transport: Maze Hill Rail or Cutty Sark DLR
Open: daily 10.00–17.00
Admission: free

The first Palladian villa in Britain, and a building truly deserving of the hackneyed phrase architectural gem, the Queen's House seems destined to have been underappreciated. It was commissioned in 1616 by Queen Anne of Denmark, wife of James I, from architect Inigo Jones, who based his design on the Medici villa at Poggio a Caiano outside Florence. Anne is said to have been given the manor of Greenwich by James, as an apology for swearing at her in public after she accidentally shot one of his favourite hunting dogs. Certainly the couple seemed mismatched, with James preferring to spend time hunting and Anne enjoying staging and performing in elaborate court entertainments, including masques commissioned from Ben Jonson and Jones. In 1612 her eldest son Henry had died of typhoid and the following year her 16-year-old daughter left home to marry the future King of Bohemia. You could say that we owe the Queen's House to empty-nest syndrome.

Building work stopped after Anne grew ill in 1618; she died the following year. A decade later her son Charles I returned to the site and by 1638 the house was completed as a summer lodge for his French queen Henrietta Maria, who commissioned ceilings and artwork from leading European painters such as Orazio Gentileschi. She described the house as a place where she could enjoy 'every pleasure the heart could desire' with 'a husband who adored me', but her idyll was short-lived. Within a decade she had fled the Civil War, leaving many of the house's artworks still uncompleted; in 1649 Charles was executed and the house's treasures seized and dispersed.

Henrietta Maria returned to live at Queen's House briefly, following the restoration in 1660 of her son Charles II. Among the subsequent occupants was John Flamsteed, who stayed here from

Queen's House

1675–76 while he waited for Flamsteed House (see page 302) to be completed. From 1689 until 1807 the house served as the official residence of the ranger of Greenwich Park. And from 1807 to 1933 it was at any one time home to some 1000 children, pupils of the Royal Hospital School for seamen's orphans. From 1937 the house has been part of the National Maritime Museum and it now holds the NMM's fine-art collection.

Elizabethan and Jacobean mansions were basically medieval buildings with Renaissance ornament tacked on; Jones, who at the point when he planned the Queen's House had just returned from a visit to Italy armed with Palladio's *Quattro Libri dell'architettura*,

'Tulip' staircase, Queen's House

reinterpreted the master's works to design integral Renaissance buildings whose characteristics are restraint and fine proportions. The extent of the revolution he introduced can be gauged by comparing the strikingly simple Queen's House – essentially a square white box – with the unwieldy plan and fussy detail of Charlton House (see page 291), designed less than ten years earlier. The domestic scale and unadorned exterior of the Queen's House are also a welcome contrast with the attention-seeking baroque of the neighbouring Royal Hospital for Seamen (now the Royal Naval College), which Christopher Wren completed for William and Mary in 1705. Wren's initial design would have obscured the view of the Queen's House from the river; when Mary objected, he was forced to slice his plan in two.

The Queen's House was originally two separate rectangular blocks – each seven bays by two – positioned parallel to one another and connected at first-floor level by a central covered bridge that gave the *piano nobile* an H plan. The bridge spanned the main Woolwich to Greenwich road and formed a private link between the gardens of Greenwich Palace and the royal park. Initially the front of the house was the two-storey park (south) side, with the downward slope enabling the palace side to have a semi-basement. The house was built of brick and faced in plaster, with rustication on the lower floor; stone was used for the window architraves, cornices and the slender Ionic columns of the recessed first-floor loggia on the north front. In 1662 Charles II commissioned Jones' son-in-law and pupil John Webb to build two flanking connecting bridges to give the first floor the square profile it has today. The two separate wings and the Doric colonnade (aligned with the former roadway, which was moved in 1667-69) that links them to the main building were added in 1807 to provide dormitory accommodation for the Royal Hospital School.

Though the house has been restored to conform to its original plan, few of its decorative features have survived. The most impressive space is the great hall, accessed via a curved double staircase from the north: a perfect, light-filled cube with a gallery at first-floor level and a black and white marble floor radiating from a central circle. The original 'tulip' staircase to the east – a spiral with an open well, its wrought-iron balustrades a pattern of tulips or fleur-de-lys – looks incongruously modern and was indeed the first centrally unsupported stair in Britain. The first-floor room to the east of the great hall (originally the queen's drawing room) retains its original decorative scheme of blue with gilded carving. The room to the west (originally the queen's bedroom) has a wonderful 'grotesque' painted ceiling. In the antechamber to the east of the hall is an exhibition about the house's history; the north basement contains a display of information about the Royal Hospital School.

Ranger's House

Chesterfield Walk, Blackheath, London SE10 8QX

Tel: 020 8853 0035

www.english-heritage.org.uk/rangershouse

Nearest transport: Greenwich DLR/Rail or Blackheath Rail

Open: Mon-Wed guided tours only 11.30 & 14.30 (prebooking
   advisable), Sun 11.00-17.00 (April to Sept)

Admission: £6/£5.10/£3

Wheelchair access: limited

Ranger's House

I remember from childhood a ciné film where my aunt superimposed
two separate holidays on a single reel, so lambs from the Lake
District gambolled aboard a cross-channel ferry. It's a bit the effect
of Ranger's House, where the turn-of-the-20th-century private
collection of diamond dealer Julius Wernher has been imported
into a turn-of-the-18th-century house whose most famous occupant
was diplomat and politician Philip, 4th Earl of Chesterfield. Yet just
as my aunt's unlikely juxtapositions and ghost images made her
mismatched effort our favourite film, so Ranger's House is no less
interesting for its curatorial sleight-of-hand.

Croom's Hill, on the western border of the Royal Park of Greenwich, was a popular site for courtiers' houses while Greenwich Palace was in royal occupation until the early 1680s. Captain Francis Hosier, who had made huge sums of money from selling his share of ships' cargoes – whether legitimate exports or booty gained by piracy – probably chose it for his new home in about 1700 because of the social contacts the area afforded, its easy access to the sea and its proximity to the newly established Royal Hospital for Seamen (now the Royal Naval College). His charming two-storey house, its seven-bay red-brick façade enlivened by a Portland stone balustrade at roof level and elaborate centrepiece (with a mask of Neptune above the door), was built to a standard early-18th-century villa design. Unfortunately Hosier had little opportunity to enjoy it: for much of the time of his occupancy he was away at sea, and in 1727 he died of yellow fever on duty in the Caribbean.

In 1740 the house was bought by John Stanhope, who on his death eight years later left it to his elder brother, the 4th Earl of Chesterfield (1694–1773). Chesterfield had at first been reluctant to take the house on, preferring the more fashionable Twickenham, where his friend the Countess of Suffolk had built Marble Hill House (see page 234). But soon after he inherited Ranger's House he resigned from government, ending his public career, and as his age and deafness increased, Greenwich's tranquillity and relative isolation became welcome. He added a single-storey bow-fronted gallery (designed by Isaac Ware) to the south side to accommodate his growing collection of old masters. Built in contrasting yellow brick and running the full depth of the house, it has a curved bay and apses each furnished with three windows, from which he claimed to enjoy 'three different, and the finest, prospects in the world'.

Chesterfield became famous for his letters of advice to his natural son, more than 200 of which were published posthumously and served as a guide for a generation of young gentleman on such subjects as table manners, deportment, food and wine, art and politics. But they had their critics: Samuel Johnson, who had found Chesterfield woefully inadequate as a patron for his *Dictionary*

'Retirement was my choice seven years ago; it is now become my necessary refuge. Blackheath, and a quiet conscience, are the only objects of my cares... I converse with my equals, my vegetables.'
Philip, 4th Earl of Chesterfield, 1755

(see page 46), complained that they taught 'the morals of a whore and the manners of a dancing-master'. Following Chesterfield's death, Ranger's House passed to a distant cousin, 'Sturdy' (Philip Stanhope, 1755–1815), who was also bombarded with letters to improve his education and behaviour. It seems the lessons didn't stick: one of the few stories of Sturdy's occasional occupancy of the house involves a drunken dinner, attended by the Prince of Wales, which ended with them both falling down the front steps.

In the 1780s lawyer and collector Richard Hulse added a north wing to the house, mirroring Chesterfield's gallery at the front but running only half its depth. From 1807 to 1813 the house was leased by Augusta, Dowager Duchess of Brunswick, the sister of George II, whose daughter Princess Caroline, the estranged wife of the future George IV, lived in Montagu House next door. Their presence made Greenwich newly fashionable. In 1815 the house was nominated as the residence of the ranger of Greenwich Park, an honorary position whose previous incumbents had occupied the Queen's House (see page 306). Subsequent residents were George III's niece Princess Sophia Matilda (from 1815 to 1844); the statesman, antiquarian and prime minister Lord Aberdeen (1845–60); Lord Canning (1861–62); Queen Victoria's third son Arthur (1862–73); the Countess of Mayo (1877–88); and Field-Marshal Lord Wolseley (1888–96). The house was acquired by London County Council in 1902 and is now run by English Heritage.

Information on the history of Ranger's House and its inhabitants can be found in a small panelled room, used in Hosier's and Chesterfield's time as the everyday living and dining room, to the right of the simple entrance hall. The rest of the rooms are given over to displaying the magnificent Wernher collection of medieval, Renaissance and later fine and decorative arts. Born in 1850 to a middle-class family in Germany, Julius Wernher amassed a fortune as a diamond merchant; his estate at his death in 1912 was the most valuable the Inland Revenue had yet recorded. He began his career as a prospector in 1871 in Cape Town, sharing a two-room canvas house with a colleague; just over 30 years later, he was the owner not only of Bath House in Mayfair but of Luton Hoo in Bedfordshire, a vast country seat set in 5000 acres that he completely remodelled at a cost of around £250,000 after buying it in 1903.

Most of the elegantly proportioned panelled rooms at Ranger's House, painted in popular Georgian colours, now form a neutral backdrop to his collection, though two have been refurbished to evoke the way the Wernher treasures were originally displayed. Wernher collected furniture and paintings for his homes as well as items that had a more personal appeal. His early success as a diamond merchant depended on examining stones for minute variations that would affect their price, and as a collector he appreciated fine craftsmanship and detailing. The first-floor red room here evokes the room of the same name at Bath House, a retreat where he could display favourite pieces that would be out of place in the fashionable rooms below. Arranging his collection – with objects grouped for effect rather than by category, and 'each vitrine... like a picture' – was a hobby in itself, and here the surprising juxtapositions and sheer density of objects crowded together create the effect of an Aladdin's cave. The ground-floor pink silk drawing room, which in Chesterfield's day was an imposing dining room, has been arranged to echo one of Bath House's grand reception rooms. Wernher's wife Alice (nicknamed Birdie) was famous for her lavish entertaining and opulent taste; social reformer Beatrice Webb, who admired Julius' unostentatious philanthropy, was more sniffy about his wife, complaining after a visit that while 'our host was superior to his wealth, our hostess and her guests were dominated by it... The setting in the way of rooms and flowers and fruit and food and wine and music, and pictures and works of art, was hugely overdone.'

Julius Wernher used his wealth to good effect at home, supporting the foundation of Imperial College in London as well as endowing several hospitals and charities, but he nonetheless made his vast fortune from exploiting black labour and land. So in a sense the story of Ranger's House has come full circle, with Wernher's adventuring abroad a 200-year-old echo of the piracy that enabled seaman Francis Hosier to build the house in the first place.

South-east Outskirts

Addington Palace

Gravel Hill, Croydon CR0 5BB
Tel: 020 8662 5000
www.addington-palace.co.uk
Nearest transport: Gravel Hill Rail
Open: occasional guided tours of ground floor
Admission: free
Wheelchair access: limited

Addington Palace

Built by Robert Mylne for alderman Barlow Trecothick, lord mayor of London in 1770–71, this Palladian villa was completed in 1778, by which time both its owner and the Palladian movement were dead. A painting used in a promotional leaflet for the current owners' country club shows a seven-bay two-storey mansion, with a central porch and pediment and mansard roof, flanked by two four-bay wings fronted by single-storey pavilions with single-storey extensions at each end, the whole built of Portland stone. The reality today is somewhat different.

In 1807 Addington was acquired by means of an act of parliament for the use of the archbishops of Canterbury following the sale of the nearby Old Palace (see page 336). Archbishop Howley (1828–48), fresh from a stint of rebuilding at Fulham (see page 172), enlarged the house to the scale visible in the painting by building up the original single-storey four-bay wings to match the height of the main building and extending them at ground level to create a chapel and library. In 1898 Archbishop Temple sold the palace to South African diamond merchant Frederick Alexander English, who engaged Richard Norman Shaw to restructure it, effectively destroying its proportions and elegance by raising the main block by a storey to allow for a double-height mock-medieval great hall and stepping it forward, presumably to create an imposing entrance space. In 1914 the house was taken over by the Red Cross for use as a hospital and in 1928 it was made into an hotel by Addiscombe Garden Estates. It was purchased by Croydon Corporation in 1951 and from 1953 was leased to the Royal School of Church Music. Its current owners acquired it in 1996 and it now functions as a venue for weddings and conferences and as a country club.

The brief guided tour leads from Shaw's misconceived great hall, complete with minstrels' gallery, to the more modest music room created by Shaw from Howley's chapel. The well-proportioned lecture room behind the great hall, its delicate plasterwork ceiling inset with Wedgwood-style medallions, leads to the library. The central staircase with its glazed cupola and wrought-iron balustrade is Shaw's most successful space. The robing room in the other pavilion was converted into a games room with a central skylight surrounded by moulded fruit and flowers; beyond it is a vaulted conservatory used by the school as a chapel. Tea and coffee are served in the common room, which mirrors the lecture room. In the basement gym the building's occupants strive to retain the grace the palace itself has lost.

Danson House

Danson Park, Bexleyheath DA6 8HL

Tel: 020 8303 6699

www.bexleyheritagetrust.org.uk/dansonhouse

Nearest transport: Bexleyheath Rail

Open: Wed, Thurs, Sun & bank hol Mondays 11.00-17.00 (April, May,
   Sept & Oct); Tues-Thurs, Sun & bank hol Mondays 11.00-17.00
   (June to Aug)

Admission: £6/£5/children free

When you look at Danson House, it's hard to reconcile its delicate
beauty and refinement with the brutality of the slave trade on which
its owners' wealth was based. Yet Danson was built by John Boyd
(1718–1800), whose father made his money from sugar plantations
in St Kitts and a slave station on Bance Island in the mouth of
the Sierra Leone. The estate he left his son, who joined the family
business in 1748, having read theology at Oxford and then made
a grand tour of Europe, included overseas properties that earned
around £9000 a year. Boyd Jr bought 200 acres of land at Danson
in 1753 and over the next 40 years increased the size of his holdings
threefold. The site of the house itself seems to have been acquired
by a dodgy deal that involved buying the freehold, for a permanent
annuity of only £100, from an almshouse trust set up in the will of
its previous owner.

   Boyd commissioned as his architect Robert Taylor, who had
designed the town house he owned near St James's Palace and was
to gain the prestigious commission to extend the Bank of England
as Danson neared completion in 1766. Boyd had married Mary
Bumpstead in 1749 and had four children, but Mary died in 1763,
just after plans for Danson began. He remarried in 1766 and moved
into the completed house with his wife Catherine, with whom he
was to have three more children.

   A perfect Palladian villa, Danson was in fact built as the vogue
for Palladianism – perhaps best exemplified by Chiswick House
(see page 162), begun some 40 years earlier – was being eroded
by such gothic extravaganzas as Horace Walpole's Strawberry Hill

Entrance façade, Danson House

(see page 254). Rising two storeys above a rusticated ground floor and faced in Portland stone, Danson is cruciform in plan, with an entrance hall, stairwell and octagonal salon along the main axis and to the sides a dining room and library, each a double square with a large elliptical bay. These bays rose originally to the top of the *piano nobile* but soon after the house was completed they were extended upwards. Unfortunately, the architect responsible destroyed some of the load-bearing trusses, causing serious structural problems that remained unresolved until the recent restoration. The house as built also had two detached wings for services and stables but these were demolished by Boyd's son and the services incorporated into the main house.

Visitors entered the three-bay hall at the front via a broad flight of steps to the *piano nobile*. Simply decorated, with a stone floor, and furnished with Roman sculptures as in Boyd's time, the space has a cool elegance. The door to the staircase mirrors the pedimented entrance opposite and to preserve the room's symmetry each of the six other openings are treated in the same way, though some lead only to service or storage space. The scallop shells on the doorcases invoke Venus, goddess of love but also goddess of the sea, perhaps in reference to the source of the family fortune.

The dining room to the west is dominated by a cycle of allegorical wall paintings by Charles Pavillon. Each wall has a male and female couple and on the fireplace wall are Pomona and Vertumnus from Ovid's *Metamorphoses*. In the story, Vertumnus disguises himself as an old woman to sing his own praises to the beautiful nymph Pomona, who so far has ignored him; when he later resumes his own form, she falls in love with him. The allegory is presumably a reference to the 48-year-old, newly widowed Boyd's courtship of his second wife, but so crude and unflattering are the paintings that it seems a miracle she recognised his charms. The fireplace is by William Chambers, whom Boyd employed to work on the interiors and landscaping once the house was finished.

Mirroring the dining room to the east is the library, painted a beautiful deep green with rich mahogany woodwork. Above the door is another image of Pomona, while the roundel over the fireplace depicts a veiled bride being prepared for her wedding. At one end of the room is a 1766 organ, indicating that Boyd sought to boost his cultural credentials by continuing the trend for domestic organ recitals pioneered by George Frideric Handel (see page 35). Though he ordered additional bookcases as work progressed, some were for display only, with shelves that are not deep enough to hold real books.

The octagonal salon, accessed directly from both the library and the dining room, is richly decorated and gilded, a small-scale jewel perfect in every detail. Its three south-facing windows look out across the park, their views reflected in gilded mirrors topped by sphinxes and in the paintings Boyd commissioned for the walls. Above the door to the library is a view of the house as originally built, with Boyd (on horseback) and his family in the foreground. The Italianate landscape above the fireplace (a replica of the original) was commissioned from Claude Joseph Vernet and correspondence shows that Boyd specified not only its dimensions but also its content. Chambers' white marble fireplace has a mantelshelf supported by caryatids and a charming central plaque depicting the marriage of Cupid and Psyche, another story of wedded bliss achieved against the odds. Though the wallpaper is a modern replica of an American design from c. 1770, much of the gilding and the blue paint on the glorious palmette frieze are original.

At the centre of the plan is an oval, top-lit stairwell typical of Taylor's villa designs. The cantilevered stone stair has elegant wrought-iron balusters and at the top is an arcaded gallery and ribbed dome painted with *trompe l'oeil* rosettes and thunderbolts. The delicate cornice moulding is repeated throughout the house's second floor.

It seems likely that the Boyd family lived mostly on the ground and second floor rather than in the grand rooms of the *piano nobile*. In addition to the unusually light and spacious double-height kitchen, presented as in Victorian times, and other service spaces, the house's lower level contained a less formal entrance hall and a

Library, Danson House

breakfast room (now the café) below the salon. The servants slept in the attic. On the second floor, the room above the entrance hall, now divided in two, was probably the family living room, with the main bedroom, now used for temporary exhibitions, above the salon. Today one of the rooms in the east bay has been recreated as a bedroom and in the other hangs a series of watercolours painted in the early 1860s by Sarah Johnston, whose father, also a businessman with interests in the West Indies, bought Danson from Boyd's son. The paintings have been used as documentary evidence for the house's restoration.

Danson's last private owner was Alfred Bean, whose company built the North Kent railway. The house was bought by Bexley Council in 1923 and gradually fell into increasing disrepair until in 1995 all the fixtures and fittings were stolen and placed in containers ready to be shipped out of the country. Luckily they were recovered, and English Heritage stepped in to save the ruinous structure and oversee the refurbishment of its interiors. Restored to its former glory, it is now run by the Bexley Heritage Trust.

Home of Charles Darwin (Down House)

Luxted Road, Downe, Nr Orpington, Kent BR6 7JT
Tel: 01689 859119
www.english-heritage.org.uk/downhouse
Nearest transport: Bromley South Rail then bus 146
  or Orpington Rail then bus R8 (not on Sun)
Open: Wed-Sun 11.00-16.00 (Feb, March, Nov & Dec), Wed-Sun &
  bank hol Mondays 11.00-17.00 (April, May, June, Sept & Oct),
  daily 11.00-17.00 (July & Aug)
Admission: £9.30/£7.90/£4.70/family ticket £23.30

'We are absolutely at [the] extreme verge of [the] world.'
Charles Darwin on his new home, 1842

As you walk through the crowded, homely rooms of Down House, it is hard to imagine that this is where the scientific theories that overturned centuries of belief about the origins of species were developed. Charles Darwin (1809–82) lived at Down for 40 years, along with his wife, ten children and a handful of servants. The house was not just a home, but also functioned as a laboratory for his experiments and a sanctuary from the world he knew was far from ready to accept his increasingly revolutionary discoveries.

Darwin and his wife Emma Wedgewood, his first cousin whom he had married in 1839, moved to Down from Upper Gower Street, London, in September 1842. Part of their motivation was to find a stable home for their growing family: two-year-old William Erasmus,

one-year-old Annie, and a third child expected at any moment. Their first weeks here were far from auspicious: Mary, born within days of their arrival, lived for less than a fortnight. But in other respects, Down, which Darwin described in letters as 'a good, very ugly house, with 18 acres', fulfilled his expectations, including his hope that it would become a home 'for the rest of my life'.

The couple had seven more children, two girls and five boys, between Mary's birth in 1842 and 1856. The youngest, Charles Waring, died of scarlet fever aged two; Darwin's favourite, Annie, died aged ten (probably of tuberculosis), a blow from which he never recovered. Emma and Charles were unusually liberal-minded parents, prepared to treat their children as individuals. Charles certainly spent more time with his offspring than most Victorian fathers, engaging their help in conducting and recording his experiments, allowing them to accompany him on his daily midday walks and playing with them in the house and garden.

Charles and Emma, it seems, were a happy couple. Like many a Victorian wife, she created and maintained the conditions that enabled her husband to work, running the household, tending the children, nursing him when he was sick, keeping unwanted guests at bay and providing emotional stability. Darwin was beset by debilitating bouts of sickness and stomach trouble, aggravated by company, changes in routine and especially by his near-constant worry about the social and philosophical consequences of his dawning realisation that human supremacy and the Victorian view of civilisation were not god-given and immutable. He had none of the iconoclasm of many of his admirers and would have happily filled the role of country squire had not his passion for the natural world and the conclusions he drew from his studies led him in new and unexpected directions. The couple shared common social principles but disagreed painfully over religion: Emma held steadfastly to the family's Unitarian beliefs and was heartbroken by her husband's increasing doubts, which grew not only as his theoretical framework took shape but also following the deaths of Annie and then of his daughter-in-law Amy soon after the birth of his first grandchild.

Downe (which added the 'e' in the 1850s to distinguish it from County Down in Ireland) was a quiet village of some 40 households, eight miles from the nearest station. Both Emma and Charles took an active part in local life, with Charles serving as a magistrate from 1857 and founding and running the Downe Friendly Society and Emma bringing food and medicine to the needy and teaching at Sunday school. Though Charles was pleased with his house's isolated position, he repeatedly took measures to extend its privacy, lowering the lane to shield the windows from prying eyes, putting up walls and hedges and buying or renting neighbouring land.

Down House itself – originally a five-bay, three-storey flat-fronted house with a parapet – was built in the early 18th century. In the 1780s businessman and landowner George Butler added a kitchen to the south side and moved the door to the north front (the right-hand side, viewed from the road). In 1837 the house was bought by the vicar of Down, J Drummond, who commissioned architect Edward Cresy (who also oversaw many of the Darwins' alterations) to renovate the interior, install a new hipped roof and render the façades. Over the course of their residency, the Darwins doubled the house's size, adding new rooms and changing the functions of the existing spaces to suit their growing family and increasing wealth. The full-height bay on the garden (west) elevation and a passage along the front half of the north elevation (which entailed moving the door to its present position) were added in 1843; the kitchen extension to the south was built in 1846; the two-storey extension to the north (originally just one room deep) was built in 1858. Darwin's final bout of work in 1876 involved adding further rooms to the road side of the 1858 extension, to give the house the shape it has today. The butterscotch walls, terracotta sashes and grey-blue trellis are matched from contemporary watercolours. Darwin may have made his house more comfortable, but it can't be said that his various alterations did much to improve its 'ugly' appearance.

The ticket office is on the ground floor of the 1876 extension, originally intended as a billiards room with a drawing room and bedroom above. Once the space was completed, however, Darwin

Darwin's study, Down House

decided to use it as a new study. The drawing room behind it (in the 1858 addition) was originally intended as a dining room, but once the building work was finished the drawing room was moved into the new wing, the former drawing room became a dining room and the former dining room was refurbished as a billiards room, which is how the spaces are presented today.

Papered with a pretty blue sprigged pattern similar to the one that replaced the original crimson and gold flock when the house was redecorated in 1876, the new drawing room is generously proportioned and light, with three full-height windows overlooking the garden. Crowded with furniture and possessions – Emma's treasured piano, a bassoon, a backgammon set (Charles and Emma had a daily game and kept a tally throughout their lives), a replica of the plant case in which Darwin made his first experiments before the greenhouses were built, books, portraits, photographs, china, and so on – it feels like the hub of family life, a space in which people with different interests lived in companionable proximity. The inner hallway, in the old part of the house, was colonised by the children as a playroom and Darwin had a slide made for the stairs by a local carpenter which he would occasionally use himself.

The dining room, with its generous bay extending into the garden, does indeed feel as if it might have worked better as a drawing room. The table sits uncomfortably in the main part of the room and the rest of the space holds an odd assortment of sofas and chairs. The walls are hung with family portraits including Darwin's grandfather Erasmus, a free-thinker and evolutionist, and Erasmus' second wife Elizabeth Pole. Darwin inherited the Wedgewood dinner service set out here – painted with a commercially unsuccessful but attractive design of large brown flowers – from his mother, who died when he was eight.

The billiards room was set up in 1859 with the proceeds of the sale of family heirlooms. Darwin played for relaxation, summoning his butler Parslow for a game when he felt the need to 'drive the horrid species out of my head'. In 1876 the room became a study for Francis, the third youngest of the surviving children, who returned to the family home with his new baby following the death of his wife in childbirth.

Darwin's crowded study was restored in 1929 from photographs and the recollections of his two surviving sons. It looks as if he had just popped out for a walk, leaving pens, papers, books, scientific instruments and the pillboxes he used for storing insect specimens scattered over the tables. The well-worn furniture includes a rectangular worktable, a baize-topped drum table and the faded blue armchair that he customised by adding cast-iron legs culled from a bedframe mounted on casters for ease of movement. The system of polished wood shelves and drawers in the corner is reminiscent of a ship's cabin, perhaps in homage to his five-year voyage on the *Beagle* (1831–36), which he acknowledged had determined his entire career. In the corner is a partitioned area with a tin bath and chamber pot that served as a makeshift privy during his bouts of sickness. His daily routine consisted of a short walk before breakfast followed by work until noon, with a mid-morning break to attend to domestic affairs with Emma. At midday he took another walk, sometimes accompanied by one or more children, returning for lunch at 1pm. He then read the newspapers, wrote letters and took a further walk before returning to his study at 4.30pm to work for another hour. After a rest and early dinner, evenings were spent with the family in the drawing room.

Darwin's work was not confined to his room, however. Over the years he conducted exhaustive studies of barnacles, seeds, tropical plants and pigeons, boiling up vats of dead birds in the kitchen or soaking the remains in a stinking brew of potash and silver oxide to remove the flesh so he could examine the skeletons. Even he had to admit that the house at times resembled 'a chamber of horrors'. He was assisted by the loyal Parslow, who stayed with the family for 37 years. Parslow's domain – the kitchen and butler's pantry – now house the tearoom. Much of their original panelling and the copious fitted cupboards are still in place. Darwin demolished and rebuilt the old service wing during his second major phase of alterations, insisting that 'it seemed selfish to make the house so luxurious for ourselves and not comfortable for our servants'. In a small hut on the terrace outside he immersed himself in cold water each morning for a couple of years and was scrubbed vigorously by Parslow in a futile effort to improve his health.

Darwin was reluctant to publish the theories he knew would attract the wrath of the establishment and so his major works appeared only in the last 20 years of his life: *On the Origin of the Species by Means of Natural Selection* (1859), *The Variation of Animals and Plants Under Domestication* (1868) and *The Descent of Man, and Selection in Relation to Sex* (1871). After he died, Emma and those of her children and grandchildren still living with her moved to Cambridge, returning to Down for the summer holidays. Following Emma's death in 1896 the house served as a school. It opened as a museum in 1929 and since 1996 has been run by English Heritage.

The upper floor of Down House contains an excellent exhibition about Darwin's life and work, crammed with artefacts that range from his notebooks, account books, letters and signed cheques, through toys, jewellery and locks of hair, to beetles, birds' eggs, seeds and three of the Galapagos finches that provided the key to his theory of evolution. In a full-scale replica of his cabin in the *Beagle* sits an eerie Darwin hologram that repeatedly examines specimens, writes in a notebook and looks up to address the viewer. In a house so saturated with the spirit of its former owner, to find him suddenly materialise at the head of the stairs hardly seems surprising.

More things to see & do

Darwin used the Down House estate, including the Great House Meadow and greenhouses, as an inspiration for his work and a test bed for his ideas, studying plant growth and pollination in the greenhouses and monitoring the proliferation of species on a patch of the lawn.

Beyond the garden is the wooded 'Sandwalk', the 'thinking path' Darwin would pace up to five times a day while working out his theories.

North front, Hall Place

Hall Place

Bourne Road, Bexley DA5 1PQ
Tel: 01322 526574
www.hallplace.com
Nearest transport: Bexley Rail
Open: Wed-Sat 10.00-16.00, Sun 11.00-16.00 (Jan to March);
   Mon-Sat 10.00-16.45, Sun & bank hol Mondays 11.00-16.45
   (April to Nov, Nov closing time 16.00); Tues-Sat 10.00-16.00 (Dec)
Admission: free

Hall Place is a dramatically schizophrenic house. Its two halves, built a century apart, sit back to back as if to shun any connection and its main elevations – the quirky north front faced in black and white chequerboard stone and the later red-brick south front with its regular bays of windows – could not be more different.

The house began life as a relatively modest manor built by city merchant Sir John Champneys in about 1537. Unusually, it was constructed of rubble masonry with flint infill, perhaps because as a recent lord mayor of London, Champneys had access to large quantities of medieval stone made available by Henry VIII's destruction of religious buildings. His house consisted of a central great hall with two wings in a U plan: the west wing had a parlour and small chapel with bedrooms above and to the east was a service wing. Following Sir John's death in 1556, his son Justinian enlarged this part of the house to its present form, extending the chapel and adding a long gallery above it.

In 1649 Justinian's son sold the property to merchant Robert Austen, who more than doubled its size by mirroring Champneys' house. Building entirely in red brick, Austen extended the existing side wings to the south and connected them at their tip by an impressive 11-bay front. The three ranges surround an internal courtyard that backs on to Champneys' great hall. The house remained in the Austen family until 1772, when it was inherited by distant relative-by-marriage Sir Francis Dashwood, founder of the licentious Hellfire Club. He spent little time here and after his son emigrated to South Africa in 1789 the house was rented out as a school for some 70 years. In the 1870s Francis' grandson Maitland and architect Robert William Edis made Hall Place once more a desirable residence, installing much of the panelling and parquet flooring in place today. The house was then let to tenants, including early-20th-century music-hall star Denise Orme. It was the home of the Countess of Limerick from 1917 to 1943; from 1935, when her son-in-law sold it to Bexley Council on condition she be granted a lifelong tenancy, it was one of Britain's grandest council houses. It was used as an intercept station by the US Army's signal corps at the end of the war and as a school from 1957 until its restoration as a museum in 1968.

Originally lined by open cloisters, Austen's courtyard is dominated by a dramatic staircase tower topped by a fashionable 'prospect room' from which to view his estate. His new building's ground floor was used mainly as service space and the kitchen in the west wing is now an introduction room giving an outline of the house's history. Visitors then enter the central hallway between the two houses, which looks authentically Tudor but was in fact fitted with some of its beams and half-timbering by Lady Limerick, who went to great lengths to 'restore the ancient appearance of her house's interior', according to a 1922 article in Country Life.

Apart from the great hall, the main room on the ground floor of Champneys' house was a parlour, now lit by a dramatic bay probably installed in the late 19th century and lined from floor to ceiling in beautiful wood panelling. The chapel beyond was originally a small space dominated by a gothic window; you can still see some of the 16th-century panelling and traces of original paintwork at the point where Justinian's extension begins. The large bay window was added at a later date, and the new extension, with no fireplace or natural light, was probably used for storage or services.

John Champneys' great hall was originally divided by a screen into a grand double-height space lit by the large bay window at its western end with a smaller buttery or service space to the east, with a gallery above. It was probably Justinian who opened it up to create a more impressive room, adding another window to give the façade, if not the hall itself, its present crowded symmetry. The kitchen in the east wing was enlarged by Justinian but the central fireplace was inserted by Lady Limerick, who used the space as a dining room.

The upper floor of Champneys' east wing has been converted into a gallery for contemporary art. The west wing still has two impressive rooms: the great chamber, above the parlour, and the long gallery, above the chapel. It was Austen who created the great chamber's glorious compartmented ceiling, decorated with an eclectic mix of grotesque figures and classical curlicues in imitation of Inigo Jones, and Lady Limerick who installed the imposing 17th-century fireplace. The long gallery has a more simple 18th-century barrel-vault ceiling and marquetry floor. Both rooms are accessed by large double doors fitted when cumbersome hooped dresses became fashionable.

Rooms on the upper floor of Austen's house, some of which still have their original beams and panelling, now contain the Bexley Museum Collection, donated by local people. The range of objects, which includes Egyptian pottery, Roman vases, African lutes and Victorian paintings, is as eclectic and unexpected as the house itself.

More things to see & do

Hall Place is surrounded by 65 hectares of formal gardens and landscaped parkland on the banks of the River Cray. Its grounds include some impressive chess-piece topiary, rose and herb gardens and a sub-tropical plant house.

The new visitor centre has a riverside tearoom with indoor and terrace seating. In addition to the collection of the Bexley Museum and occasional changing exhibitions, the house also hosts an extensive programme of events, art-based activities, concerts and theatre. See *www.hallplace.com* for details.

Old Palace, Croydon

Old Palace Road, Croydon, Surrey CR0 1AX

Tel: 01883 742969

www.friendsofoldpalace.org

Nearest transport: East/West Croydon Rail then tram or 15-min walk

Open: occasional 2-hour tours during school holidays

Admission: £7/£6/£3, including tea

Wheelchair access: limited

The Old Palace, Croydon, is certainly impressive, but anyone whose schooldays were the bane of their lives should go prepared to sit at classroom desks and chairs, listen with attention to the tour guide and participate in the compulsory break for tea and cake.

The palace was the last in a series of staging posts set up on the road to London by the archbishops of Canterbury after their acquisition of Lambeth Palace towards the end of the 12th century. In 1780 it was sold by the church because of its 'low and unwholesome situation'. A century later they were reluctantly given it back, on condition it was made into a place of education. It has been a school since 1889.

The palace today consists of irregular ranges of buildings, mostly from the 14th and 15th centuries, grouped around two small courtyards. The tour begins in the great or banqueting hall – the most impressive room of the complex as it stands today – built in its present form in about 1450 by Archbishop John Stafford. Though considerably less dramatic in scale than its near-contemporary at Eltham Palace (see page 293), the lofty space, its original oak arch-braced hammerbeam ceiling supported by Spanish chestnut tie beams installed in 1748, has a magic the school stage and chairs have not destroyed. It was here that Archbishop Thomas Cranmer reluctantly condemned to death Protestant martyr John Frith for denying transubstantiation in 1533; Cranmer was a frequent visitor to Croydon, where he installed the woman to whom he was secretly married and accommodated Catherine of Aragon between her divorce and her death three years later – a poignant period no doubt, since Catherine and Henry had spent a lot of time here before their marriage.

The adjacent guardroom, used as a withdrawing room after banquets in the hall, was built by Archbishop Thomas Arundel around 1400 and is one of the earliest uses of brick in Britain. The name probably dates from 1412, when the young James I of Scotland was a prisoner here. The dramatic barrel vault was Arundel's attempt to create the impression of the upturned hull of a ship (a popular metaphor for the church). The room next door, with a fine low-moulded Tudor ceiling, was built as a private dining room by Archbishop John Morton at the end of the 15th century.

Morton also built the passageway linking this wing of the palace with the chapel at the other side of the north courtyard. Here you can see an allegedly haunted Jacobean staircase and a windowpane etched with placement instructions to the Elizabethan glazier: 'next ye chapel'. Probably built by Archbishop Bourchier (1460–80), the chapel has a fine carved screen installed by Morton and a raised pew built for Elizabeth I by her mentor Archbishop Matthew Parker in the 1560s. The west pews and altar rail date from the time of Archbishop Laud, who embellished the chapel, moved the altar from the centre (as decreed by Reformation lore) to the end and repaired the stained-glass and crucifix, all of which was used as evidence against him leading to his execution for endeavouring to 'overthrow the Protestant religion' in 1645. Note the four negroid heads that form part of the coat of arms of Archbishop Juxon (1660–63) on the east pews, suggesting a shameful family connection with the slave trade.

After tea in the Norman undercroft, the oldest surviving part of the palace, now distinguished by a mass of exposed heating pipes, the tour continues through the bedroom used by Elizabeth I, which retains its original Tudor ceiling but not much else, to the long gallery. Used for dancing, exercise and entertainment, this dates from the late 15th or early 16th century and is thought to be one of the oldest of its kind. It was here in 1587 that Elizabeth made Sir Christopher Hatton lord chancellor (he was said to be a fine dancer).

Red House

13 Red House Lane, Bexleyheath, London DA6 8JF

Tel: 020 8304 9878

www.nationaltrust.org.uk/main/w-redhouse

Nearest transport: Bexleyheath Rail

Open: Wed-Sun & bank hol Mondays, booked tours at 11.00,
11.30, 12.00, 12.30 & 13.00 or self-guided viewing 13.30-16.45
(March to Nov); Fri-Sun same times as above (Dec)

Admission: £7.20/£3.60/family ticket £18

Wheelchair access: ground floor only

'Pilgrim's Rest', Red House

The idea of Red House was hatched by three men in a boat during a
rowing trip down the Seine in summer 1858: William Morris (1834–
96), architect Philip Webb, whom Morris had met two years earlier
during his year-long apprenticeship with gothic-revivalist architect
G E Street, and Charles Faulkner, a Birmingham mathematician
whom Morris had met at Oxford through his friend Edward Burne-
Jones. At the time Morris had abandoned architecture to pursue
the pure art of painting at the behest of pre-Raphaelite artist Dante

Gabriel Rossetti, with whom Burne-Jones was a pupil. In February 1858 Morris had become engaged to Jane Burden, a groom's daughter he and Rossetti had spotted at an Oxford theatre and asked to model for the frescoes Rossetti was planning for the new debating hall of the Oxford Union. Though the project proved disastrous – the paint began to rub off before the job was finished and Morris' contribution was so amateurish it made his mentor laugh – through it Morris not only met his future wife but also discovered his vocation for decorative arts when he was allocated the job of painting the ceiling.

Red House was conceived by Morris as a home for his future wife and family and a 'small Palace of Art of my own'. He hoped it would satisfy the dreams of communal living and purpose first given shape in an abandoned idea for a monastery that he and his friends were to found after they left Oxford (see Water House, page 354). It seems that the five years he and Jane lived here – from the summer of 1860 to November 1865 – were indeed the happiest of their lives: their two daughters Jenny and May were born in 1861 and 1862 respectively and the house was filled each weekend with such friends as Webb, Faulkner, poet Algernon Charles Swinburne, the Burne-Joneses (Edward had married Georgiana, the vivacious daughter of a Methodist minister, in June 1860), Rossetti and his wife Elizabeth Siddal (who committed suicide in 1862), and Rossetti's mentor Ford Madox Brown. As well as producing furnishings, hangings and murals for the house, the friends spent time playing bowls, touring the countryside in the medieval-style coach Morris had built, eating, drinking and talking. 'It was the most beautiful sight in the world', wrote Georgiana Burne-Jones, 'to see Morris coming up from the cellar before dinner, beaming with joy, with his hands full of bottles of wine and others tucked under his arms.'

The solitary occupation of painting had made the gregarious Morris irritable and miserable; in the collaborative nature of the decorative arts he found a profession more suited to his temperament. In 1861 Brown had the idea of formalising the friends' ad hoc crafts activities and the commissions he, Burne-Jones and Webb were receiving for furniture and stained-glass by founding with Rossetti, Faulkner and P P Marshall, a surveyor friend, the firm of Morris, Marshall, Faulkner & Co. It was hoped that by taking part in the production and sale of their designs, the artists would avoid the division of manual and intellectual labour that according to Ruskin produced a society of 'morbid thinkers, and miserable workers'. The firm – established in 1861 using the £900 per annum Morris received from shares in a Devonshire copper mine inherited from his father plus a loan of £100 from his mother – was to revolutionise 19th- and 20th-century design, but its development proved the death knell for Morris' dream. In the early years it ate steadily into his inheritance and though by 1865 its prospects were improving, its expansion now required new premises, while the effort of managing the London enterprise from Red House was becoming increasingly taxing. At first Morris suggested adding another wing to the house for the Burne-Joneses and buying land for workshops nearby. But following the death of their newborn second child from scarlet fever, Edward and Georgiana Burne-Jones withdrew, and Morris, whose own recent attack of rheumatic fever had made the daily journey to London impossible, was forced to choose between home and business. His grief was so great he never saw Red House again.

Morris had married Jane for her beauty rather than her personality; Swinburne stated frankly that he should have been content to have 'that wonderful and most perfect stunner of his to look at or speak to. The idea of marrying her is insane.' It seems that while Morris was very much in love with her, she found his wildly oscillating enthusiasms and irascible personality difficult to deal with and retreated into defensive, enigmatic silence, aggravated by nervous rheumatism. (Henry James, writing in 1868, described her as 'an apparition of fearful and wonderful intensity... this dark silent medieval woman with her medieval toothache'.) Just two years after the couple left Red House, Rossetti asked Jane to model for him again and fell passionately in love with her. Morris was generous to a fault, taking out a joint tenancy with his rival of the Manor House in Kelmscott, where Jane and their daughters spent much of their time, and retreating through journeys to Iceland – his latest passion – and his friendship with Georgiana Burne-Jones (whose husband was having an affair). It seems that Jane and Rossetti continued their liaison for about a decade, after which she ended it. The marriage survived, though Jane was to take other lovers while William threw himself into ventures that included Morris & Co, the Socialist League and the Kelmscott Press (see Kelmscott House, page 186).

Red House was a three-dimensional statement of Morris' principles: a challenge to the dominance of the machine and a call for a return to traditional craftsmanship and human values embodied in a rosy vision of the medieval age. Drawing on the forms and materials of vernacular English country architecture – a massive, barn-like tiled roof, red brick, and irregular fenestration that expresses what lies within rather than conforming to the demands of the façade – it was a marked contrast to the neoclassical regularity and painted stucco then fashionable. The exterior is that of a fairytale cottage writ large: the asymmetrical façades, the heavy overhanging roofs punctuated by projections and recesses, the turrets, towering chimney stacks and porches with gothic arches contribute to the appearance of a house that has grown up organically. Like a monastery or medieval castle, Red House encloses a private world rather than presenting a series of façades for public display.

As with the house's architecture, Morris seemed determined to rethink its interior decoration and furnishings from scratch. So visits by the couple's friends turned into working parties in which Burne-Jones and Rossetti painted glass, tiles and furniture – most of it designed by Webb – Morris drew flower patterns for hangings that Jane and her sister Bessie embroidered and Faulkner painted the geometrical ceiling patterns laboriously picked out in the wet plaster. Though Morris' most lasting legacy is the wallpaper that lines the house today, originally all the walls were to be covered with murals or hangings. The L-shaped plan places the principal rooms facing north and west, as if to eschew direct sunlight; rather than being a rejection of Victorian gloom and clutter, these rooms were envisaged as dark and richly furnished, though sadly many of Morris' grand schemes for them remained unfinished when he left.

The main entrance is near the middle of the northern wing and the entrance hall runs its full depth, connecting with the western wing, which originally housed the kitchen, scullery, pantry and larder. The dining room is in the outer corner of the L, and on the other side of the hall are two smaller rooms, labelled waiting room and bedroom in Webb's plan. These are flanked on the garden side by a passage that culminates in a porch which Morris called the Pilgrim's Rest, in a Chaucerian reference to the house's location on the old London-to-Canterbury road. The lawn at the inner angle of the L – its main feature a well with a conical roof – was originally an outdoor room enclosed by the trellis that inspired Morris' first, clumsy wallpaper design, a drawing of which hangs beside the back door.

Visitors enter the house through the service wing and proceed into the entrance hall. Like the exterior, the space eschews symmetry and grandeur, its differently scaled doors arranged in accordance with the demands of the rooms around it. The walls were to be covered with paintings by Burne-Jones of scenes from the Trojan War re-enacted in medieval costume; the white ceiling has a grid of small holes made when the plaster was wet to provide a guide for future decoration. The Webb-designed settle-cum-bureau has traces of Morris' amateurish, unfinished paintings of his friends, with himself as a lute player entertaining his wife.

The passage leading to the Pilgrim's Rest has windows decorated with delightfully quirky birds painted by Webb and flowers by Morris. One of the two small rooms now holds a collection of objects found during the recent restoration work, including a sympathetic letter from Webb written after the collapse of Morris' dream of making Red House an artists' commune. The glazed screen was installed in the late 19th century to keep out the

Drawing room-settle, Red House

draught; some of its panels are scratched with the names of visitors brought to the house after Morris moved out, including Arthur Lasenby Liberty.

The dining room, originally decorated with terracotta walls and deep green panelling, must have been considerably darker, despite its three large windows; plans for 12 full-sized embroidered hangings of illustrious women were never completed. Along the back wall is a Webb-designed dresser stained and lacquered in Morris' favourite dragon's-blood red, its relatively conventional base surmounted by a typical reinvention and amalgamation of traditional forms including a canopy adapted from medieval ceremonial chairs. By contrast, the oak staircase, with its tapered newel posts and minimal carving, seems refreshingly simple, and the bold geometrical pattern on the ceiling has a muscularity lacking in Morris' typically more delicate designs.

Lit by three tall casement windows to the north and a charming oriel to the west, the first-floor drawing room, its ceiling extending into the roofspace, was intended by Morris to be 'the most beautiful room in England'. The tall red-brick fireplace was probably inspired by those of French Renaissance châteaux. The massive settle was designed by Morris for his previous home in Red Lion Square in London; Webb added a platform cum canopy to provide access to the loft. The idea was to imitate a minstrels' gallery, but in fact there is not enough room to stand upright. On the walls are three of seven planned paintings by Burne-Jones, one of which depicts William and Jane crowned at a wedding feast, standing in for the medieval subjects of Froissart's romance 'The Tale of Sire Degrevaunt'. Hidden behind the panelling is a wall painting by Morris of a repeating pattern of trees and parrots with his motto 'Si je puis' (If I can).

William and Jane's bedroom above the hall is a long, thin, north-facing room originally hung with blue serge embroidered by Jane and Bessie in a pattern of daisies taken from a medieval illumination. In the cupboard are fragments of a mural on the theme of the Garden of Eden begun by Elizabeth Siddal. Morris'

L-shaped studio is nestled in the corner of the north wing. Like the entrance hall, it gives the impression of being designed according to need, with the door and fireplace off centre and the two tiers of mismatched windows seemingly placed wherever space could be found. Today the foot of the L is filled by a wonderfully simple De Stijl-flavoured workstation designed by architect Ted Hollamby, the house's last private owner.

Red House's owners in the first half of the 20th century included two of the editors of the design magazine *Studio*. From 1952 until their deaths in 1999 and 2003 respectively, it was the home of Ted and Doris Hollamby, whose children sold it to the National Trust. The Hollambys shared the house first with Mary and Dick Toms, like Hollamby an architect at the LCC, and then with David and Jean Macdonald, all of whom contributed to its restoration. Morris' dream of a purpose-designed home and studio may not have materialised for him, but it seems to have worked well for another family who spent almost half a century appreciating the home in which he spent only five years.

East

Dennis Severs' House, see page 349

East

18 Folgate Street
(Dennis Severs' House)

18 Folgate Street, London E1 6BX
Tel: 020 7247 4013
www.dennissevershouse.co.uk
Open: Sun 12.00-16.00, Mon evenings 18.00-21.00 (booked visits
   only), Mondays following the 1st & 3rd Sun of the month 12.00-14.00
Admission: Sunday £8/Monday lunchtime £5/evenings £12
Nearest transport: Liverpool Street LU/Rail

18 Folgate Street was bought by Californian Dennis Severs in 1979. At the time Spitalfields was still a wholesale fruit, vegetable and flower market rather than a conglomeration of art and jewellery outlets, and the surrounding area housed newly arrived immigrants and downmarket printers rather than refugees from the City. Severs scavenged food along with the area's many tramps and camped with his chamber pot, candle and bedroll in each of his house's ten rooms, trying to discover the key to its particular atmosphere. Eventually he invented the Jervises, a family of Huguenot silk weavers who fled France soon after Louis XIV repealed the law allowing Protestant worship in 1685, bought the Folgate Street house when it was built in 1724, and whose descendants lived here until 1914. Over the course of 20 years until his death in 1999 at the age of 51, Severs created and furnished the rooms the Jervises lived in, each frozen at the moment when the inhabitants, startled by the intrusion of modern-day visitors, beat a hasty retreat.

Visitors are asked to remain silent for the duration of their stay, and certainly the absence of embarrassed sniggers at the stale

'The late 20th century may be a fascinating place to visit, but surely... nobody would want to live in it.' Denis Severs

urine in the chamber pots or irrelevant exclamations at the beauty of some of the house's objects helps keep the 21st century at bay for those willing and able to suspend their disbelief. The most intrusive element for me was the haranguing notices asking you not to touch anything or explaining why children are unwelcome, presumably erected by the keepers of Severs' flame to coerce visitors into experiencing the house as they believe he would have wished. Don't be put off either by Severs' own text on the website: there's no doubt that his installations deserve the status of 'art' rather than theme park, but the key to appreciating them lies in allowing your senses to take over rather than trying to deconstruct the psycho-babble with which the experience is described.

The three-storey flat-fronted three-bay house with basement and attic is built to a standard L plan. The ground-floor front room – in which a programme for the coronation of William and Mary in 1689 hints at the occupants' Protestantism and the date of their arrival in the country – is set up as a dining room. A heavily italicised notice explains the plot: 'Eighteenth-century silk master Isaac Jervis – his family and descendants – are all still around you somewhere in the house. As you approach – they depart, as you depart – they re-enter, but all so that by not actually seeing them your Imagination might paint a series of pictures: of the various domestic scenes your arrival has forced them to abandon.' And indeed if you are able to keep your scepticism under wraps, then the smells of food that waft around the abandoned dining table and the soundtrack of domestic exchanges, street noises and cockcrows combined with the chirping of a real caged bird produce an atmosphere that at the least could be described as uncanny.

The most spine-chilling room for me, however, is the first-floor back, where Severs has painstakingly created the scene that might have followed the drunken all-male party depicted in Hogarth's 1733 painting *A Midnight Modern Conversation* (which hangs above the mantelpiece here) once the protagonists had left. The abandoned jackets and newspapers, the disordered furniture, the overturned glasses and decanters, the overpowering smell of cloves from the empty punchbowl, the fire's dying embers and the morning-after-the-night-before gloom are eerie enough, but what is most disturbing is the feeling that the myriad details have been provided with such precision and completeness that the space is in fact fully inhabited, and the visitor an unwelcome intruder. The notice asking 'Would you recognise art if it fell out of the frame at you' seems supremely irrelevant.

On the landing a stunning crystal chandelier hints at the more genteel atmosphere of the drawing room. But the most potent indication that we are entering the domain of the woman of the house is the change in smell – from the punch dregs of the Hogarth room to a refined lavender. Presided over by a portrait of Mrs Edward Jervis (presumably the daughter-in-law of the Mrs Isaac Jervis whose picture hangs in the dining room below), the orderly room is set for tea, with a fan draped on what one presumes is the mistress' chair, the tea locked in a caddy at her feet, and the startled departure of her guests indicated by the upturned sugar bowl and a broken cup. On the table is a book of entertainments dating from 1740, a point at which the halt on imports following the start of the 1740–48 war with France led to a surge in demand for locally produced silk and the prosperity of Spitalfields reached its zenith.

The second floor belongs to a less affluent age. Abandoned wooden toys gather dust at the top of the stairs and the back room is a combined bedchamber/sitting room where the smell of stale urine from the half-filled chamber pot mingles unpleasantly with the odour of half-eaten food and dregs of tea. The clanking, creaking soundtrack – footsteps, servants emptying slops, or perhaps simply the house groaning around us – is more evocative than any words. The date is 1821, a time when the number of silk weavers dramatically outflanked demand for their product and the influx of veterans from the protracted war with France that ended in the Battle of Waterloo in 1815 had led to social instability and unrest.

The front bedroom has a magnificent display of Delft above the mantelpiece but somehow our attention is diverted to the clockwork monkey hanging from the bedpost, which clicks as it swings from side to side. Another Mrs Jervis dominates the room through her portrait, clothes, toiletries and the chair that seems to hold the impression of her body and might still feel warm to the touch. Disconcertingly, beside the fireplace are a pair of 20th-century men's shoes and socks and tucked away behind a screen are a jumper and sweatshirt. It's a discrete reminder that this was also Severs' room and that he chose deliberately, masochistically, to efface his own needs and live in obeisance to a woman created by his imagination.

The attic landing is hung with greying underclothes, and a quotation from Dickens' *Oliver Twist* – 'The House to which Oliver had been conveyed was in the neighbourhood of Whitechapel. It was very dirty' – hints that we are now in the late 1830s. Padlocks on the doors indicate that the rooms are occupied by lodgers; in contrast with the ordered symmetry of the drawing room below, the oddments of furniture are arranged pragmatically, with no pretence at elegance. Several people obviously sleep, cook, eat and live in each of the rooms – a pan of cabbage warms by the fire; the table is littered with plates of empty mussel shells.

The cluttered ground-floor back parlour is late Victorian, by which time gentility has reasserted itself. The basement kitchen is warm and bright, with a blazing coal fire and griddle cakes done to a turn. And in the hall hangs a fine display of black leather jackets of the kind once found in abundance in the area's gay pubs and clubs.

Water House

William Morris Gallery (Water House)

Forest Road, London E17 4PP
Tel: 020 8496 4390
www.walthamforest.gov.uk/william-morris
Nearest transport: Walthamstow Central LU/Rail then 15-min walk
Open: closed for refurbishment until summer 2012,
    please check website for details
Admission: free
Wheelchair access: ground floor only

William Morris' family – his mother Emma, plus two older and two younger sisters and four younger brothers – lived at Water House for only eight years, during most of which time William (1834–96) was away from home, first at school at Marlborough and then at Oxford. But the house provided the backdrop for two dramatic announcements to his long-suffering mother which were to transform the course of his life and arguably of late-19th- and early-20th-century design. These were his decision to turn his back on the church – a vocation he had chosen at Marlborough, perhaps inspired by the romance of singing Elizabethan church music in the neo-gothic chapel newly designed by Edward Blore – in favour of a career as an architect and then to quit architecture for the pure art of painting.

The Morris family had moved to Walthamstow from their huge Woodford mansion in 1848, following the death of Morris' bill-broker father. It was a step down from heady affluence to respectable prosperity, thanks to the fluctuating value of the family's shares in a Devonshire copper mine. At the age of 14, Morris junior was sent to Marlborough – a 'progressive' school with little organisation, no prefects and no uniform, where the boys were allowed to ramble and birdnest at will. His first stay at Water House was for the Christmas vacation of 1848–49. Three years later, following a rebellion at the school, William was brought back to Walthamstow to prepare for Oxford under the guidance of the Reverend F B Guy, with whom he spent some of the following year in Devon. In 1853 he went up to Oxford's Exeter College, where on his first day he encountered Birmingham grammar-school boy Edward Burne-Jones. Through Burne-Jones he was to meet the group of friends – mathematician Charles Faulkner, also from Birmingham, and painters Dante Gabriel Rossetti, Ford Madox Brown and William Holman Hunt – who through the pre-Raphaelite brotherhood and the arts-and-crafts movement were to stamp their mark on 19th-century art and design. By the time his family left Water House in 1856, Morris had attained his majority, giving him access to an annual income of £900, and was articled to gothic-revivalist architect G E Street, in whose office he met Philip Webb, designer of his arts-and-crafts manifesto Red House (see page 338).

Morris' time at Oxford – where he became known as much for his explosive rages as for his purple trousers, swaggering bow ties and rampant curly hair and beard – shaped many of his ideas. Through the Birmingham contingent he met people who had first-hand experience of the inhuman conditions in which workers lived following the industrial revolution – this tempered his romanticism and inspired his future socialism as well as fuelling a common desire for a return to a pre-industrial age. The friends would spend long evenings reading aloud (poetry, particularly Tennyson, was seen as a relevant and revolutionary activity) and it was probably here that Morris established his preference for the writers who from 1890 he would publish using typefaces of his own design through his Kelmscott Press (see Kelmscott House, page 186). In 1855 the brotherhood set aside some of Morris' inheritance to found a magazine (the scheme superseded a previous notion of establishing a monastery and living together in chastity), in which William published the first examples of the poetry that was to reach its critical peak in The Earthly Paradise (1868–70). And on holidays to France with Burne-Jones, the friends discovered the Italian pre-Raphaelite art and gothic-cathedral architecture that were to influence their painting and stained-glass design.

Though Water House and Walthamstow lacked some of the romantic appeal of Epping Forest, which Morris had explored avidly in his early childhood, the moat at the back of the house (which gave it its name) provided opportunities for swimming, sailing, skating and fishing, its central island a fantasy fairyland on which the children spent most of their days. The handsome, three-storey nine-bay brick mansion with symmetrical three-bay bows at either end was probably built in the late 1740s; an early reference describes a 'new built capital brick messuage or tenement' valued at £200 and owned by Catherine Woolball on her marriage to Sir Hanson Berney in 1756.

The year after the Morris family left, Water House was bought by Edward Lloyd, whose *Lloyd's Illustrated London Newspaper* (later *Lloyd's Weekly News*), founded in 1842, had by 1863 reached a circulation of 350,000. In 1876 he bought the *Daily Chronicle*, which he transformed into a paper of national importance. The father of 24 children, he left Water House in 1885 because the new houses being built in the area 'did not provide the right kind of companions for the social life of his growing children', according to the daughter of a former employee. It was a sentiment echoed by Morris, who in later life described Walthamstow as 'once a pleasant place enough but now terribly cocknified and choked up by the jerry builder'.

Water House was given to the council by Edward Lloyd's son Frank in 1899, at which point it was almost derelict. In 1911 it became a school clinic and dental surgery and in 1950 opened as a museum. At the time of writing it was undergoing a major refurbishment promising enhanced displays of the extensive collections relating to Morris' life and works.

Sutton House

2 & 4 Homerton High Stret, London E9 6JQ

Tel: 020 8986 2264

www.nationaltrust.org.uk/suttonhouse

Nearest transport: Hackney Central Rail

Open: Thurs-Fri 10.00-16.30 & Sat-Sun 12.00-16.30 (Feb to Dec),
    Mon-Wed 10.00-16.30 (Aug)

Admission: £3/£1/family ticket £6.90

Wheelchair access: ground floor only

Preserved in an attic room in Sutton House is a red-and-black mural of an eye, believed, according to the caption, to date from 1985 and to be 'the emblem of the rock group P.S.I.' Two floors down, the parlour is one of only three London rooms (including one at Hampton Court, see page 214) completely lined with 16th-century linenfold panelling. That either has survived is something of a miracle – the panelling because it was dismantled by thieves who moved in following the eviction of the squatters who painted the mural, sold, and then restored to the National Trust by a wary dealer. The mural because the policy underlying the house's restoration in the early 1990s seems to have been to uncover the many layers of its history rather than simply fix on a set period to preserve.

Sutton House was built by Sir Ralph Sadleir, a privy councillor to Henry VIII, in 1535. Like Eastbury (see page 365), it follows a standard Tudor H plan, with the rear legs of the H, which flank the south-facing courtyard, skewed to accommodate existing buildings. The bar of the H was occupied by the great hall, entered via a screened passage to the east with a dais to the west and the great chamber above; the service wing was to the east and the family wing to the west. In the attic were rooms for servants and children.

Sadleir had started his career at the age of 14 in the Fenchurch Street household of Thomas Cromwell, soon rising to become the king's chief advisor's right-hand man. Attracted perhaps by Hackney's reputation for clean, healthy air, Cromwell was in the 1530s rebuilding a house in nearby Clapton known as King's Place, for which purpose Henry had given him 100 oaks from the royal forest at Enfield. Though Sadleir's relatively modest house, unusually, was of red brick – hence its original name of 'bryk place' – it's likely some of this timber found its way into the frames of its heavy mullioned windows and the bargeboards of its four gables.

Following Cromwell's execution in 1540 for refusing to sanction the king's marriage to Anne of Cleves, Sadleir managed to disassociate himself sufficiently from his past master to survive in office until midway through the reign of Elizabeth I. Meanwhile in 1550 he sold his house to John Machell, a wealthy wool merchant and sheriff of London, whose family lost possession when their acquisition of a large estate in Cambridgeshire led them into debt. From c. 1630 the house was owned by silk merchant Captain John Milward, who was forced to surrender it following the collapse of silk prices. For almost a century from 1657 it was a girls' school.

In 1741 John Cox took over the house with the intention of modernising it to earn higher rents. He transformed Sadleir's Tudor pile into an elegant Georgian manor, replacing the mullioned windows with sashes, concealing the gables behind a parapet, removing the large Tudor chimneys and adding a small cottage to the rear. Luckily most of his alterations were done on the cheap, so the traces of the Tudor building – including many of the original fireplaces and some decoration – were left in place behind them. On the death of his first tenant Mary Tooke, the widow of a prominent Huguenot merchant and the first of many occupants of French Protestant descent, he divided the house in two, with most of the great hall going to the western house and the cottage to the eastern portion. For much of the 19th century the latter functioned as a school. In 1896 Canon Evelyn Gardiner bought both halves and reunited them into St John's Church Institute, a recreational club for local men. The house was bought by the National Trust in 1938 and was used as offices for charities, Hackney Social Services and the trades union ASTMS until the 1980s. In 1990–94, after a public campaign to prevent it from being developed into flats, it was restored to its present form.

The entrance in the eastern corner of the central recessed front is via the original front door, moved to this position by Cox. Though the façade of the east wing was rendered in the 19th century, the west side retains its Tudor brick and some diaperwork. The space that was once the great hall is still divided much as it was by Cox and is now occupied by the reception area, which retains its 18th-century panelling, and the entrance corridor. The linenfold parlour at the front of the west wing is completely lined in 204 individually carved panels, to breathtaking effect. The panels date from about 1535 and were probably moved here by Machell from his previous house, as was common practice. The simple oak furniture allows the beauty of the varnished wood to dominate – presumably a return to form after the excesses of Milward, whose decorative scheme of corn yellow, emerald green and mahogany red can still be glimpsed. The rear of this wing is occupied by the present café.

In the damp-smelling cellar is a display of recuperated building materials including the original carved bargeboards. In the stairwell, overlooking the internal courtyard and therefore ignored in Cox's showy remake, is one of the original mullioned windows. The staircase itself was probably installed by Milward. Towards the top are fragments of his stencilled gold murals including a faux strapwork frieze and a pair of griffins intended to resemble elaborately carved newel posts. The remains have all the poignant romance of a ruin, as well as providing a strong flavour of how the house must have looked after his sumptuous decorating spree.

The gallery above the café has also been left in a suspended state of discovery, with layers peeled back to reveal the original brickwork, a Tudor stone fireplace decorated with Milward's coat-of-arms hiding behind a staircase installed by Cox, and fragments of late-18th-century wallpaper. The little chamber above the linenfold parlour has an original stone fireplace and plainer panelling dating from the late 16th century, some of which swings open to reveal the fragile lath and plaster beneath. The majestic great chamber beyond, also fully panelled, gives a sense of the grandeur the house once possessed. Opposite a full-length painting of the swaggering Sir Ralph are portraits of his descendants by Mary Beale (1632–99), one of the first professional female portrait painters.

Vestry House

Vestry Road, London E17 9NH
Tel: 020 8496 4391
www.walthamforest.gov.uk/vestry-house
Nearest transport: Walthamstow Central LU/Rail
Open: Wed-Sun 10.00-17.00
Admission: free
Wheelchair access: ground floor only

Though little different in plan or appearance from a contemporary five-bay double-fronted family home, Vestry House was in fact a purpose-built workhouse expected to accommodate 30 to 40 'paupers' in six of its eight smallish rooms. It was built in 1730 by the vestry – an assembly of all the ratepayers of the parish, which was responsible for many aspects of local government including providing for the poor – just eight years after an act of parliament first permitted the construction of workhouses. A workroom was added to the rear in 1756 and the vestry meeting room to the left of the entrance was almost doubled in size in 1779 by extending it into the front yard (it was also given its own separate entrance). The rear extension was used as a police station for 30 years from 1840, when the paupers were moved to the new Union Workhouse (now Langthorne Hospital) in Leyton, and subsequently as an armoury for the Walthamstow Volunteers and as a builder's yard. From 1882 the front part of the building was the headquarters of the Walthamstow Literary and Scientific Institute and from 1892 it was a private house, occupied first by the Maynard family and then by Constance Demain Saunders, who gave it to the council in 1930.

The ground-floor rooms to the left of the entrance (now a gallery) were originally the vestry meeting room, with the workhouse-master's room – in which he and his wife would cook and eat – at the rear. The paupers cooked and ate in the two kitchen areas to the right (now offices and a shop). The bedrooms above the gallery are now one long space with displays of Victorian household objects. Those above the paupers' kitchens house toys and games and a reconstructed Victorian parlour, its polished furniture and multitude of homely ornaments a reminder of the middle-class norms enjoyed by those who kept the poor in such miserable conditions. By the 1820s Vestry House accommodated more than 80 poor, issued with clothes with the badge 'W.P.' (Walthamstow Poor) sewn on the shoulder, three primitive meals a day washed down with beer brewed on the premises, medical care and basic education for their children. Both adults and children had to work for their keep (the plaque above the entrance bore the legend 'if any would not work neither should he eat').

The transition between the original building and the rear extension, roofed over in the early 19th century, has a chilling display of truncheons. The extension, panelled in wood taken from the 1596 Essex Hall, demolished in 1933, now houses cases of clothing and uniforms, though an original police cell, complete with graffiti, has been preserved. The area to the left, roofed over in 1934, was formerly an exercise yard surrounded by a 4-metre wall. The space above the panelled room – originally a paupers' dormitory accessed only by a ladder – is now a local-history archive.

'If any would not work neither should he eat...'
Vestry House

East Outskirts

Eastbury Manor House

Eastbury Square, Barking IG11 9SN

Tel: 020 8724 1000

www.nationaltrust.org.uk/main/w-eastburymanorhouse

Open: Mon, Tues & first two Saturdays of each month 10.00-16.00

Admission: £2.50/65p/family ticket £5

Nearest transport: Upney LU

*'A great house, ancient, and now almost fallen down, where tradition
says the Gunpowder Treason Plot was at first contriv'd, and that all the
first consultations about it were held there.'*
Daniel Defoe, 'A Tour throughout the Whole Island of Great Britain', 1772

Eastbury Manor House – a red-brick Tudor mansion obviously
designed to impress – today sits on a roundabout surrounded by
unprepossessing semis. At the time of writing it was undergoing
an extensive restoration programme that promises new displays
about its history along with reconstructions of some of its murals
and spaces. What follows is a bare-bones description of a work-
in-progress.

Originally on rising ground surrounded by marshes, with views
of the Thames, Eastbury was built in the 1560s by wealthy merchant
Clement Sysley on land that until the reformation had belonged to
Barking Abbey. Though Sysley had intended his house to become a
family seat, in 1592 his son Thomas leased and then sold it to his
step-brother Augustine Steward to pay off his debts. The rumour
of a connection with the 1605 gunpowder plot is probably through
conspirator Francis Tresham, whose brother Lewis was married to
the Spanish Catholic stepdaughter of John Moore, who leased the
house from the Stewards. Certainly both Lewis and his wife Maria
Perez were living at Eastbury at the time of Moore's death in 1603.
As Defoe's description implies, the house was subsequently to hit
hard times, and during the 18th and 19th centuries it was leased to
a succession of tenant farmers. It was bought by the National Trust
in 1918 and is now run by the local council.

365

Like Sutton House (see page 358), built about 30 years earlier, Eastbury has an H plan, with a great hall in the bar of the H connecting ranges to the east and west, each two bays wide and seven bays long. At the back of the house these ranges flank a walled courtyard from which you can fully appreciate the impressive chimney stacks and English bond brickwork with diaperwork patterns. Vertical circulation was via two octagonal stairtowers in the inner corners of the courtyard, one for servants and one for the family. The eastern turret was demolished in the early 19th century and has recently been rebuilt, but the servants' staircase, a spiral of solid oak, is one of the most evocative remaining spaces.

The entrance porch on the north front would originally have led via a screen directly into a three-bay great hall; today this and the painted chamber above have been reduced in size to make room for a staircase added in the 19th century. At the eastern end of the hall was a dais where the family would sit to receive visitors; if you look up the chimney you can see a priest's hiding hole, more evidence of the house's Catholic connections. The east wing once housed the family's summer and winter parlours and in the west wing were the steward's room, still lined with 17th-century panelling and with a raised floor to accommodate the cellar, and the kitchen (now a café).

In the painted chamber above the great hall are remnants of the 17th-century frescoes of fishing scenes that once covered the walls. The bedroom in the south-west corner, with a closet and garde-robe (toilet) opening off it, was probably Clement Sysley's. The long gallery above the parlours was originally divided into several smaller rooms and still has its original beams and one of its Tudor fireplaces. In the glorious, light-filled attics, with their rollercoaster floors and exposed roof timbers, you get a true sense of Eastbury's age and of the miracle of its survival.

Valence House Museum

Becontree Avenue, Dagenham, Essex RM8 3HT
www.lbbd.gov.uk/heritage
Nearest transport: Chadwell Heath Rail then bus 62 or
    Becontree LU then bus 62
Open: Mon-Sat 10.00-16.00
Admission: free

The only surviving manor house in Dagenham, Valence House is located at the edge of Valence Park within the Becontree Estate, an ambitious suburban housing project begun by the London County Council after World War I to provide 'Homes for Heroes'. The house takes its name from Agnes de Valence, granddaughter of the French wife of King John, who spent 19 years of widowhood here following the death of her third husband in 1291. The last occupants were the May family – three generations of formidable women and a shadowy farmer patriarch – who lived here from 1879 until the house was acquired by the LCC in 1921.

Still partly surrounded by a moat, Valence House is an L-shaped building with charmingly irregular white-painted elevations. The earliest part of the present timber-framed structure dates from the 1400s, though the cellars and foundations show signs of previous work. A survey of 1649 – at which point Valence was confiscated by Cromwell from the Dean and Chapter of Windsor – reveals a much larger building than today, boasting 15 hearths, and there is evidence that a west wing was demolished in 1863.

On the ground floor are the great parlour, lined with wooden panels dating from the late 16th century, a gallery containing information about the house's history, and the Fanshawe gallery, hung with a collection of portraits of the local Fanshawe family, including Peter Lely's portrait of the foppish Sir Thomas and his wife. Up the 17th-century oak staircase is the O'Leary gallery, which contains displays on the people and communities of Barking and Dagenham. Also on view on the upper floor are recently discovered wall paintings dating from c. 1600.

Index

Index

To order our books:

The following titles are available from our website:
www.metropublications.com (p&p free)

Alternatively, please send your order along with a cheque made payable to Metro Publications Ltd to the address below (p&p free). Or you can call our customer order line on 020 8533 7777 (Visa/Mastercard/Switch), open Mon-Fri 9am-6pm.

metropublications ltd
PO Box 6336, London, N1 6PY
www.metropublications.com / info@metropublications.com

Also in this series:

LONDON'S PARKS AND GARDENS
COVER MORE THAN TWENTY-FIVE PERCENT OF THE CAPITAL – THAT'S A LOT MORE GRASS BETWEEN TOES THAN ANY OTHER CITY IN EUROPE

LONDON'S HOUSES
FROM WORKHOUSE TO ROYAL PALACE, COME IN, CLOSE THE DOOR AND STEP BACK IN TIME...

LONDON'S MONUMENTS
FROM BOUDICCA AND BYRON TO GUY THE GORILLA

LONDON'S CITY CHURCHES
SEE THE SCORCH MARKS OF THE GREAT FIRE, OR VISIT AN ALTAR BY HENRY MOORE

LONDON'S HIDDEN WALKS
THE LONDON YOU KNOW IS JUST THE SURFACE!

LONDON'S CEMETERIES
SPEND THE DAY WITH KARL MARX, ENID BLYTON, KEITH MOON AND MANY MORE

Museums & Galleries of London
4th edition

Veggie & Organic London
2nd edition
Russell Rose

METRO GUIDES
Book Lovers' London
4th edition

METRO GUIDES
The
the London Market Guide

4th edition
BARGAIN HUNTERS' LONDON

THE LONDON THEATRE GUIDE

'A Joy'
Nigel Slater
Food Lovers' London   Jenny Linford

LONDON ARCHITECTURE
FORWARD BY MAXWELL HUTCHINSON

The London **Cookbook**
Recipes
Stories
History
Jenny Linford

Image Credits